Urszula Clark
Staging Language

Language and Social Life

Editors
David Britain
Crispin Thurlow

Volume 13

Urszula Clark

Staging Language

Place and Identity in the Enactment,
Performance and Representation
of Regional Dialects

DE GRUYTER
MOUTON

ISBN 978-1-5015-2450-9
e-ISBN (PDF) 978-1-5015-0679-6
e-ISBN (EPUB) 978-1-5015-0669-7
ISSN 2192-2128

Library of Congress Control Number: 2018959331

Bibliographic information published by the Deutsche Nationalbibliothek
The Deutsche Nationalbibliothek lists this publication in the Deutsche Nationalbibliografie;
detailed bibliographic data are available on the Internet at http://dnb.dnb.de.

Typesetting: Integra Software Services Pvt. Ltd.
Printing and binding: CPI books GmbH, Leck

www.degruyter.com

Acknowledgements

There are many people to whom I am indebted in assisting me in the realization of this volume. First of all, I wish to thank two UK research grant awarding bodies, the Leverhulme Trust who awarding me a Leverhulme Research Fellowship and the Economic and Social Sciences Research Council (ESRC), including the anonymous reviewers, for awarding me a further two grants. Thanks are also due to the performers and all the other people who participated in the project, and to all the research assistance I received over the years. Many warm thanks to the series editors and the anonymous reviewer of the initial proposal, without whose support this volume would not have seen the light of day. I wish to thank Lara Wysong and the editorial team at De Gruyter. And last but not least, thanks are due to my colleagues, family and friends for their support and understanding throughout the whole process.

https://doi.org/10.1515/9781501506796-201

Contents

1 Staging language: Place and identity in the enactment, performance and representation of regional dialects

1.1 Introduction

My overall aim in this book is to investigate the relationship between a specific discursive practice – that of creative and imaginative performance played face to face by local performers in front of a local audience – and any connections such performance may have with language and identity linked to place. In line with recent research (Trester 2012; Jaffe 2015; Jaffe et al. 2015; Vigourouz 2015 among others) largely undertaken in relation to languages other than English, I investigate the role of dialect use in English in creating and maintaining specific cultural, social and regional identities in the context of contemporary, localised, live spoken word events performed by regionally based performers and attended by local audiences. In so doing, I also consider issues related to creativity and imagination, by taking account of the degree to which dialect use is incorporated in tune with the locality in which performances take place, together with the wider cultural, historical and socio-political contexts within which they are performed. Such considerations allow for an examination of the beliefs, values, assumptions and ideologies that underpin the performance contexts and dialect use therein, and the nature of the dialectic relationship between linguistic form and function, linguistic ideology and interactional practice.

The lens through which dialect use is viewed in this book then, is not so much concerned with either a comprehensive linguistic analysis of identified dialect features or a discussion of perceived attitudes and beliefs in relation to social and regional dialects of English. Rather, I am concerned more with how performers in a specific region of England, in this instance that of the West Midlands, engage creatively and imaginatively with dialect features in their performances. Firstly, in relation to the ways in which social identities linked to place are constructed and secondly, how such identities align with social class and power structures in contemporary society. Following Eckert (2000), Coupland (2007) Johnstone (2011) amongst others, such consideration is set against the background of the wider historical and socio-political contexts within which language is used and the sets of beliefs, values, assumptions or ideologies that underpin these contexts.

Identification of dialect features then, rather than being an end in itself, acts as a catalyst for examining their role in the discourse within which it takes place. Auer (2013) has made the point that in traditional dialectology, the focus

https://doi.org/10.1515/9781501506796-001

has been largely upon language as it links directly to space, with speakers themselves largely left out of the account. He attributes this to two main assumptions, namely that speakers only speak one language (or dialect) or only the dominant one is taken account of and that speakers are bound to places in immobile ways. However, in an age of globalisation, people's mobility comes increasingly to the fore, through space as well as time, as Chapter 4 demonstrates. An interactional perspective upon dialect use also entails conceiving of alternatives in language "......not as 'variants' of underlying abstract (or more basic) structural units that are distributed in a contextually determined versus free form fashion, but rather as resources in their own right...." (Couper-Kuhlan and Selting 2018: 548).

Equally, a corresponding consideration of the social forces governing or underpinning any individual's spoken language use has also largely been ignored. It is also often assumed that speakers who draw upon regional accent and dialect in their speech will do so in relation to one dialect and its corresponding accent. For example, in the performance context, a performer born and brought up in the English city of Birmingham to indigenous white parents of a low socioeconomic class but who has, by virtue of education and/or employment become in adult life a member of a higher socio-economic class, may speak standard English with a Birmingham (Brummie) accent. S/he may also, though, enregister specific features of that accent to index Birmingham, known locally as Brum and being Brummie. Locally based performers and in urban areas particularly, may also draw upon a range of accents and dialects from different places both within England and beyond in crafting their personae in their performances. This is evident in Chapter 4, where I discuss performers of Jamaican heritage from the Jamaican community within Birmingham who draw upon Jamaican Creole, Patwa and Brummie in their performances. In this way, performers draw upon what Auer (2011) in the context of mainland European languages has called a *linguistic pool* and Cheshire et al. (2011) a *feature pool*, whereby a range of accent and dialect features are used to index different aspects of identities – individual, local, regional, national and global. Such performers may be said to create a new multiethnolect (Clyne 2000) discussed further in that chapter.

My focus also includes examining the ways overt stylization in creative performance sheds light on the multiple social indexes being performed by any performer(s) through a multiplicity of voices; the ways in which audiences react to them and how performers draw upon dialect to challenge hegemonic practices associated with standard English. The face to face performance contexts of the kind I discuss in this book, can be seen as a kind of 'in-between' zone between casual face to face conversation and the type of heavily scripted language of most traditional spoken media. Live performance is particularly interesting in terms of the relationship between performers and their audiences. This is because live performance is interactive in nature, ranging from close proximity between any one performer or performers and their audiences in small venues such as rooms in public houses to the distance created between a stage and auditorium in a theatre, amateur or professional. In such settings, and particularly in relation to semi-improvised performance such as comedy, feedback flows from the audience to performer who, in turn, may make adjustments in to what they say response. Discussion of performances therefore, is accompanied by a consideration of what performers in the case of comedy and sketches, playwrights in the case of scripted plays, and members of their audiences have to say about specific performances, and particularly in relation to the reflexivity and metapragmatic awareness (or lack of) involved in preparing and enacting a performance. These conversation interviews provide a 'behind the scenes' view of linguistic performance scenarios. They offer insight into the extent to which performers deliberately draw upon certain features of dialect as a resource in not only creating characters and scenarios but also with the iterative dynamic between performances, audiences and the places and spaces within which performances are enacted. Whilst the extent to which individuals do this in the course of day to day interaction has been the focus of much recent sociolinguistic research, my focus is upon the ways performers draw upon dialect use in their staged performances to create and maintain difference from standard English. Particularly, this focus is upon the ways such use can be said to juxtapose the norms and values of those 'within' a given community with those 'outside' it, thereby subverting traditional notions of linguistic – and thereby social – hierarchy. Consequently, I examine how such overt stylization sheds light on the multiple social indexes being performed by any individual performer through a multiplicity of voices. In so doing, I also address issues of reception in considering the reaction of audience members to performances and performers.

In addition to the performances themselves, conversation interviews were undertaken with the performers and, wherever possible, members of the audience who attended the performance. To supplement these, conversation interviews were also held with playwrights, poets and other people known either nationally or locally for their affiliation to the region. These conversations provide a 'behind the scenes' view of the linguistic performance scenarios, offering greater insight into the reflexivity and metapragmatic awareness (or its lack), in preparing and enacting a performance. The main aim of these conversations was to investigate the extent to which audiences have any affinity with the dialect use shown by performers and the ideology produced and reinforced by them and the nature of the relationship between performers of any kind (artists, writers, poets, comedians, broadcasters) and the communities they purported to represent. A further aim was to ascertain if any evidence could be found for the claim that speakers draw upon dialect use dialect associated with a traditional place identity when confronted with social and economic change speakers as a way to resist that change.

The kinds of staged performances I analyse range from stand-up comedy events given as part of variety type performances by single and multiple performers; performance poetry; professionally produced plays to medieval mummers' plays. The location of the performances in the West Midlands region of England centred upon the four shire counties of Shropshire, Staffordshire, Warwickshire, Worcestershire and a fifth metropolitan country superimposed upon the region called, confusingly, the West Midlands Metropolitan Borough. This latter area encompasses Britain's second largest city, Birmingham. The region as a whole comprises a landscape made up of large swathes of countryside with small towns and villages through to urban sprawls such as Birmingham, the Black Country, Coventry and Stoke on Trent that have, over time, swallowed up what were once themselves small towns and villages.

As Crul (2016) has pointed out, international migration has dramatically changed large West European cities such as Birmingham in the space of two generations in ways that challenge established sociological theories such as segmented and new assimilation theory. Such change can be accounted for more by Vertovec's (2007) sociological notion of *superdiversity*, explored linguistically by Blommaert (2010). Such diversity has led to new forms of linguistic use that go beyond traditional notions of bilingualism, code-mixing or code switching such as that first identified by Rampton (1995) as a more reflexive 'crossing'. Increasingly in modern, urban societies in particular, people may draw upon features of more than one language that point to plurality in language use. These include, among others, 'translanguaging' (Garcia 2009a; Blackledge and Creese 2010; Wei 2011; Garcia and Wei 2015), 'polylingual languaging' (Jorgensen 2008a; Moller 2008) and 'metrolingualism' (Otsuji and Pennycook 2010; Pennycook and Otsuji 2015) as well as the formation of multiehnolects as discussed above. Such research also intersects with work undertaken on *styling* in the work undertaken by Coupland (2001, 2007) and Bell (2011) and Bell and Gibson (2011) amongst others, discussed further below. The focus of such endeavour has been mainly upon how people marry multiple ways of speaking with different personae to accomplish certain things.

Such a view of language use put agency at the forefront of sociolinguistic research, including the ways in which people draw upon dialect in different and varying ways as resources in identity construction (e.g. Beal 2009; Johnstone et al. 2006). I explore the impact of such superdiversity upon new forms of linguistic usage, specifically in the context of staged performances enacted by male performers within the Afro Caribbean Jamaican community in Birmingham in Chapter 4. This is alongside the staged performances given by adult ethnic white performers, male and female, discussed in Chapters 3 and 5. Here too, globalised discourses can be seen to be present, by way of references being made to contemporary American popular culture and ethnicities other than English in juxtaposition with locally referenced people and events.

As a social activity, performance is inherently reflexive, constructed discursively and may function as a mechanism of helping performers and their audiences make sense of the rapidly changing world in which we now live. The performances discussed illustrate ways in which dialect use can serve to reinforce reflexivity in striving to maintain a sense of a distinctive working class culture through the lens of the present day, in ways that connect the present with the past, anchor time and space to place and relocate disembedded social institutions back into local communities. Following Giddens (1991), Appadurai (1996) identifies the world in which we now live as one that is very different from all kinds of pasts, a difference or rupture he attributes to the twin forces of media and migration, particularly electronic mediation that has transformed the ways in which we communicate with one another. He points to the ways in which electronic media audiences are no longer bound by local, national or regional spaces, and few of us do not know anyone who is either living or traveling elsewhere. Recent patterns of migration also mean that many of us live in places that are different from those of our parents or grandparents. For example, a striking feature of the performers discussed in the chapters that follow, is how so few of them can trace their ancestors' places of birth beyond the last one or two generations. In this sense, both persons and images often meet unpredictably, outside the certainties of home and the comfort zone of local and national media effects. As he says: "This mobile and unforeseeable relationship between mass-mediated events and migratory audiences defines the core of the link between globalisation and the modern" (1996: 4).

Imagination, and particularly the creation of imagined communities within the fictional worlds performers create, is central to creative performance. Those discussed share a common theme of viewing an increasing globalised world through the eyes or mirror of a regional place. They illustrate how locally based performers annexe the global and its electronic mediatisation through the prism of the local and its impact upon their audience's lives, often in comic and semi-serious ways.

1.2 Dialect and style

Two key concepts related to performance and performativity are dialect and register or style. As Biber and Conrad (2009) point out, two main kinds of language varieties can be identified in any speech community. Firstly, varieties that are dialects associated with different speaker groups, further subdivided into geographic and social dialects. Secondly, varieties that are registers associated with different uses of language. Traditionally, studying variability in dialects has related to linguistic form and in register in relation to its function. Thus, for example, dialect research in traditional Labovian sociolinguistics centres upon a linguistic variable that has several variants which by definition, preserve meaning and do not relate to function. In dialect studies, linguistic variables are more often than not conceived of as a choice between two variants. To use Biber and Conrad's example, pronouncing the word *car* as either [kar] or [ka] indexes membership of different groups but does not affect the word's meaning and there is no functional difference between them. The extent to which either group uses either variant is given as a proportionate score showing a preference for one over the other and in relation to a certain geographic or social dialect. By contrast in register studies, the higher the rate of occurrence for any one linguistic feature is interpreted as showing a greater need for the function associated with it. Biber and Conrad (2009: 12) point out that it is possible to study functionally motivated linguistic variation across dialects, but provocatively say that most sociolinguists are prevented from so doing because of their theoretical stance that the meaning potential of all dialects is equivalent to their communicative one.

In traditional linguistics, the difference between dialect and register is often taken to be that distinctive formal patterns characterising a dialect cannot be shown to be motivated by the circumstance of speech correlating with it, whereas distinctive formal patterns characterizing a particular register can be shown to be motivated by the factors that correlate with register distinction. Agha's (2007) definition of register however, differs from such a traditional understanding of the term, in that linguistic forms are inextricably linked with the context in which they occur. As with register, so with style. As Johnstone (2019) also points out, if a linguistic form means anything to anyone, then it is because it has become enregistered. (Chapter 2 discusses this in more detail). Thus, in locally based performance events, performers may evoke a range of genres and associated registers within which dialect features are used in motivated – enregistered – ways because of the very nature of the context within which they are performed. They also, as discussion in the following chapters makes clear, portray ways of being that are rooted in the region and its economic and sociocultural past. It is thus not accidental that in closely knot communities the more local the audience, such as those of the Black Country and the Staffordshire Potteries, the more dialect features are enregistered that are in tune with the locality in which they are being performed. It is also evident that in performance contexts, the further away from the region, the fewer are drawn upon by the performers. A relatively rare occurrence of a few and restricted set of phonological, morpho-syntactic and lexical features can serve as an important indicator of dialect differences. It can be possible to study linguistic variability in a way that encompasses both notions of dialect and register, that come together in the concept of 'style' and the ways in which dialects can be viewed as 'social styles' (Coupland 2007).

The term *style* as it is used in sociolinguistics often refers to the ways in which individuals pattern language in distinctive ways in terms of both dialect and register in what Coupland (2007: 30) calls "...an agentive possibility for social identification – how we can style ourselves." Such a concept of style refers to the ways in which the speech of any one individual varies according to the nature of the interaction of any social situation in which an individual is engaged – in other words, according to its register. Eckert (2008) also takes issue with the traditional definition of sociolinguistic style as different ways of saying the same thing. As she says: "...style is not a surface manifestation, but originates in content" (2008: 456). Eckert's view of style, and one which I share, is that style precludes the separation of form from content, on the grounds that: "...the social is eminently about people's lives. Different ways of saying things are intended to signal different ways of being, which includes different potential things to say" (2008: 456). Thus, many of the people interviewed that are discussed in later chapters, talk about the extent to which they are conscious of the ways in which they accommodate their speaking styles in relation to their interlocutors, including modifying their use of accent and dialect. At home with the family or out in local settings such as public houses, people may speak with a regional accent and accent in predominantly unconscious ways and in mainly informal registers to one another, but modify their accent and dialect in particular, when speaking to people outside of such contexts and venues such as in the workplace and/or occasions elated to the workplace such as conferences and social occasions. Issues of performance and performativity then, are thus examined in the chapters that follow in relation to individual performer styles, in relation to accent and dialect and register.

Take, for example, Jaffe's (2015) work on staging language in Corsica, where she considers improvised performance in relation to a *Casa di a Lingua* 'Language House' event as part of a Corsican language planning programme. She refers to the Bakhtinian concept of 'double-voicing' discussed in the next Chapter in that it "... captures the historical, interdiscursive links between the voices of actors and the real people/figures they animate" (2015: 162). She argues that such reflexivity and the 'meta' dimension of language use relates to Bauman's (2000) work in relation to reflexivity and performance vis a vis identity. She extends such a notion of reflexivity to be an inherent property of contemporary sociolinguistic circumstances which in her case is that of Corsican as a minority language.

Thus, the heteroglossia evident in performance is not bracketed off as a special feature of performance but is also evident and generalized beyond the performance event as a feature of both individual and collective identity and practice in day to day contexts. The same is also evident in the heteroglossia evident in the performers use of English in the West Midlands, both on and off stage, discussed further in Chapter 2. In relation to her research into the Northern American dialect of Pittsburghese, Johnstone also makes the point that:

> People's response to language is always partly aesthetic: we are always attending to how language sounds (or looks on the page) as well as attending to what is said...In this sense we could say that all language is performance in the sense that we are always putting forth some kind of persona, playing some sort of part. But there are times when speakers and hearers are especially attentive to what talk sounds like...Speech that is performed calls attention to and takes responsibility for its multi-voiced quality, the way, in other words, in which speakers' "normal voice" is juxtaposed with a performed voice that may represent some other person or person.
> (2013: 197)

Recent sociolinguistic research into issues of performance, mediatization, dialect and style have been largely undertaken in relation to a context where twentieth century cultural and economic developments have had the effect of diminishing the relevance of geographic place in our lives in the twenty first, as discussed above. Although the dynamism of modern life has largely separated place from space and removed social reality from local contexts, local, place-based communities still have a part to play in today's world.

As Honeybone says: "...languages exist...mentally, on the grounds of speakers' perceptions. People have conceptions of who speaks the same language as them – that is, of who belongs to their close or extended speech community" (2011: 176). At the same time, languages also exist imaginatively, in relation to speakers' and listeners' perceptions. Androutsopoulos (2010) in the context of media discourse draws upon Gumperz's (1982) concepts of 'situational' and 'metaphoric' code-switching to make a distinction between different ways of theorising dialect use. Situational code-switching refers to a conventionalised distribution of a code to situations. Androutsopoulos, in the context of media discourse, gives the example of local media regularly include a small part of their content in dialect in a symbolic way. In a more localised context such as that discussed in Chapter 3, is an example of graffiti on a wall opposite the coach station in Birmingham: 'welcome to brum babs' where 'brum' is local token for the city Birminghan and 'babs' a local token for a female of any age. In vox pop clips such as those in news programmes, local dialects linked to local activities are often in direct contrast to the language of the newsreader. By contrast, metaphorical code switching

captures linguistic evocations of localness typically short and often unique in the course of a text or program: a show host switching to the local vernacular in order to caricature a social type or to address a caller; a politician in a talk show switching into dialect to claim an understanding of local affairs; a newspaper report casting direct speech by elderly locals in the dialect. This is a wide, largely uncharted territory, in which language often indexes spaces and associated social types by means of double-voicing and stylization.
(2010: 247)

Analysis of linguistic forms he argues, needs to be complemented by the analysis of *contrasts* between local speech and other linguistic resources in their discourse context, the *genres* in which local speech occurs, the *voices* local speech is allocated to or presented as owned by, and the *identities*, i.e. social categories, which are represented or evoked through local speech in discourse. Such an approach is fundamental to the analysis I undertake in relation to localised live, creative performances, where localness is not simply a matter of using a local code but of doing so in ways that evoke places and foreground 'cultural icons' associated with them. Attention is thus shifted away from varieties to styles and stylizations and from linguistic forms as such and more upon the ways in which they intersect with other dimensions of discourse.

1.3 Mediatization and performance

Particularly relevant to the discussion throughout this book is the notion of 'imagined communities' as first proposed by Anderson (2006 [1983]) and to which Appadurai refers, as discussed above. Although Anderson coined his term in relation to nation states, the concept can be equally relevant to regionally based communities located within nation states. Just as the concept of a nation state exists in the minds of a nation's community, so too does the concept of a geographic region within that nation exists in the minds of its inhabitants, whether they continue to reside in the region or move away from it to other parts of the world. In Cohen's terms a boundary "encapsulates the identity of the community, and, like the identity of an individual, is called into being by the exigencies of social interaction" (1985: 12). The specific region considered in this book is that of the English West Midlands, as outlined above. Within this region, borders between shire counties and various towns and cities remain undisputed, apart from those that separate Birmingham and the Black Country.

Birmingham and the Black Country refer to a specific geographical place, and there are distinct differences in how boundaries are drawn between the two communities. The Black Country has no agreed physical or political boundaries, being defined instead by what it is not, and by its residents primarily in opposition to Birmingham. It is thus a good example of Anderson's concept of an 'imagined community.' An important aspect of this concept for Anderson is that of simultaneity, as a means of 're-representing' the kind of imagined community that is the nation or in this case, the region and sub-regions within it. Anderson invokes the structure of an old-fashioned novel as a device for the presentation of simultaneity in what he calls "homogenous, empty time" (2006: 25).

All of the performances discussed in the chapters that follow are performed by actors at the same calendrical time in front of audiences who are by and large unaware of one another outside of the performance space but who live in the locality, in a 'novelty' of an imagined world conjured up in the audience's minds by the performer(s). Appadurai (1996: 5–9) distinguishes between three different aspects of the role of the imagination in today's world. Firstly, imagination is no longer confined to the space occupied by the expressive arts, myth and ritual, and has become part of the mental work of ordinary people as we become ever more self-reflexive. Secondly, there is the distinction between imagination and fantasy, and the fact that the consumption of mass media throughout the world provokes irony, resistance and selectivity – in other words, *agency*. He cites the example of terrorists, to which that of lone mass shooters can be added, who model themselves on Rambo-like figures. (The degree to which any one of us understands the reference of course also places us in a particular relation with the media, especially film, social media and television). Further examples are Muslim families listening to recorded, or, nowadays, streamed sermons by Islamic leaders and housewives reading romance novels and watching soap operas on television as a way of helping to both construct and understand their own lives. Thirdly, is the distinction between the collective and individual sense of the imagination. Mass media makes it possible for people to imagine and feel things together, because of the way it is consumed through collective reading, watching, criticism and pleasure, in what Appadurai calls "communities of sentiment" (1996: 8). He cites Anderson in reminding us that print capitalism – and now media capitalism – can be an important aspect for people who have not nor may never be in contact with one another to think of themselves as American, British, English, Indian, Somali and so on and thus belonging to a nation.

Nations are made up of regions, divided in countries such as Australia and the USA by states and in the UK by different countries that in turn are made up of shire counties whose boundaries date back centuries and some of which have been redrawn in recent decades to accommodate changing populations. What is true of the nation is also true of smaller spaces of which it is comprised. Where once whole communities lived and worked in close proximity to one another, also spending their leisure time together meant virtually all of its members were known to one other, this is no longer the case. In an area such as the Black Country region which has no defined geographic borders, delineating its physical boundaries is an imaginary act on the part of people who live within it, particularly at its margins, and are a source of largely goodhearted banter by those living within the region. Equally, the superimposed metropolitan borough of the West Midlands is one that exists in the minds of bureaucrats rather than of those living in the region. Created artificially in the 1970s to accommodate local government administration, people living within the area so designated still think of themselves in terms of shire county identity. Thus, within a nation such as England, the performances given by regionally based local performers in front of a local audience create a community of sentiment centred upon a specific locality through references to a shared collective past. Such references are interspersed with ones to the media, for example reference being made to 1970s American cop shows and Clint Eastwood in his role as a policeman in the film *Dirty Harry* by a Black Country comedian in his persona of a policeman as discussed in Chapter 3. Although performed in an expressive space, the performances lie largely outside of the mainstream, which, given the proximity between performer and their audience, is highly dialogic between the two. Where a performer's staged performance is anchored in place, it thus occurs in both physical and imagined space, with the performer drawing upon various local, national and international social characters and stereotypes whom the audience 'meets' through the performer and his/her performance. In this way, the imagined communities evoked by performers in their performances can be said to be discursively constructed and mediated by their performances.

The boundaries of an urban region such as Birmingham and the Black Country and that of the West Midlands Metropolitan Borough also extend beyond its physical reality in England to an imaginary one across its entire community of users that includes people no longer resident in it but live instead in other parts of the country or across the world. Contemporary dialect use can thus be said to transcend physical borders, and thanks largely in part to greater geographic mobility and technology, dialect use associated with a particular region is no longer confined to the region in which it originates. Thus, in the Black Country for example the local newspaper, *The Black Country Bugle*, has an international circulation and features stories, poems and letters written in dialect, as does *The Black Countryman*, a journal associated with The Black Country Society, which also has its own website (Clark 2013b). There is a Black Country Living Museum, which attracts visitors from all over the world and where copies of the Old Testament written in Black Country dialect can be bought.

Alongside these, there is a thriving local community arts scene centred upon the spoken word, in folk music, poetry, comedy, drama and song performed by locally based performers, many of whom draw upon the region's linguistic features in their performances both locally and further afield, of which the ones discussed in this chapter are but a few instances against a backdrop of many. A mobile app has been invented which 'translates' standard English into a wide variety of UK English varieties, including those of Birmingham and the Black Country, available to anyone, anywhere in the world. In today's technological age then, social interaction across individual lines of difference transcends physical boundaries, where members of a 'speech community' associated with a geographic region may live anywhere in the world and their social networks are many and varied.

Dialect also features in public display around the region and in common with others in the UK such as the North East (Beal 2009) and Pittsburgh in the USA (Johnstone 2009), a range of commodities can be found, including T-shirts, caps and sweatshirts that feature local dialect words. This is particularly the case in the city of Birmingham and its neighbour, the Black Country. For example, the Birmingham Museum and Art Gallery, the Birmingham Repertory Theatre and the Black Country Living Museum also display artefacts for sale such as mugs displaying a local word such as *bostin* meaning good, and *tay* (tea) towels featuring the Black Country alphabet. T-shirts are commercially available with dialect words printed on them such as an alphabet design – *f is for fettle; z is for stripey 'oss* and the ten commandments in Black Country *spake* (speak). In the Staffordshire Potteries, a website called Staffordshire Potteries sells Potters' greeting cards that feature a cartoon of a man greeting a women with the words with the greeting 'ay up duck' (hello my dear) and mugs with the slogan *keep calm and dunna panic duck* (keep clam and don't panic dear) and *keep calm and dunna worry thee sen* (keep calm and don't worry yourself). As both Beal and Johnstone point out, local speech becomes commodified in this way in regions where people have not only become aware of dialect difference but also choose to draw attention to it in such artefacts, known as third order indexicality discussed in Chapter 2. In contrast, other areas in the region such as Coventry lag behind the processes of commodification and enregisterment despite this city undergoing the same 19th century growth of industrialisation and its subsequent decline in the 20th century. This is largely due to differing patterns of demography and social networks and not least because Coventry suffered the most bombing during the second world war and was nearly annihilated as a city.

Features drawn from local dialect appear not only on such commodities but also in the linguistic landscape of the city of Birmingham, in graffiti and names of touring buses. Until recently, people alighting from coaches at the Birmingham coach station were greeted by graffiti on a large wall opposite the station that said: WELCOME TO DIGBETH, BABS. Digbeth is the area in Birmingham in which the coach station is situated and a well-known Irish quarter of the city, whilst 'babs' or 'bab' is a local term of endearment and positive politeness, used mainly in addressing women and girls and still in use today, both unconsciously in everyday social interaction and through its enregistration as illustrated above. The bus which takes tourists on tours of the city is called 'The Big Brum Bus', with Brum being the local word for Birmingham and people born and living in the city known as Brummies. At the annual Christmas Market imported from Frankfurt in Germany that is held annually in the city centre, had a large neon sign at one of its entrance points in 2017 that read: 'HAPPY CHRITMAS BAB.' In 2014, the Black Country established its own 'Black Country Day' of July 13th, that marked the beginning of a 'Black Country Week,' with a number of cultural events taking place across the region, including spoken word performances. Taken altogether, such instances demonstrate not only the extent to which a self-reflexive linguistic conservatism permeates the fabric of social life in the region, but also the degree to which it is celebrated. They also reinforce the link between dialect use and regional identity at a time of ever greater dialect levelling. It seems that in the face of such levelling, people from within communities such as those in the West Midlands are 'holding onto' an albeit restricted set or range of dialect features which are enregistered to index a place identity that permeate discursive practices across the region, particularly creative ones. The ways in which I investigate dialect use in creative performance then, is interactional in nature, taking account of the wider histori-cal and socio-political contexts as well as the sets of beliefs, values, assumptions or ideologies that underpin its use. In so doing, I also take account of the ways in which the performances discussed are *mediated*, in the sense that they have been rehearsed and range from partly to fully scripted ones, but *unmediated* in the sense that they occurred in face to face settings where no third party broadcast or virtual medium is involved such as the internet, film, radio or television.

Ever since Bell's seminal work on audience design (1984) there has been increasing interest in the role of dialect use in general as it relates to both 'tra-ditional' and 'new' media, such as television, newspapers, film and online that Antroutsopoulos (2014, 2016) amongst others (see, e.g. Bauman 1986, 2001; Bell and Gibson 2011; Coupland 2009, 2012, 2014; Gibson 2011; Johnstone 2011; Paizza et al. 2015; Queen 2015) has identified as the *mediatization* of discourse. Whilst the concept of mediatization in sociolinguistic terms remains diffuse, as Androutspoulos (2016) points out, it can be said to relate to the ways in which language is mediated in various ways between the producer and the receiver at one remove in ever increasingly diverse forms, from radio through to social media such as blogs and chat fora and across a whole gamut of genres, from film through to game shows, computer games and political debates. For Androutsopoulos the concept of mediatization can be viewed in one of two main ways: as either refer-ring to the ways in which processes of communication align (or not) with those of commoditization or as: "... large scale, metaprocesses of social and cultural change through the development of communications media" (2016: 294).

Linked to this are questions related to how changes in the media impact upon and change human cultural and linguistic practices and their social formations. Both interpretations include mediation, and point to how mediatized messages are linked with mediated communication. The performances I discuss in this book are thus mediated, in the sense that they have been rehearsed and range from partly to fully scripted ones, but unmediatized in the sense that they occurred in face to face settings with no third party broadcast medium is involved such as radio, TV, film or internet. At the same time, it is very clear that mediatized discourse is drawn upon by the performers throughout their performances. As Androutsopoulos goes on to say (2016: 295), the exploration of which is a key theme in this book: "This association is constituted through metapragmatic stereotypes, which link speech forms with recognizable speaker stereotypes and social contexts of use." It also includes the ways in which typical or exemplary speakers are discursively constructed, and how they can change over time. Androutsopoulos also discusses how mediatized forms of vernacular speech proliferate in a variety of genres that are present in audio visual media such as commercials, film, reality TV shows or soap operas. Fictional genres regularly draw upon register contrasts (discussed further below) as a way of mediatizing their presentation of social types and interpersonal relations, whilst commercials often commodify features of regional dialect by linking them to an advertised product.

Such a perceived vernacularization of English has been the focus of recent research in cultural, media and literary studies, and a corresponding perception of an increased democratization of both linguistic uses and media production itself (Heyd 2010; Hodson 2014; Turner 2010). Hodson in her work on dialect in film and literature, argues for the analysis of dialect use to be an integral part of the fictional world in which it appears, rather than in terms of its real-world accuracy, 'authenticity' or consistency. Drawing upon Coupland's (2007) work, she goes on to argue that issues relating to authenticity in particular should be analysed and explored through the discourses that surround dialect representation, and in their own right. She says that

> I am not proposing that we simply dispense with notion of stereotyping and authenticity. There is clearly space for approaches that attempt to assess how close specific literary or filmic representations are to 'real world' dialects. However, we need to abandon the idea that such judgements can ever be absolute, as well as the idea that representations which lay claim to some real-world 'authenticity' are therefore inherently 'better'. Instead, we need to explore how authenticity is being constructed in particular instances, and investigate who gets to decide what is authentic or not.
> (2014: 236)

To literary or filmic representations can be added representations in live performance. Performers enact different personae, and the Bakhtinian concepts of double-voicing, heteroglossia and polyphony, discussed briefly above and further in Chapter 2, are of central importance to the analysis undertaken in forthcoming chapters, since all performers and writers who draw upon dialect use enact and create fictional worlds through their performances and writing in multi-voiced ways. Bell (2016) also points to the importance of Bakhtin in relation to considering linguistic diversity and a dialogic theory of language. As he points out: "The stabilising, centralising impetus of linguistic standard and convention seeks to define and name languages and is always in tension with the decentralising, momentary, creative use of language" (2016: 8) Chapter 2 picks up on this point further.

1.4 Performance and performativity

For many linguists and linguistic anthropologists in particular, the concept of 'performance' is linked with social constructivism and the construct of 'performativity' (e.g. Baumann and Briggs 1990; Butler 1990, 1997). These concepts have been very influential in the discipline of pragmatics and in discourse analysis more generally. Performance under such a view, encompasses not only 'artful' or 'poetic' uses of language of the kind used in the staged performances at the heart of this book, but also the ways in which language use – and thus dialect use – in general is tied to social action. As Baumann and Briggs say: "A given performance is tied to a number of speech events that precede and succeed it (past performances, readings of texts, negotiations, rehearsals, gossip, reports, critiques, challenges, subsequent performances and the like" (1990: 61).

'Performativity' refers to the ways in which an act of linguistic performance is 'normalised' or 'regularised' through the social systems that construct what it means to be say, a judge, registrar, husband or wife in any given society. It also extends to include the ways in which social norms are constructed and imposed in relation to gender, for example. As Sali (2002: 56) explains, whilst: "… performance presupposes an existing subject, performativity contests the very notion of a subject…there is thus no 'I' outside language, since identity is a signifying practice, and culturally intelligible subjects are the effects rather than the causes of discourses that conceal their workings." Under such a view, the day to day identity construction with which we all routinely engage through social interaction that includes our linguistic performance is thus also performative, since it involves the ritualization and regulation of identity enactment – and sometimes, its disruption.

For the purposes of this book however, issues of 'performance' relate to overt face to face creative, staged performance contexts rather than what might be called routine everyday performance. 'Performativity' relates to the ways in which performers in their performances self-consciously draw upon dialect use in creating various personae as part of the fictional worlds they evoke that in turn, is tied to the speech events that precede and succeed it, any rehearsals that may have taken place and so on. Focusing on live staged performance, the performers who create them and the audiences that receive them, opens up possibilities for investigating the relationship between a performer and his or her audience. This is because performances occur as interactive settings, with feedback from the audience flowing to the performer, and the performer in turn adjusting what they say and how they move, based on the feedback, or lack of it. Such performance and performativity can thus be seen as a kind of 'in-between' zone between casual, face to face conversation and that which is more heavily scripted in relation to most traditional spoken media.

In analysing any performance then, consideration is given to establishing what social events any text is part of, the social practices within which it is framed (Trester 2012; Bauman and Briggs 1990), and whether the performance is part of a chain or network of events. Analysis thus pays attention to considerations such as whether a given performance is situated in a genre chain and/or involves genre mixture; what genres the performances draw upon and their characteristics in relation to the performers' activity and interpersonal relations. It also includes identifying performances orientation to difference in whether or not there is openness and/or acceptance of it; if any attempts are made to overcome difference and if any 'bracketing-off' or consensus of difference can be identified. Vigouroux (2015: 244) points out that any genre is "... intrinsically relational, as it creates indexical connections that extend beyond the setting and the production and reception of performances". Such an approach allows for the assessment of dialogicality and related Bakhtinian concepts of double voicing and polyphony: that is, how far relations between different voices are set up. Such concepts are explored in more detail in Chapter 2. Analysis of performer interviews allows for the performers to have a say for themselves in relation to how they perceive their performances orientation. Analysis of audience interviews allows for investigation into the concept of framing, discussed further in Chapter 2, where how something is presented to an audience influences choices they make about how to process the information received.

1.5 Researching dialect as staged language

Bauman and Briggs (1990) argue that for any analysis of performance to be an adequate one, it requires sensitive ethnographic study of both form and meaning and how both taken together index a broad range of discourse types or genres.

They say that: "Performance-based research can yield insights into diverse facets of language use and their interrelations...studying performance can open up a wider range of vantage points on how language can be structured and what roles it can play in social life" (1990: 61). Although Baumann and Briggs were writing about performance in relation to its everyday use, their words also hold for staged performance, especially in regard to its metapragmatic and reflexive nature. Consequently, the data upon which the analysis upon chapters of this book draw was undertaken through ethnographic study, discussed further in Chapter 2.

Localised performance events are to be found throughout the UK, particularly in densely populated urban areas of the UK, such as those found in the West Midlands region. In addition, other media, especially on the radio, broadcast shows that are targeted at local audiences. For example, until recently, a radio show was broadcast every Sunday evening featuring Black Country poets, writers, musicians, and storytellers, subsequently available as a podcast; a long running BBC Radio West Midlands programme broadcast on Sunday mornings that ran until 2015 was hosted by Carl Chinn, a locally well-known Professor of Social History at the University of Birmingham and dedicated to local affairs and a weekly programme is broadcast on Black Country radio every Sunday afternoon called *omma n chain (hammer and chain)* that comprises locally based music, plays and poetry hosted by a well- known, local singer and songwriter.

Some of the performances discussed in this were performed in the format of established British tradition of Music Hall or Variety shows, similar to American Vaudeville theatre and are indicative of a large part of locally oriented performance activity in the Black Country and Birmingham regions of the West Midlands in particular. Such performances bring together a variety of different acts which together formed an evening of light hearted entertainment. Although similar types of entertainment had been going on for many centuries, Music Hall can be traced back to eighteenth century London's coffee houses and taverns or public houses particularly, which by the early nineteenth century had rooms devoted to musical and performing clubs. Such rooms also became a feature of public houses in rapidly expanding urban areas of the country, including those in the West Midlands. The growth of halls was rapid across Britain through the middle decades of the nineteenth century until changes in the law made a dancing and music licence a requirement for their operation. Even so, they continued as a popular form of entertainment into the early decades of the twentieth century when the advent of radio and television led to their dwindling and eventual dying out. Nevertheless, Music Hall still exist in some parts of the country, of which the English West Midlands is one. 'A Black Country Night Out' is a touring Variety show, that is nostalgic in nature, regularly touring venues in the Black Country and the surrounding West Midlands area. On the third Wednesday evening of every month, poetry readings by local poets are held at Wednesbury Library and similar events occur at other local libraries. The performances discussed in this book then, took place against a wide range of similar activities across the region and as part of its social life.

The performances and related activities were to be attended and recorded within the four west midlands shire counties of Shropshire, Staffordshire, Warwickshire and Worcestershire. Once mainly agricultural and comprised of small towns and villages, from the nineteenth century onwards migration from the neighbouring countryside and beyond to towns and cities had led to a density of population centring particularly upon the areas two major cities, Birmingham and Coventry and their major automobile and aerodynamic industries that continued into well into the twentieth century. This concentration and density of population became such that in the 1970s, a metropolitan borough was superimposed upon those parts of the shire counties in which the urban conurbations of Birmingham and Coventry were located that straddled three of the four counties and called, confusingly, West Midlands. The area covers a region that is approximately 902 square kilometres and at the last census date of 27th March 2011, had a population of 5.6 million, an increase of 6 percent from 2001 when it was 5.3 million. Just under half this number is located in the West Midlands metropolitan county. Also included within these four counties is a region to the west of Birmingham that stretches to the Staffordshire city of Wolverhampton known as the Black Country, as discussed above. Identification of these sites allowed for a comparison to be made in terms of performance activity between the more rural areas of the four shire counties in contrast with the urban areas of Birmingham and the Black Country that existed within them.

Both in demographic and geographic terms then, the region arguably represents the whole of England in microcosm in terms of its mix of urban and rural areas; densely populated cities and sparsely populated villages; flat valleys and ranges of hills; canals and rivers; industrial, rural and technological economies; age profiles and ethnic mix. Staffordshire encompasses within its borders some of the poorest and most affluent areas of the UK, whilst Shropshire, Warwickshire and Worcestershire are made up of large market towns and villages. The one geographic aspect it does lack, however, is the presence of a major river estuary that would have enabled development during the nineteenth century industrial revolution of the kind that took place in other major English cities such as London, Bristol, Newcastle and Liverpool. In its place, a significant network of canals exists across the region that used at one time to transport goods to all areas of the country. Today, the canals and boats that use them, following a period of decay and neglect, are given over to tourism. It is thus the most landlocked region of the UK, with Birmingham being England's second largest city in terms of population.

The intention in the four shire counties had also been to identify two performances to sound record within each of them, one performance in the major town or city of each county and a smaller town or village bordering one of the other counties. However, it soon became apparent that in focusing upon locally based live creative performances as the main focus of data collection, traditional sociolinguistic methods of sampling simply did not work. Identifying performance locations was determined by where the performances actually took place, which turned out to be mainly in the urban centres of Birmingham, the Black Country and the Staffordshire Potteries and rarely in smaller towns and villages. In Shropshire and Worcestershire there was a significant amount of creative activity centred predominantly around folk clubs, writing circles, summer folk festivals. Suh activity though, was found to be non-region specific, in the sense that songs and related performances centred upon past rural and seafaring ways of life that were not tied to any specific British region but rather told stories of rural and sea faring life in general. Performances in rural areas tended to be advertised as localised events but in effect brought together performers from across the country. Any dialect use was thus representative of the areas from which the various performers were drawn, namely from across the UK, rather than tied specifically to the locality in which they took place. No localised performances which were for the local community by locally based performers were found in the more rural counties of Shropshire, or Worcestershire.

This was in stark contrast to the urban areas of Birmingham, the Black Country and the Staffordshire Potteries and to a lesser extent in the city of Coventry, the Warwickshire town of Leamington Spa and neighbouring villages. These urban regions have an industrial heritage dating back to the eighteenth century, centring around close knit communities whose adult population worked mainly in small factories and cottage industries such as chain making (the Black Country) and pottery (Staffordshire Potteries) jewellery in Birmingham amongst host of other trades that led Birmingham to be known in the early part of the 20th century as the city of a thousand trades. This is not in any way to imply that the cultural, economic, social and political processes associated with modernity have not affected rural areas or that 'rural' and 'urban' are perceived of as opposites. Rather, as Britain (2017) observes, it is that their impact is less visible and does not manifest itself in the same ways as it does in urban areas, especially in relation to localised creative performances. The exception to this is the performance of Mummers' plays, discussed in Chapter 5.

The performances discussed in the following chapters were all performed at local venues within the West Midlands region; the performers giving the performance were from the locality and the content of the performance also related to the locality. The demographic from which performers are drawn is such that the majority were white, and predominantly male, with the exception of two all-female theatre groups one of which is discussed in Chapter 3 and black male performers in Birmingham discussed in Chapter 4. The demographic profile of the performers themselves was also dictated by who was actually doing the performing, rather than through any superimposition of traditional sociolinguistic sampling categories of age, class, ethnicity or gender.

Once performers had been identified and contacted via local contacts or through fieldwork visits to all the various localities, meetings took place between a research team member and the performer in advance of any performance being recorded at least once, if not several times. Either myself or a member of the team attended the performance events as members of the audience, and the performance sound recordings were supplemented by conversations about the performance that had been recorded with the performers themselves and wherever possible, members of the audience. Here again things did not go entirely to plan, particularly in relation to talking to members of the audience. It had been envisaged that members of the team would approach members of the audience at events attended, obtain contact information and talk to them at a later date. However, the time frame of events did not lend itself to such a method of data collection. Members of an audience who come to watch a performance are not known in advance and leave as soon as a performance has ended, making it difficult to make contact personally. To mitigate against this, forms were distributed with stamped addressed envelopes, inviting members of the audience get in touch should they be willing to be interviewed but this was met with limited success. As an alternative, 'celebrities' associated with the region both locally and nationally such as actors, playwrights and poets were interviewed instead, to give an additional perspective to that of the performances, on the grounds that they contribute a great deal in terms of public perceptions of accents. These celebrities ranged from Julie Walters and Mark Williams, both internationally acclaimed and recognised actors; Benjamin Zephaniah, a nationally renowned poet through to local playwrights Malcolm Stent and Allan Pollock.

Issues also arose as to what actually counted as a performance. What had at first sight seemed unproblematic and obvious, turned out to be a much more complicated phenomenon. This is because the nature of the performances attended and recorded varied considerably and was not of a homogenous nature. They can be grouped into four different types, in relation to their audiences, the locality and the spaces in which they were performed. Firstly, there are professional performances given by a performer or group of performers as one single event (with an interval) such as the play *Too much pressure* by the local playwright Allan Pollock performed at the Belgrade Theatre in Coventry discussed in Chapter 5 or the semi-professional events recorded at *The Drum* discussed in Chapter 4.

Recordings of such performances were also fraught with permission issues, since permission to record had to be obtained from the playwright and the theatre's production team as well as the actors themselves. Secondly, performances given by a performer as part of a multi-performance event such as an open mic night at a local comedy club often held in public houses or as part of a variety-type event that featured a range of performers with performances linked by a compere. Again, permission issues arose, this time in relation to performers who were not from the region taking part in the performance and whose permission we had not been able to obtain beforehand. Thirdly, during conversations about their creative endeavours with performers or celebrities and especially poets, performers would break into poetry as part of the conversation, as discussed in Chapter 4. Finally, one performance, the Mummers' plays discussed in Chapter 5, was repeated several times in the course of a few days in the town of Leamington Spa and neighbouring villages.

Such issues notwithstanding, over a period of three years, from 2009 until 2012, contacts were made and established with performers, and several meetings and conversations took place between the fieldworkers and performers, and very often, performances attended before any actual recording of a performance took place. The total spoken data set collected was as follows:

a) Performance data: 36 performance events were recorded (31.5 hours in total), the majority of which were in the locations of Birmingham, The Black Country, Coventry, the Staffordshire Potteries, Leamington Spa and its neighbouring villages in Warwickshire.

b) Conversation interview data 1: 28 recordings of performers (20 hours) talking about their performance;

c) Conversation interview data 2: 19 recordings of members of the audience (7.5 hours) talking about the performance they had attended;

d) Conversation interview data 3: 36 recordings (21 hours) of local and national public creative artists and personalities talking about the dialect in question in relation to their own experiences.

The discussion that follows from Chapter 3 onwards, clearly demonstrates that different speaker groups and the individuals that comprise them, do indeed rationalise dialect features in ways that can carry different ideological meanings for individuals and different groups. Dialect features can also be exploited and rationalised in performances to expose different ideological meanings, largely through performers subverting or reversing conventional stereotypes associated with the region in question in their performances. Locating the research within specific discourse practices allows for linguistic variables associated with both dialect and register manifested in performance to be identified and examined in the context of that performance. Accompanying analysis of conversations with the performers, members of the audience at their performances and well-known artists associated with the region, identifies the extent to which audiences, performers and other artists are aware of dialect being used in enregistered ways.

The next chapter, in addition to elaborating further on the Bakhtinian concept of double voicing and polyphony discuss other related theoretical concepts that are relevant to both the ways in which data was collected and subsequently analysed. In contemporary English, it is clear that dialect use has become increasingly double voiced and polyphonic. The twin concepts of 'indexicality' and 'enregisterment' are particularly relevant in this regard, and are explained further in the next chapter. Building on the work of Bauman and Briggs (1990) and used most recently by Trester (2012) in the context of language play amongst a community of improvisational (improv) theatre, I draw upon the concepts of 'framing' and 'intertextuality' in examining how performance texts are shaped and reshaped, decontextualized, encontextualised and recontextualised and cued through framing. 'Intertextuality' refers to the relationship between texts and like Trester, I draw on the work of the literary theorist Bakhtin (1981[1971], 1984a, 1948b) understood by Kristeva (1980), Fairclough (1992) and Johnstone (2002) as intertextuality. Trester (2012: 238) in the context of improv, discusses intertextuality in relation to the ways in which performers notice 'incidents' in their day to day interactions, shelve or store them to be recalled and retrieved at a later date and woven into performances. She draws upon Baumann and Briggs' (1990) terminology and identification of the process of intertextuality by which paying attention to texts renders them extractable (entextualising them); moving them from their original interactional context (decontextualising them) and using them again as and when the opportunity arises (recontextualising them).

Chapters 3 to 5 focus on performances and related conversation interviews from within specific areas of the West Midlands region. Chapter 3 discusses comedy performances in a predominantly white ethnic context of Birmingham and The Black Country whilst the focus of Chapter 4 is a black ethnic context in Birmingham. This chapter also discusses the emergence of a hybrid dialect from across different geographic places around the world, notably Birmingham, London and The Caribbean, I have called *Black Brum*. Chapter 5 moves on to consider the performance of dramatic plays in two different contexts, those of a professional theatre performance and an amateur performance of Mummers' Plays performed several times in public houses on consecutive nights in the Warwickshire town of Leamington Spa and surrounding villages. Chapter 6 brings discussion to a close, identifying common threads throughout the performances and accompanying interview conversations.

2 Further theoretical considerations

2.1 Introduction

In this chapter I provide theoretical framing over and above that outlined in Chapter 1 which further underpins discussion in the ensuing three chapters. Beginning with a discussion of grounded theory and ethnography, the remaining sections discuss key concepts that have emerged from the data in addition to the overarching perspectives discussed in Chapter 1. These are: indexicality and enregisterment; heteroglossia, polyphony and double-voicing; reference, frames, the burlesque and carnivalesque. Discussion of specific dialect features in the chapters that follow then, are considered in the light of this conceptual framework. The chapter ends with a discussion of a theoretical issue related to data preparation, namely that of transcription.

2.2 Grounded theory and ethnography

Grounded theory as originally conceived by Glaser and Strauss ([1967]1999) is one that presupposes research should have no *a priori* assumptions from its outset (see also Hammerlsey 2006, 2007a and 2007b). However, one has to start somewhere and scholars such as Hutchison, Johnston and Breckon (2010) support using knowledge that is generally discipline based (see also Charmaz 2014; Martin and Gynnild 2011). Charmaz and Mitchell (2007: 160) point out that one of the main advantages of grounded theory is that it allows for flexible strategies to be developed in relation to both theoretical perspectives to be employed in relation to frameworks for data analysis and preparation as well as the collection of data itself. They say that grounded theory builds upon a: '…symbolic interactionist theoretical perspective and constructivist methods that assume existence of multiple realities, the mutual creation of knowledge by researchers and research participants, and aims to provide interpretative understanding of the studies world.'

Grounded theory research is thus not linear, allowing for moments and flashes of insight and instant realizations of analytic connections to occur at any time during the research process, up to and including writing it up for publication in a book such as this. Its methods aim to provide flexible yet systematic guidelines for the collection and subsequent analysis of qualitative data, thereby allowing for theories to be constructed from analysis as well as being applied to it. Grounded theory thus begins with inductive data, and includes the use of iterative strategies going back and forth between literature reviews, methods of data

https://doi.org/10.1515/9781501506796-002

collection and identifying frameworks for data analysis, of the kind discussed in this chapter and the previous one. Above all, it keeps the researcher constantly interacting and engaging with literature, data and emerging analysis. It thus allows for an interactional approach to be a fundamental one in every part of the research process, both in terms of how data is collected and subsequently analysed. An inductive enquiry method such as grounded theory also allows for an interdisciplinary approach to analysis, since concepts are chosen for what they bring to the study of the data via consideration of the data itself, rather than any set of predetermined categories.

An ethnographic approach to data collection also allows for an interpretative dimension to the study of everyday social practices in ways that take account not only of the wider social practices and structures within which any study takes place but also how such practices and structures are discursively constructed (Copland et al. 2015; Hoey 2013; Rampton 2011; Tusting and Maybin 2007; Johnstone 2002, 2004; Eckert 2000). Social life is constructed through and in discourse, and a combination of linguistics and ethnography brings together, as Rampton, Maybin and Roberts (2015) say, contexts for communication that should be investigated rather than assumed, with the internal organisation of semiotic resources being examined in detail. In ethnographically oriented research of the kind discussed here, the nature of the relationship between the researcher and researched is conceived in terms of co-participation, in that the researcher is part of the discursive event which they are researching, in this case, face to face creative performance. The researched, in turn, is also a participant in the research.

However, one danger of both grounded and ethnographic approaches is that openness can lead to considering every possible theoretical option being considered in relation to data collection and analysis that can prove very time consuming and unsystematic. Another drawback is, that without a predetermined data set to be collected, the sheer volume of that collected can become overwhelming. Like Trester (2012: 238–9), writing in relation to her experiences with improvisational theatre performers in Washington, D.C., I found the ethnographic process of discovery was accompanied by periods of confusion and found myself getting lost at various junctures in the process. Grounded theory helped me overcome issues that are often raised in relation to ethnographic fieldwork, namely seeing data everywhere and nowhere. This can lead to the gathering of mountains of unconnected data, much of which is left undigested and can lead to its analysis being little more than low-level description. Strategies drawn from grounded theory can thus help ethnographic research by emphasising comparative methods such as comparing data from the beginning of the research and not waiting until after it has all been collected, and to compare data with emerging categories to demonstrate relations between concepts and categories. Ethnographic methods have tended to separate data collection from its subsequent analysis, whilst grounded theory allows for an open-ended approach to studying the empirical world. It also adds a degree of rigour in building in checks into collection and analysis, as described later in this section. Grounded theory thus mitigated against identified issues that dog an ethnographic approach such as lengthy, unfocussed forays into fieldwork settings, the random, superficial collection of data and identification of coding categories. Grounded theory also allows for ethnography as a research process to be iterative rather than linear, and allows for the possibility of changes to the original research design to be accommodated.

Even with ethnographic research undertaken in a grounded theory paradigm one has to start somewhere, and choices have to be made in terms of research design which in this instance, were in relation to identifying fieldwork locations centred upon instances of creative performances performed in local contexts; access to the number of performances to be attended and recorded and access to performers and members of the audience to be interviewed. My original research design had been configured in a more traditional sociolinguistic paradigm, with sampling frames devised that related to the age, gender and ethnicity of the performers. However, through engaging with an ethnographic approach it quickly became clear that the social world of creative, face to face entertainment does not lend itself very easily or readily – in fact, not at all – to the imposition of such sampling frames. An ethnographic approach to research supported by grounded theory has the value of allowing for issues such as fieldwork locations and sampling to be re-thought and accommodated as part of the research process. For example, my original intention had been to record two staged performances in each of five fieldwork locations within the West Midlands, as outlined in Chapter 1, one urban and one rural. However, during the course of visiting potential fieldwork locations, it became apparent that there was a stark contrast in performance activity between urban and rural regions, discussed in more detail in Chapter 5. I found a stark polarity between urban regions and the countryside in relation to instances of staged performance that linked to place. In the shire counties of Shropshire and Warwickshire in particular, there were plenty of folk clubs and folk festivals to be found. However, the acts that performed at such events were not particularly local since they drew in performers from a wide area and, in the case of folk festivals, from across the UK. Their unifying factor was that the acts performed celebrated largely rural ways of living that had existed in the past and live on through the life of the imagination wrought by such events. One such performance discussed in Chapter 5 performed in the Warwickshire town of Leamington Spa and neighbouring villages is the performance of Mummer's Plays. In stark contrast to such events, performances by local performers that were designed to be performed in front of a local audience were found in densely populated urban areas of Birmingham, the Black Country, Coventry and Stoke-on-Trent. Equally, sampling in relation to age and gender also proved problematic, since performers were drawn mainly from an age range between early 20s and late 60s and in relation to gender, were largely male. The one unifying factor across all such performances was in relation to social class, in that all performers or playwrights self-reported being born to working class parents or having lived from an early age in working class communities but had become, through education and employment, affiliated with the middle class.

A grounded theoretical approach meant that identification of dialect features has emerged from the transcription of the data and its subsequent analysis, rather than through having a pre-determined set of linguistic features superimposed onto it. Specific dialect features therefore are considered in the context of the discussion of performances as they appear, rather than being listed here. Further key categories for analysis then, briefly touched upon in Chapter 1, are firstly *indexicality* and *enregisterment*, particularly as these relate to the metapragmatic and reflexive nature of dialect use present in performances and identifying the linguistic tokens through which the concepts are manifested. Secondly, the work of the cultural theorist Bakhtin complements these categories through a consideration of the essentially *dialogic, discursive* and *polyphonic* and *multi-voiced* nature of language use vis a vis the hegemonic forces that maintain, perpetuate and uphold the social forces underpinning the largely negative attitudes and prejudices people hold towards regional dialect use, especially that of the West Midlands region. The very fact that some people feel the need to accommodate their speech while others do not and the extent to which some people dialect-switch and others not, points to the underlying hegemonic forces that govern accommodation theory but also to its resistance. Thirdly, since dialect occurs in a creative, discursive context of staged performance that invites imagined communities, then concepts drawn from discourse analysis and stylistics, namely *frame* and *perspective* and the *burlesque* and *carnivalesque* are also drawn upon as relevant in relation to how different personae and identities are constructed and how linguistic tokens are indexicalised and enregistered. The following sections take each of these conceptual categories in turn and elaborates on them further.

2.3 Indexicality and enregisterment

The twin concepts of indexicality and enregisterment have come increasingly to provide ways to account for the complex interaction between linguistic variation and social and geographic mobility. They identify the degrees to which speakers and writers draw upon language as belonging to a specific social group in varying degrees of metapragmatic awareness and self-reflexivity ways as well as the linguistic tokens themselves (Agha 2003; Adams 2009; Beal 2009; Clark 2013b; Johnstone 2016, 2019). Traditionally, dialect use has been perceived in terms of relatively stable sets of linguistic conventions or rules that can be mapped onto social and physical spaces. *Dialects* map onto geographic space and *sociolects* onto demographically defined groups that are generally linked at a national, rather than regional, level. Through the range of linguistic features any one of us employs in relation to both dialect and register, we can thus be identified with a specific place and/or group onto which any regional or social dialect maps. However, sociolinguists' work over the past ten years or so has led to a greater degree of problematization. As Johnstone (2014: 290) says: "We now ask questions about why people use features of one variety or another, rather than assuming that people inevitably speak the way they first learnt to speak, and the answers we arrive at have to do with identity and agency rather than only with geography and demography." The key question then, is not only to establish the ways in which particular words, pronunciations, grammatical patterns and prosodic features such as intonation point to – or index – particular activities and identities, but also *why*. Drawing upon semiotics and the works of Roman Jakobson and Charles S. Pierce, anthropologists Silverstein (1992, 1993, 2003) and Agha (2003, 2007), have developed a framework that links linguistic choice to social meaning and how sets of linguistic choices can be construed as varieties of linguistic use that relate to both dialect and register as discussed in Chapter 1.

The concept of indexicality as proposed by Silverstein refers to the essential connection between micro-analytic and macro-analytic phenomena and frames of analysis. Micro-analytic phenomena are those identified in specific utterances in speech or lexical/morphosyntactic items in writing, and subsequently analysed in relation to linguistic frameworks associated with conversation/discourse analysis and pragmatics. Macro-analytic phenomena include social categories such as age, ethnicity and gender or social partitioning and associated cultural values such as rich and poor, citizen and alien. The interconnection between the micro- and macro- phenomena is an essential one, in that the micro-order is neither autonomous nor independent of the macro-order but rather embedded within it. The wider socio-cultural contexts within which indexicality is marked, therefore and as discussed in Chapter 1, is as important as the individual or sets of linguistic variables themselves.

The contexts in which micro-phenomena occur, whilst being embedded within the wider macro-order, can be said to be mediated through an intermediate or mezzo-analytic contexts and phenomena (Androutsopoulos 2010). That is, the groups or networks to which individuals belong, from the immediate family or primary carer group to widening (or narrowing) familial groups across an individual's life span together with the varying communities of practice and social networks with which any one individual' also engage across their life span. Mezzo-phenomena thus interconnect with both macro- and micro- phenomena at any given moment in a person's life. At the same time, interconnections may change across a person's life span.

Ochs' (1992) theory of indexicality, although related specifically to gender, shares many similarities with that of Silverstein. Och writes that the relationship between language and gender "...is constituted and mediated by the relation of language to stances, social acts, social activities and other constructs" (1992: 337). The same can also be said of the relationship between language and any social category, since arguably they are all constituted and mediated in and through discourse. As Och goes on to point out, anthropological and sociological studies of language assume that (a) language across a whole range of social contexts varies in systematic ways that can be studied in relation to their linguistic meaning and (b) variation is part of the meaning indexed by linguistic structures and gives rise to social meaning. Thus, as discussed in Chapter 1, two or more phonological variants of the same word such as a long /a/ or short /a/ in a word such as *bath* may share the identical referent of the word *bath* but convey different social meanings. In this case, in the UK, the long /a/ has long been associated with being from the South and more 'posh' and middle class than the short /a/ which is associated with being from the North and working class.

A more salient example is that of the pronunciation of the sounds /g/ and /s/ at the beginning and end of the word *genres*. The word is French in origin, pronounced in French with a soft /g/ with the /s/ left silent and voiceless. British people who retain the French pronunciation when speaking the word index an education of which learning a modern foreign language and French in particular, has been a part. Generally speaking, it is also an index of a more cultural sophistication associated with the middle classes than the pronunciation of the word with a hard /g/ and the /s/ pronounced. Such a pronunciation indexes an education in which learning French had little or no part and usually indicative of a working class background, even where the speaker has an undergraduate degree in media studies and teaches secondary school English where the study of genre/s looms large.

The social meaning of such differences in pronunciation is not hard to fathom out. As Och points out, competent members of any community interpret such meanings by and large unconsciously as part of the processes of socialisation. However, dialect features can also be drawn upon in deliberate, self-conscious ways to enact and evoke particular social meanings that also point to people's acute awareness of socialization processes, as the performances discussed in this book show. One of the consequences of increased access to education and ensuing social mobility for example, has led to a destabilising or disruption of traditional social categories such as those of age, ethnicity, gender and social class (Llamas and Watts 2009; Bigham 2012 amongst others). Whilst earlier sociolinguistic research correlated dialect use with non-linguistic variables such as social class, changes in social organisation and structure from the mid twentieth century onwards have led to this correlation being loosened and weakened. For example, many of the performers, as well as audience members and celebrities discussed in the later chapters of this book, self-reported as having both a working- and middle- class affiliation. The working-class affiliation was given in relation to the social class into which they had been born, their family backgrounds and histories, in contrast to the middle class affiliation they had come to hold in adult life through educational opportunity and social mobility of the kind that previous generations had been denied.

Dialect use in such performances thus indexes a geographic place, an industrial working- class family history and a middle-class present *at one and the same time*. Such use can function indexically to trigger an association with a place, its largely past working-class culture and industrial heritage. Enregistered features thus may also stand in place of the dialect as a whole. In this way, an urban working-class identity once manifested through manual labour has in contemporary post-industrial times, transferred to language instead. For example, a local West Midlands newspaper called *The Black Country Bugle* undertook a survey in 2011 into aspects of Black Country identity. The response with the greatest number was identity in relation to the area's accent and dialect. It is also clear that the extent to which performers draw upon any one dialect feature also alters situationally, as the conversations with performers, audience members and celebrities testify. Some performers may accommodate their dialect use the further away from the region they perform and use it less; others, like the Jamaican poet Benjamin Zephaniah, ensure that they are retained. The general public at large, it would seem, and especially those who come from a working-class background, are all too well aware of the ways in which they accommodate their speech to the situation in which they find themselves, or dialect switch accordingly. The closer to family and home, the greater the use of regional accent and dialect; the further away or more public the context, such as work and work related functions beyond the immediate region, the less they may feature and disappear altogether, or not.

People may thus choose, either consciously or unconsciously, to level out any previously existing dialect in their speech or, in the case of celebrities such as the British actress Julie Walters, the Afro Caribbean poet Benjamin Zephaniah or Carl Chinn, Professor of Social History and well known locally in Birmingham, deliberately enregister region specific variables in their speech to index a place identity and resist accommodation. Thus, dialect use in the context of creative performance is always highly indexical, since it is drawn upon in double-voiced and self-reflexive ways, as the performers themselves testify. Indexicality can also account not only for the ways in which individual variables linked to a single place connect across and within a standardised form of a language such as English, but also multiple places and spaces, as Chapter 4 explores further.

Whilst indexicality refers to general processes and stages of linguistic aware-ness and reflexivity, Agha's (2005, 2007) concept of *enregisterment* refers to the specific forms used in discourse. Specific regional forms are enregistered – for example Pittsburghese /aw/ (Johnstone & Keisling 2008) or Brummie /ing/, discussed further in Chapter 3, to mark a sense of place identity and dislocated from social immobility. Enregistered forms are thus drawn from highly codified lists to perform local identity, which in performance are often drawn upon in comic, mocking, ironic or semi-serious ways to undercut dominant ideologies linked to linguistic and social hierarchies, as the following chapters make clear. As Adams (2009: 116) has pointed out, the relationship enregisterment con-structs between theory and detail is an invaluable one, since it brings together and synthesizes virtually every aspect of studying speech in whichever dialect of English is under scrutiny, including the historic, cultural and methodological aspects, alongside linguistic elements of discourse, style, phonology, lexis and syntax. Enregisterment also allows agency and structure to be taken into account in considering the conscious use of dialect in creative performance that can be seen as an act of indexing identity through the enregistering of specific linguis-tic variables, particularly if used by legitimate speakers of the dialect. Johnstone in particular has explored how linguistic variation can be enregistered with identities, personas and styles. She develops Agha's (2007) notion of the 'charac-terlogical figure' and takes up Agha's point that: "...a linguistic feature or a set of features can be ideologically linked via enregisterment with a way of being and acting associated not just with a social identity in an abstract sense, but with its embodiment in a character, imagined or actually performed" (2016: 285).

For example, through an analysis of two talking dolls called the *Yapping Yinzers* and the website advertising them, Johnstone discusses how their social identities are represented in fictional biographies, and how they invite their consumers "...to re-enregister a set of forms that are already enregistered with place known as 'Pittsburghese' with a particular communicative style and stance associated with a post-industrial stereotype of the working class" (2016: 290) She shows how their characterlogical figures can be evaluated in at least one of two ways, namely as a positive valorization of a working class Pittsburghese past or as an image of the stigmatization of post working class Pittsburghese. In the performances discussed in the following three chapters, personae are enacted in ways that are very similar to Johnstone's characterlogical figures of the Yinzer dolls. However, rather than the polarisation of the evaluation identified by Johnstone, I show how performers and writers link dialect and place whilst *at the same time* also subvert the ways in which the social stereotypes they enact are represented by dialect itself. Furthermore, use of dialect in the performances discussed often juxtaposes the norms and values of those 'outside' the community – in terms of both social class and geographic distance – with those 'within' it, thereby identifying with a cultural and social normativity which may be at odds with those from 'outside' it. They do this in ways which aim to subvert ideologies of social class and linguistic 'correctness', through the use of the very phenomenon which is stigmatised: enregistered forms of the dialect itself (Clark 2013b). Valorizations of a working class urban, West Midlands past and present are often accompanied by a self-reflexive increase in enregistered dialect features that also indicate its stigmatiziation, as discussion shows.

2.4 Linguistic hegemony, heteroglossia, polyphony, double- and multi-voicing

A further theoretical aspect of the research is in relation to the ideological implications underpinning discursive practice and the contexts in which it takes place. A useful concept here in terms of the relationship between language and ideology can be thought of in a more developed way is through taking account of concepts such as 'hegemony' drawn from the work of the Italian philosopher Antonio Gramsci (1995 [1971]); those of 'unitary language', 'polyphony', 'double voicing', 'multivoicing' and 'dialogicity' attributed the Russian cultural critic Mikhail Bakhtin, also writing under the pseudonym of Voloshinov. I also draw upon Bakhtin's concept of 'polyphony' that also contribute to Kristeva's (1996) notion of 'intertextuality' and Bakhtin's concept of 'double voiced discourse' (1984). Kristeva developed Bakhtin's spatialization of literary language, arguing that: "...each word (text) is an intersection of other words (texts) where at least one other word (text) can be read" (1996: 65). That is, all manifestations of language, whether spoken or written, are in dialogue, are dialogic, linking in and across one another across time and space in a tissue and web of intertextuality.

One important intertextual element of dialect use in performance is how such use intersects with standard English and its underlying hegemonic ideology. Despite the fact that the ideological nature of the standardisation of English in England has been well documented (e.g., Agha 2007; Crowley 2003 [1989], 1991, 1996; Clark, 2001; Hackett 2012) and that dictionaries and grammars of English are now corpus based upon how language is actually used, the underlying hegemonic ideology of standard English still persists in the minds of the public at large. It is also very clear that the linguistic norms associated with standard English are predicated upon and replicate white, cultural hegemony. Yet, at the same time, the disruption of hegemony is evident in the linguistic landscapes surround us physically and materially in the places where we live (Blommaert 2010; Coupland 2007; Scollon and Scollon 2003), particularly urban ones. As Coupland and Garret says: "Linguistic landscapes are visualisations of (mainly urban) modernity, and they can bring very different qualities of the contemporary urban experience into focus" (2010: 78).

Linguistic landscapes that draw upon dialect features of a regional dialect or words and script from other languages, especially in public displays such as shop signs, writing on mugs and t-shirts, posters, graffiti and so on, often link language to place. This can be as localised as the *Welcome to Brum, Babs* graffiti opposite Birmingham coach station in the centre of the city as discussed in Chapter 1 to the signage of a men's barbers' shop in an ethnically diverse suburb that offers its services in a range of different languages and their associated scripts. Equally, the voices we hear in entertainment and public broadcasting, far from being homogenous as they once were, now celebrate both global and regional diversity in English accents. However, such a broadening only goes so far, and is largely confined to the world of entertainment and has not as yet permeated many other dominant discourses such as those of the law and government with a few notable exceptions.

Language then, is involved in the production of a sense of place rather than an 'expression' of it. On the one hand place can signify a specific physical and material reality expressed linguistically through linguistic features associated with a particular place location and national and/or regional identity, be it the USA, Canada or India for example. On the other hand, indexes of place such as shop signs, those found on religious buildings and so on can signify a connection to a physical space that is in an entirely different geographic location. Consequently, the notion of community or place as being bound physically by material space is no longer tenable in today's world. Within say, Australia, Europe (including the UK) and USA, streets within a community – especially in large towns and cities – relate more to countries of origin than to their host community, to the wider neighbourhood and the nation within which they live. Communities are also subject to demographic change, and in addition to the post working class communities who draw upon dialect to maintain a link with their working-class past, so too do performers of black Afro Caribbean origin to create new, urban dialects of English, such as that discussed in Chapter 5, and identified as *Black Brum*. Performers who were born in the West Midlands city of Birmingham of Afro Caribbean heritage, interweave aspects of Jamaican patwa of their parents' generation with a restricted set of features drawn from the accent and dialect of their peers in both Birmingham and London.

In today's world and in the case of a country such as England, it is less and less likely that speakers speak consistently in a regional accent and dialect of that language. It is far more likely, depending upon any one individual's backgrounds, that s/he will either draw upon both to varying degrees (most likely if from a working-class background) or speak standard English consistently (most likely if from a middle-class background with English as a first language or as bilingual with English and another language from birth). As Chapter 1 has discussed, such a polyphonic use of language (discussed further below) has been the subject of much debate and different conceptualisations such crossing, translanguaging and metrolingualism. Such debates all point to a shift in our conceptual thinking about language(s) and dialects in ways that challenge the concept of linguistic hegemony and the notion that a language such as English or any dialect of it is perceived as: "... static, 'fixed', totalised and immobile to being thought of as dynamic, fragmented and mobile, with the focus upon mobile resources rather than immobile languages" (Blommaert 2010: 197). Blommaert's view that languages are ideological constructions which shift according to changes in hegemony and associated historical events and cultural practices are echoed by others such as Pennycook and Otsuji (2015). Such work is reminiscent of Bakhtin's through the emphasis upon the inherently social construction of both spoken and written language behaviour, and that part of the meaning of any utterance (whether spoken or written) is its social history, as well as its present and future. In relation to studying dialect use then, Bakhtin's theory of language in particular is an important one, since it brings to it a historical dimension of social meaning.

Bakhtin (1981), writing in his essay *The Dialogic Imagination*, makes the point that: "A common unitary language is a system of linguistic norms. But these norms do not constitute an abstract imperative; they are rather the generative forces of linguistic life..." (1981: 61). In other words, the norms that constitute a standard form of a language and its related sociolect such as English are not intrinsic to the language itself. Rather, they have developed over a long period of time, supported by mediated hegemonic practices and regulated and reproduced through education, the media, publishing and so on. In contrast to the concept of unitary language, Bakhtin goes on to say that: "At any given moment in its evolution, language is stratified not only into linguistic dialects in the strictest sense of the word... but also...into languages that are socio-ideological: languages of social groups, 'professional' and 'generic' languages; languages of generations and so forth" (1981: 271–2). Although Bakhtin was concerned with literary representations of language in the novel, his concept of unitary language is a useful one here in that it underlines the ways in which language varieties are associated with different social groups with different ideological perspectives.

The term Bakhtin uses for the multiplicity of language varieties is *heteroglossia*. He argues that any language exists in a state of continual tension between the hegemonic forces that promote unity in a language he terms *monoglossia* and the multiplicity of dialects of which it is actually comprised. Regional dialects and sociolects that comprise of language such as English then, are in a constant interplay of tension of which the performers and writers discussed in the chapters of this book are perfectly aware and which they exploit to the full in their performances and written texts.

Bakhtin also makes the point that utterances may have several *voices*, in so far as there can be a speaker's or writer's voice, the voice of someone referred to within the utterance, the voice of another on whose behalf a message is being relayed and so on. In this way, the voices of any speaker/writer and that of others can be blended in the course of any utterance and become part of the social meaning indexed as part of it. Bakhtin calls this phenomenon *double-voiced discourse*. Although Bakhtin considered this concept in relation to the study of drama and literature, he was also keenly aware of the ways in which double voiced discourse can also occur in the day to day speech of our ordinary lives, and he often related the language of literature to that of everyday speech genres. Double voicing is thus to do with identifying different semantic intentions uttered by the same speaker or writer, and is to be found within all forms of cultural production whether literate or non-literate, highbrow or popular, verbal and nonverbal.

Baxter (2014) draws upon Bakhtin in relation to her work on language and gender in institutional settings, and makes the point that the significance of double voiced discourse has much to offer in relation to sociolinguistic research and not been as fully appreciated as it might have been to date. As Baxter goes on to point out, identifying double-voicing in discourse is not as straightforward a task as identifying its grammatical, lexical and phonological components or indeed its pragmatic ones, since it is highly bound by its context, and identifying it requires a certain amount of ethnographic and localised knowledge. Thus, whilst double voicing might make use and draw upon linguistic features such as impersonation, hedging, humour, politeness, and paralinguistic ones of intonation, pauses, pitch, volume and so on, none of these are *in or of themselves* instances of double voicing. However, there is a sense in which double voicing is present in any staged performance, since performers are taking on voices of someone else in their performances. More often than not, especially in stand-up comedy, performances are multi-voiced.

Bakhtin, like other influential social-constructivist theorists such as Vygotsky and Halliday, do not take a Saussurian perspective of separating language from consciousness or thought. Rather, he views consciousness as inherently dialogic in nature, constructed through assimilating and hearing the discourses and words of others with whom we as individuals interact from the moment we are born such as parents, siblings, peers, co-workers, members of political and religious groups, the media, social media and so on. As individuals, we assimilate and processed dialogically the discourses with which we are surrounded so that they become part of any one individual's repertoire, drawn partly from discursive practices with which any individual engages and partly their own (Bakhtin 1981: 345). As a person matures, an individual's language works in more discriminate and experimental ways, albeit generally within the dialogically discursive and pragmatic norms within which any speech act occurs. Double voicing can also be found at all levels of discourse, from the micro-level of an individual's *inner speech* and interpersonal relationships through to the meso-level of any individual's interaction with members of a community, social group or network through to the macro-level of changes in language and social movements. Every time a person speaks or writes, s/he is negotiating an identity and in relation to the context within which the speech act takes place, whether professional or social, by using a range of discourse strategies such as authoritative language, humour, politeness and so on to achieve their goals. Choice of discursive strategies in turn, links to and signifies wider social-cultural aspects of an individual's identity such as age, ethnicity, gender, social class and status in ways that may either constrain or enhance their interactions with others (Baxter 2014; Clifton 2012). The difference between such day to day performative acts of identity construction in which we all as individuals engage and performers' creative performance is that the latter is self, rather than unconscious.

Double-voicing can thus also be thought of in terms of multi-voicing, since double-voicing implies a binary relationship between two discourses, when in fact Bakhtin's concept of heteroglossia and others such as polyphony point to plural or multi-voiced dimensions of discourse. More relevant, perhaps, is the concept of polyphony in relation to heteroglossia and the power issues implicit therein. Whilst Baxter has drawn upon Bakhtin's work in relation to language and gender in institutional settings and others such as Rampton (1995, 2011) to adolescent multi-ethnic groups, like Vigouroux (2015) I draw upon it in relation to face to face staged performance performed in a variety of adult group settings, since it is particularly relevant to the ideological/power dimension of dialect use. There is a sense in which any performer in enacting a creative performance is double- or multi-voicing in the sense that they are an individual taking on different personae as the performance contexts demands. Often, but not always, performances are also draw on the comic genre in undercutting the ideological aspects of linguistic hegemony.

2.5 Comedy, parody, humour, the burlesque, carnivalesque and dialect

In terms of genre, all of the performances considered in this book are in the overarching form of fictional narratives. Fictional narratives that draw upon dialect use tend to be dubbed 'working class', in opposition to those spoken or written in standard English that are 'middle class'. Such a distinction serves to isolate the dialogue in a text unnecessarily from its broader sociological context, and monologises that which is essentially dialogic. However, speaking or writing in dialect – or in literary terms the demotic or vernacular (Turner 2011) – can be viewed as a direct challenge to conventional assumptions about the ways in which narratives in standard English mediate the world. Narratives employing dialect mediate the world in a different way and through a different social lens than those spoken or written entirely in standard English. Rather than dubbing such narrative 'working class', they can be viewed in terms of not only Bakhtin's concept of the *carnivalesque* (1968/1984) but also Burke's (1984 [1937/1959]) notion of *burlesque* and the corresponding *frames* of acceptance and rejection.

The performances I discuss in Chapters 3 and 4 can be classed poetically as comedy. One very obvious way in which comedians subvert dominant ideologies in their performances is through the use of humour. Linguistically oriented theories of humour focus particularly upon ambiguity and bi-sociation. As Goatly (2012: 21) points out, ambiguity has long been recognised as essential for most kinds of humour and bi-sociation stresses the incongruent nature of humour. He cites the work of Attardo (2001) where a situation or an idea is represented and intended to be perceived in two self-consistent but habitually incompatible frames of reference, in ways that are similar to the discussion of frames and reference discussed above. These frames are also referred to as 'scripts' or 'schemas', in relation to the ways in which we store stereotypical knowledge about events, actions and beliefs in and about the world. Humour more often than not involves telling jokes, the structure of which includes a setup, an incongruity and a resolution, in which a disjuncture or punchline introduces an incongruity (Goatly 2012: 22). In a similar vein and in the context of discussing performing Pittsburghese in relation to comedic performance on the radio, Johnstone says that such performance: "... creates multiple possibilities for the enregisterment of unexpected linguistic forms, so that different audience members may draw on different cultural schemata to make these forms meaningful" (2013: 212). She goes on to make the point that linking locally occurring linguistic forms onto multiple models of action, behaviour and speech can act as a centrifugal force. That is, performances may extend the range of potential meanings associated with particular language forms. This is particularly the case when linguistic forms as well as performance content in comedy are used satirically, and the extent to which performers invite audiences to look beyond the laughter to any underlying satirical message.

The performances discussed in Chapters 3 and 4 also accord with Bakhtin's concept of the *carnivalesque* about which he wrote in relation to his work on the novelists Rabelais and Dostoevsky. In these works, Bakhtin emphasises the tradition of folk humour in the grotesque aspects of Rabelais' writing which he traces to a 'folk spirit' that is anti-authoritarian, dissident and subversive strand of medieval and Renaissance culture that found expression in vents like Bacchanalian excess, May Day celebrations and working-class riots. The multi-voicedness Bakhtin attributes to the carnival folk spirit can be seen to run contrary to the monologic discourse of authority that emanates from the standard language of the 'centre of power', whether that be the Church, the Law or in Bakhtin's case, the excesses of Stalinist political oppression. As Scott (2016: 319) writes: "Against this official language of the centre arises a Babel-like cacophony of voices and discourses which compete with and feed from each other in a complex and ever-evolving discoursal system." In Saussurean terms, Scott goes on to say, carnival can be viewed as both a signifier and a signified. It can be the object of representation and more crucially, its means: the sketch and its narrative method As Scott says:

> The link between these two aspects of carnival – the inherently-rebellious aspects of popular culture and the conversations of style and narrative technique – could be defined as follows: so-called classical realism and its modes of representation came to be associated with what Vice refers to as the 'specular' (1997: 182) or transparent, aspiring to a form of objectivity and narratorial covertness, and, by inference, with discourses of authority: the hegemony of standard English, third-persona, past tense narrative voice which intones 'THIS IS WHAT HAPPENED. THIS IS HOW IT WAS.' We see through the windowpane of the heterodiegetic narrative voice, straight into the fictional world that lies beyond...The carnival, in its infiltration of both the object and mode of representation, attempts to show this assumption about how narrative fiction works to be false. It infects the pseudo-specular, standard English narrative discourse with the demotic vernacular of both its object and its subjects or constituency: characters and readers.
> (2016: 320)

Or, in the case of live performance, characters and spectators rather than readers. Drawing attention to dialect, or in literary terms the demotic or vernacular, functions as a direct challenge to conventional assumptions about the ways in which narratives in standard English mediate the world. Scott's arguments are made in relation to the English Midlands author Alan Sillitoe, whose work represents lives of working class people and is thus dubbed 'working class fiction.' He argues that to dub such narratives as 'working class' is to isolate the text unnecessarily from its broader sociological context, and to monologise that which is essentially dialogic. Rather than 'working class', he argues that the works of a writer such as Sillitoe be seen as carnivalesque. Performances given by performers who draw upon dialect can also be viewed in the same way. For example, in the first performance discussed in Chapter 3, the comedian Paul Jennings in his persona as the policeman Harry Pardow, evokes the lawlessness associated with working class estates through his portrayal of being a Black Country policeman, enregistering dialect features in his portrayal of being from such an estate himself.

2.6 Frame and perspective

Discourse is at the heart of communication and social interaction, and in live performances involves active participation and differing of roles between speaker and listener. In order for successful communication to occur, interaction has to be built upon common ground, in that participants in an interaction assume and share a certain degree of similar knowledge. Thus, whilst implicit in communication is social interaction that occurs in physical social space through sound and gesture, it is also cognitive in nature. Two concepts Ensink and Sauer (2003) identify as central to the cognitive dimension of discourse analysis are those of 'frame' and 'perspective'. 'Frame' refers to: "...the fact that discourse participants need a shared sense of the way in which discourse is framed; i.e., an overall sense of the function not discourse in the social situation" (2003: 4) 'Perspective' refers to the context of discourse which is necessarily displayed from some point of view.

The use of the term *frame* as so defined is thus metaphorical, evoking a spatial context such as the separation of a painting by a literal frame, and also structures time, as where the opening and closing of a curtain or use of music constitutes the frame in which theatrical performance is perceived in time and separated from events that occurred before and after. The concept of frame thus accounts for the human need to set up structural understandings of the ways in which the world functions (Fauconnier and Sweetser 1996). Ensink and Sauer distinguish between two different kinds of cognitive frames: knowledge and interactive, with perspective adding a third dimension. Knowledge frames are to do with what we already know about the world and how that knowledge is used in our understanding of it. The example Ensink and Sauer draw upon is that if a child reads a story that begins: *Mary was invited to Jack's party. She wondered if he would like a kite;* and asked what the kite was for, then the likely answer would be as a birthday present, even though gift or present has not been mentioned. A 'party-invitation' frame is evoked in the readers' mind and attached to 'terminals' of the frame such as what clothes to wear, where the location of the party is to be and so on. The concept of frame, sometimes also called *schema* or *script*, as Ensink and Sauer say '…accounts for coherence in knowledge as used for the representation and understanding of the world' (2003: 5).

Interactive frames pertain to our behaviour in different social settings. Participating in interaction requires a shared sense of the kinds of activity in which participants are engage, such as awareness of personal space, conventions associated with turn taking, interruption, pauses, forms of address and so on. Such a use of the term frame has been applied to the analysis of interaction in many different situations and is similar to Goffman's (1981) concept of 'footing'. The concept of 'perspective', whilst similar to that of frame, is different from it in that it is concerned with the literary stylistic perspective of point of view (Simpson 1993). Implicit in any communicative act is the point of view or perspective that is being presented by interlocutors in speech (or authors and their readers in writing). Discoursal or textual aspects that contribute to the analysis of perspective then, include use of active or passive voice; lexical choices that express different opinions and deixis: that is, the ways speakers and writers fit discourse to the time and place within which it is produced and in the analysis of narrative, the point of view of the narrator. Concepts such as frame and perspective then, add a cognitive dimension to the analysis of discourse that complements that of enregisterment.

Kenneth Burke (1984 [1937/1959]) is an author whose work continues in dialogue with Bakhtin and the concept of frames and who has been particularly influential in film, TV and video studies. Burke discusses how, in order to cope with the injustices of life in particular, people tend to position themselves in relation to the human condition or situation as being either 'friendly' or 'unfriendly'; accepting the universe or protesting against it, as acceptance and rejection. Burke draws upon the work of the American philosopher and psychologist William James, in whose view action and results did not stem from purely utilitarian principles. This is because to choose a lesser evil can be viewed as an act, if such a choice leads to the eventual opportunity to choose an even lesser evil. Burke write that

> In the face of anguish, injustice, disease, and death one adopts policies. One constructs his notion of the universe or history, and shapes attitudes in keeping. Be he poet or scientist, one defines the 'human situation' as amply as his imagination permits; then, with this ample definition in mind, he singles out certain functions or relationships as either friendly or unfriendly. If they are deemed friendly, he prepares himself to welcome them; if they are deemed unfriendly, he weights objective resistances against his own resources, to decide how far he can effectively go in combating them. … call a man a villain, and you have the choice of either attacking or cringing. Call him mistaken, and you invite yourself to attempt setting him right.
> (Burke, 1959: 3–4)

Burke draws on the concept of frames and extends it further. Frames construct human perception discursively, as discussed in the section above. However, Burke divides the concept of frames into two, namely those of acceptance and rejection. He defines frames of acceptance as "...the more or less organised system of meanings by which a thinking man gauges the historical situation and adopts a role with relation to it" (1959: 5). Frames of rejection are defined as taking their "... color from an attitude towards some reigning symbol of authority, stressing a *shift in the allegiance* to symbols of authority" (1959: 21). Frames of acceptance correspond to the epic, tragedy and comedy, that includes *carnivalesque*, whilst those of rejection include burlesque, elegy, grotesque and satire. Individuals and groups are criticised through the burlesque frame by negatively caricaturing them rather than through challenging their argumentation. Burlesque thus criticises the behaviour of others and in ways that amplify their stupidity. Carnivalesque invites audiences to question established hierarchies; burlesque, by contrast, appears as a rejection of the dominant group's authority. The use of carnivalesque in verbal art releases audience members from communal norms and allows people to resist symbols of authority and power, thereby allowing the audience to think freely about the world; to laugh, and through laughter, disrupt social order. Thus, whilst carnivalesque mocks a community as a whole, burlesque targets the individual.

However, Burke acknowledges that the comic cannot of itself promote social change, and is thus only ever at heart a 'frame of acceptance.' It can though, help people to understand or make sense of the modern world, acting as a coping mechanism, a means of understanding the current social order and any one's individual place in it. Bonstetter (2011) draws upon Burke's concept of frames in her discussion of two films produced by Mel Brooks, *Blazing Saddles* (1974) and *History of the World Part 1* (1981). She discusses how Burke's categories and Bakhtin's concept of the carnivalesque can be used to explore two different modes of satiric discourse that aim to critique a specific person, stereotype or social norm. When satiric discourse is punitive and unsympathetic, then its mode is burlesque, offering a frame of rejection that make no attempt to get inside the psyche of its victim. However, when operating through comedy in particular and a connection is made with the victim's psyche, then the discourse becomes framed as one of acceptance, that warns against the dangers of pride and where the shift is from crime to stupidity. She says that:

> recognising the satiric elements of texts as *socially* critical (as opposed to just making fun of textual elements) and deciphering what mode(s) they are operating through can assist audiences in better understanding ironic texts and the criticism a text is lodging. The degree and placement of irony and its 'correct' reading can vastly change a satiric message. (2011: 29)

The performances discussed in the forthcoming chapters create a space where imagined communities are constructed through enregistered, double-voiced dialect use to differing degrees and in relation to the kind of frame being evoked, serving comic and satiric purposes in terms of trying to make sense of the forces of modernity, and in particular through mocking shifts in current social order. The performances discussed in the chapters that follow illustrate some of the ways that regional performers draw upon frames and references in burlesque and carnivalesque ways, subverting dominant ideologies in their performances not only through the use of humour, but also that of dialect, to revert and subvert the dominant social order and their underlying ideologies. The chapters also, as the following chapters demonstrate, the audience's responses to such stylization and presentation in performance is by no means homogenous, and the degree to which they accept or reject the frames evoked by the performance links in turn to their own experiences.

2.7 The politics of transcription

Locating the study of dialect use in its discursive contexts and situational practices has inevitable implications for its transcription. Transcription means that language used in one medium, that of speech, is transformed into another, that of writing. There is no such thing as an 'objective' transcription, since the transcriber creates the transcribed text in ways that have ideological implications for the end result: that is, the transcription itself. Equally, interpreting a recording for the purposes of transcription is also never a neutral event but always has a point of view. Transcription is thus in and of itself a form of social action (Jaffe et al. 2012) that involves both interpretative and representational aspects that have to be taken into account (Bucholtz 2000; Green et al. 1997). Transcription, as Lapadt and Lindsay (1999) amongst others point out, is problematic, not least because when researchers are making choices about transcriptions they enact the theories they hold. Walker (2014) also makes the point that within conversation and discourse analysis, standard transcription conventions on the whole conflate form with function, whilst sociolinguistic analysis, particularly that concerned with representing dialect, separates out these two dimensions. The central concerns at the interpretative level of transcription then are the decisions that lead to determining *what* is transcribed and at the representational level *how* it is transcribed. Issues relating to transcription of the data discussed in the following chapters, therefore, involved making decisions in relation to both *what* was to be transcribed, in terms of what was and was not to be included in the transcript, and *how*, in terms of the notation to be used to represent in writing that which had been spoken. Auer (2014), whilst broadly agreeing with Walker's position that form and function in conversation analysis should be kept separate, the amount of detail in a transcript is determined by the research questions. Consequently, no amount of detail in a transcript can ever be exhaustive.

The transcription notation system used for orthographic transcription was that of Gesprächsanalytisches Transkriptionssystem (discourse and conversation-analytictranscription system, GAT, given as Appendix 1), with a limited addition of project-specific notations. GAT follows the conventions and principles of Jeffersonian style transcription, in that is readable and can be understood by linguists and non-linguists and has additional ways of marking prosody that allows for three levels of delicacy: minimal, basic and fine. It does not entail any special mode of representation for speech, and is intended to be unambiguous in that transcription symbols represent only one phenomenon. Transcription symbols follow iconic principles, designed to be as non-arbitrary as they can possibly be. The transcription system aims to be relevant, in that it allows for the notation of phenomena previously shown to be relevant for analysis and interpretation of verbal interaction and the notation conventions aim for form-based transcription. Instead of interpretive or meta comments such as, for example, 'surprised', the specific parameters on which such interpretations are based are represented individually on the basis of their form (Selting et al. 2011).

The software used for transcription was that of Extensible Markup Language for Discourse Annotation (EXMARaLDA).[1] Originally developed in 1999 for use with multilingual data, EXMARaLDA has since been developed to allow for corpus assisted transcription, annotation and analysis of a wide range of spoken interaction including conversation and discourse analysis, language acquisition and attrition, multilingualism, phonetics and phonology, dialectology and virtually any other area of linguistic and sociolinguistic research related to spoken data. It supports time-aligned transcription of both video and audio data and has a flexible annotation system for freely choosable categories. It thus provides the means by which dialect variables could be both transcribed and analysed in relation to their discursive context, thereby marrying together practices associated with conversation/discourse analysis with linguistic variability. The program includes a searchable function, enabling the transcripts to be searched for both discourse features and occurrences of phonetic as well as morphosyntactic and lexical variation (Ruhi et al. 2014; Schmidt & Worner 2016).

The issue of what was to be transcribed was a central one, since the sound recordings had been of performance events in total which were not edited in any

---

1 EXMARaLDA is freely available from: http://exmaralda.org /en/

way for meta performance data such as introductory music and in the case of variety type shows, compere performance between different acts and different acts themselves. By far the most difficult decisions were those that needed to be made in terms of *form*. Because the research focussed upon dialect use, this led to discussions about how such use should be transcribed. A first rule of thumb for transcription in either conversation or discourse analysis is in regard to representing recorded speech as close and as it is faithfully possible to be. This includes paying attention to and transcribing what is actually said. However, it is impossible to transcribe in such a precise way that captures all the detail of the speech being transcribed and to recreate the full sound of the recording. Constraints of time and finance mean that decisions have to made with regard to the unavoidable limits of transcription. Use of eye-dialect and re-spelling of the kind used to represent dialect in writing was considered, but this type of representation too is exceptionally hard to read. Thus, following Preston (1982, 1983, 1985), the use of nonstandard orthography to represent nonstandard usage was rejected, in all but a limited and restricted set of commonly used features such as – *g dropping*, which was incorporated into the orthographic transcription. Each performance was thus transcribed orthographically in its totality in standard English as a baseline, with no attempt made at representing accent or dialect features heard. This meant that any dialect feature was 'ironed out' or 'corrected' into standard English. A second layer or tier of transcription was then added where IPA notation was used to indicate where phonetic and morphosyntactic variation occurred, rather than transcribing the whole transcript into IPA.

In the chapters that follow, the IPA notation in all the examples given is in the context of the orthographic GAT transcription, thereby allowing for a discussion of dialect features to be undertaken in the discursive context in which they occur and in ways that can be understood by the wider academic community.[2] The features chosen for discussion in the chapters that follow were those that occurred most frequently across performance and performer interview data. Frequency of occurrence of any one feature does not in and of itself signal its enregistration. The extent to which any feature is enregistered and functions indexically is discussed in the following chapters in relation to (a) the discourse context in which the feature occurs and (b) through discussion with the performers.

---

2 The recordings and accompanying transcriptions can be accessed via the Aston Corpus of West Midlands English website: http://www.aston.ac.uk/lss/research/research-centres/ccisc/discourse-and-communication/acwme/

3 Staging language in performance: Comedy and parody

3.1 Introduction

In this chapter I discuss comedy acts performed by amateur and semi-professional performers in local venues for local audiences in the Birmingham and Black Country areas of the West Midlands region of England. This discussion also includes conversation interviews with the performers about their performances, members of the audience who attended the performances and local and national celebrities associated with the region. The acts range from those performed as part of a variety stage act at public house that had transformed itself into a local arts venue to an 'open mic' night at a local public house. The first section below identifies a set of dialect features identified from across performance and conversation interview data discussed in this chapter. For each performance and conversation interviews discussed thereafter, identified dialect features are considered in the context of their use and in relation to indexicality, enregisterment, frames, referencing, double-voiced and polyphonic discourse, the burlesque and carnivalesque as discussed in Chapter 2. This discussion is set against wider sociocultural contexts as discussed in Chapter 1 in relation to modernity and imagined communities. In this way, analysis of performances and accompanying conversation interviews reveals not only the extent to which dialect features are present, but the part they play in terms of indexing place, enregistering social identities, the kinds of social realities they evoke and the ways in which standard language ideologies are subverted.

The extent to which any one of the dialect features identified below can be said to be enregistered in performances or any performer's speech also depends upon whether or not the performer is deliberately drawing upon any one of them or several in combination, to index a specific aspect of identity that links to place. A linguist such as myself may draw conclusions informed by data analysis. The extent to which enregistration is identified by both members of the audience and the part it plays in the frames and references evoked by the performer can also be partly judged by a researcher through the ways in which audiences as a whole react. Live performances have the advantage that they create an opportunity for researchers to talk to performers, playwrights and members of their audiences, to shed further light on any conclusions a linguist such as myself have drawn.

https://doi.org/10.1515/9781501506796-003

3.2 Features of Birmingham and Black Country dialect in performance

As Clark and Asprey (2013) have identified, morphologically and phonologically, Birmingham and The Black Country lie in a Midlands transitional zone between the so-called North-South linguistic divide in England. This zone forms a pan-regional variety distinct from either North or South, that also shares some features in common with Northern English, for example the shortening of the /a/ vowel in tokens such as *bath* and *grass* to rhyme with that in *hat*. Other features in relation to vowel sounds are discussed in more detail below. In relation to consonants, the most salient variants across the data are 'h- and g- dropping', 'glottal stopping' and what is called 'velar nasal plus', all discussed further below. 'Rhoticity' is the term given to the pronunciation of the /r/ sound which in the region is normally non-rhotic; that is, /r/ is not sounded at the end of tokens such as 'year' and after vowel sounds in tokens such as 'bird' as indeed the case across the data with the exception of the Birmingham born performers of Jamaican descent, discussed in the next chapter. There is also evidence of the T-R rule where a token such as 'matter' is pronounced 'marrer' or 'marra'. This second pronunciation also evidences an ER-A rule, where the [er[at the end of a token is pronounced as /a/, so that 'mother' is pronounced 'motha'.

The most salient morphosyntactic dialect features are in relation to the declension of the verbs 'be', 'can' and 'do' and the absence of negative forms of these verbs. This is particularly the case with the Black Country performances discussed in this chapter. Another feature is adding –s to the first-person form of verbs, for example 'goes' in place of 'go' in 'I goes'. The reverse is also true, where an –s ending is deleted, such as in the utterance 'A couple of year ago.' In relation to lexis, very few region- specific tokens were found in the data, apart from tokens to describe 'Birmingham' as 'Brum'; hailing from Birmingham as being a 'Brummie'; 'tarra' in place of 'goodbye' and females of any age called 'bab' or 'babs'. The sections below focus upon the linguistic variation evident in the data with regard to phonology and morphosyntax.

3.2.1 Phonology

In relation to consonants, of all the features of Birmingham and Black Country consonant phonology identified by Clark and Asprey (2013), by far the most frequently occurring across all the data in the data were *h- and g- dropping, glottal stopping,* and the *velar nasal plus. H- dropping* occurs when the word-initial /h/ is not pronounced in tokens such as *how* to give *ow* represented in IPA as

/aʊ/. The phenomenon often referred to as *g-dropping* occurs when the velar nasal sound represented in writing as 'ng', typically in words ending with the inflectional suffix – *ing*, is pronounced as the alveolar nasal /n/. This variant is conveyed orthographically as *n'*, so the RP pronunciation represented as *going* becomes *goin'*.

Glottal stopping is the term given to the abrupt silence that replaces the sound represented by the letter *t* in words such as *right* or *little* where the *t* is not pronounced, represented in IPA as /ʔ/.

H- and *g- dropping* and the *glottal stop* are all features that are commonly found in non-standard English speech, but its salience in the data is in its frequency of use. An aspect of consonantal variation specific to Birmingham and the Black Country is the feature known as *velar nasal plus*. *Velar nasal plus* relates to the presence of /g/ in the pronunciation of words such as *sing*, *fling* or *hang*. A distinctive feature of Birmingham and Black Country accents is also the realisation of all three variants of the cluster represented in writing as *ng*, again typically in words ending in the suffix *-ing* (Grant et al 2017). This feature occurred across the data regardless of performers' age, gender or ethnicity. In order of their occurrence across the data, the three variants are:

G-dropping as discussed above. For example, pronouncing *speaking* as [spi:kɪn], and represented in writing as *speakin'*.

The velar nasal sound, where the /g/ is pronounced, represented in IPA as /ŋ/. It can occur more than once in a word, for example, the standard English pronunciation of *singing* which in IPA is [sɪŋɪŋ].

The velar nasal plus realisation, found in some English accents, including those of the West Midlands region of the UK. Where this occurs, the velar nasal /ŋ/ is 'over-articulated', being immediately followed by the sound /g/. For example, in *Birmingham* ing- is pronounced [ɪŋg], making the pronunciation more like *Birming-gam* or [bɜ:mɪŋgəm] in IPA, which also renders the *h* silent. Its most common occurrence was in relation to the pronunciation of the token *Birmingham*. Finally, there is the pronunciation of /d/ as more of a /j/ in words such as *dead* pronounced as *jed* [dʒed], used mainly in the performance by the women's theatre group *Fizzog* in their personae of elderly middle-aged women from the Black Country. In terms of saliency then, the table below summarises the features considered in more detail in the data, shown below in Table 3.1.

In relation to vowels, the features of note here are those that relate to the ways monophthongs and diphthongs are realised. Vowel sounds that are heard as single sounds in tokens such as *mend* or *hat* are called monophthongs. As discussed above, a feature Birmingham and Black Country dialects share with

Table 3.1: Consonant features.

Dialect indexed	Feature	Example
Birmingham and Black Country	h-dropping	Merry Hill as Merry _ill
Birmingham and Black Country	g-dropping	[gɪvɪn] giving
Birmingham and Black Country	Glottal stop	[əlrɑɪʔ] alright [pʊ[] put
Birmingham and Black Country	Velar nasal plus	[bɜːmɪŋgəm] Birmingham
Black Country	/d/to a/j/sound: 'dead' to 'jed'	[dʒed] dead

those of Northern English is shortening of monophthongs in words such as *bath* and *grass* to rhyme with *hat*. When one vowel sound glides into another one in any one syllable it is called a *diphthong*, for example in tokens such as *coin* or *loud*. In The Black Country, but not so much in Birmingham, the diphthong in tokens such as *like, price* and *quite*, the vowel sound represented in writing as /i/ and lengthened by the addition of /e/ at the end after a consonant, is realised in *like* as *liyek* [lɔɪk] and 'quite' as *quiyet* [kwɔɪt], rather than the RP [kwaɪt] and [laɪk] so that the [aɪ] sound is more often than not pronounced as [ɔɪ]. In a token such as *face* the /a/ sound is pronounced more like *fayce* [æɪ]. The token *you* is often realised as *yow* [jəʊ]. The RP of the single vowel in words such as *Dudley* or *run* is more like the sound represented in writing as *oo*, found for example in *foot*, for example *doodley* and *roon* represented by the IPA symbol [ʊ].

A further feature of vowel pronunciation in Birmingham and the Black Country is the exchange or transposition of the vowel sound in a word such as *mum* pronounced in RP as *mum* [mʌm] to Birmingham and Black Country *mom*. (A third variant is that of *mam*, found more in the North of England). *Mon* is also heard instead of *man* and *shap* in place of *shop*. An example of the degree of enregistration of the *mom* pronunciation as indexing a Birmingham place identity is that given by a Birmingham MP for the Yardley Wood district, Jess Phillips. In a television interview given in December 2016 as part of a daily politics show, she insisted that in Hansard, the official record of all speeches given in Parliament, the spelling of the word *mum* to *mom* be changed in transcripts of the speeches she has given, saying:

(1) i_m from Birmingham and i say mom (.) it annoys the hell out of me when they change
  it to mum

Public figures such as Jess Phillips who come from working-class backgrounds but who through education and occupation have become middle class, illustrate how an individual may refuse to bow to hegemonic pressures to change the ways they speak away from dialect to standard English. Here, dialect-switching can be said to function metaphorically, or even metonymically, where the use of one word, 'mom', stands for the dialect as a whole.

Finally, three further features found throughout the region are the tendency to pronounce RP *my* or *myself* as *me* or *meself*; *take* as *tek* and ER-A in tokens such as *mother* or *brother*. The table below gives a summary of the features discussed:

Table 3.2: Vowel features.

Dialect indexed	Feature	Example
Black Country	like quite	*liyek* [lɔɪk] *quiyet* [kwɔɪt]
Black Country	face	*fayce* [æɪ]
Black Country	you	*yow* [jəʊ]
Birmingham and Black Country	lucky put	*Looky* [lʊki] *poot* [pʊt]
Black Country	Transposition of vowel sound	'mom' for 'mum'; 'mon' for 'man'; 'shap' for 'shop'
Birmingham and Black Country	'my' or 'myself' as *me* or *meself*	*mislef* [mɪsɛlf]
Birmingham and Black Country	take	*tek* [tek]

3.2.2 Morphology and syntax

The Black Country dialect, far more so than Birmingham, retains many distinctive morphosyntactic features. Of all those that have been recognised in the literature, the ones drawn upon most frequently by performers discussed in this chapter are in relation to declension of the verbs *be* and *do*. The present tense of *be*, particularly second person singular, *you am*, is often contracted to *yowm* and when asking a question, *am you* (Clark and Asprey 2013; Clark 2013a, Clark 2007). This feature is enregistered in performance through the policeman persona portrayed by Harry Pardow and the womens' theatre group *Fizzogg* in their role as elderly Black Country women, discussed in more detail below. Another distinctive feature is in making what is negative in standard English positive, for example in phrases featuring the verbs *be* and *do* such as *we ay* for *we aren't; I don't like it* to *I doh like it*. Other examples are *dun you know* for *don't you know; they day* for *they don't; bay British* for *be British; cor* for *can't; wor* for *weren't* and *ay* for *isn't*. −s endings can also be added to the first-person form of verbs, such as *I knows* in place of *I know*. Conversely, -s endings can be absent, for example, *a couple of year ago*. In a verb such as *come*, the present tense *come* is used throughout where in standard English the past tense *came* would be used, for example *I come home from work*. The pronoun exchange *her* for *she* is also evident. Table 3.3. below provides a summary.

Table 3.3: Morphosyntactic features.

Dialect indexed	Feature	Example
Black Country	2nd and third person singular and 1st and 2nd person plural 'be'	*Yowm* in place of *you are*
Black Country	negative 'be' throughout	*I ay* or in place of *I'm not* or *we ay* in place of *we're not*
Black Country	Negative 'can' throughout	*I cor* in place of *I can*
Black Country	Negative 'do' throughout	*I day* in place of *I do*
Birmingham and Black Country	-s endings added -s endings absent	*I knows;* *a couple of year ago*
Black Country	Pronoun exchange	*Her* for *she*

In the data extracts that feature in the remainder of this chapter and the two following for ease of reading, IPA notation is given in the same line immediately after the orthographic GAT transcription.

3.3 Performance 1: *I know what yowm thinkin'*... stand-up comedy

The performance considered in this section was given by the comedian Paul Jennings, in his stage persona of Harry Pardow in his persona of a middle-aged policeman. Jennings is himself a middle-aged retired policeman in real life, and the performance discussed below was the first time he had performed this persona, his more usual one being that of a banker. Both personae exemplify occupations that are generally framed negatively in working class culture or, in Burke's terms (as discussed in Chapter 2) framed by rejection, as typifying institutions and occupations designed to benefit and protect the rich at the expense of the poor. This particular event took place as part of a regular series of Black Country Variety Shows, held at what was once a pub in the village of Cradley Heath (pronounced *Cradeley* with a long *a* to rhyme with *baby*) in the heart of Black Country, that has been turned into a local arts venue. The room in which performances are given is not much bigger than an average sized living room, with an audience of around 30 people on the night in question. Such performances continue in a music hall tradition as discussed in Chapter 2, providing a space for locally based performances, comprising a mixture of amateur and semi-professional performers performing in front of local audiences drawn from the immediate locality.

For his act, Harry dressed in a dark suit, white shirt and tie. His physique is large and in appearance he evokes the national stereotypical burly English policeman, the 'bobby on the beat' which he represents. After a warm up act given by the compere, Craig Deeley from Birmingham who is discussed further below, Harry comes on stage:

(2)   1   evenin_ [iːvnɪn] everybody alright
      2   audience: evenin_<<cheering>> fine ye::s
      3   fantastic my name is harry [ari] pardow gOOd evenin_ [iːvnɪn] CRADLEY[kreɪdliː]
      4   audience member: alright harry
      5   alright [alrɔɪyt] ah settle fuckin_ [fʊkɪn] down right (.) i_ve got a [gora]
      6   confession to make my name_s harry [æri] PARdow an_ [an] for the last [læsʔ] thirty
      7   YEARs although i_m not [noʔ] now I was a policeman
      8   audience member: oh no
      9   e::R I feel like [lɔɪk] a well padded muslim on the tube now don_t [dəʊʔ] I ey
    10 I was a yes I was a policeman up [ʊp] until about [abæɪt] six months ago (.) and
    11 erm (-) so that_s a killer [killa] I always wanted to be a policeman to put [pʌr] it
    12 [ɪʔ] in perspective thirty years ago when I joined the police (–) MERRy hill [ill]
    13 was round oak steel works NEstle was nestles
    14 <<audience laughing>>
    15 SNICKers was marathons and Jordan was a country [kʊntri] instead of a cunt
    17   <<audience laughing>>
    18 I think i_ve found [faɪnd] the level
    19 A: <<laughing>> <<laughing>> <<laughing>> laughing>>

Harry's performance is redolent of carnivalesque frames and references from the start, as he evokes an imagined community centred in the Black Country but with national and global dimensions and himself as a policeman at the centre of it. In the opening lines, Harry is establishing a rapport with his audience in his stage persona Harry Pardow and he would have been known to many in the audience who had attended other performances given by him. Initial dialect features are common non-standard ones: g-dropping in the first word of line 1; h- and g-dropping in line 3. In addition, the distinctive Birmingham and Black

Country pronunciation of vowels in 'alright' as [alrɔɪyt] and 'fuckin_' as [fʊkɪn] also accompanied by g-dropping in line 5. Also in this line the T-R rule is evident with 'a got a' pronounced as [gora]. In line 6, Paul switches to his persona of a policeman. This double-voicedness is given as a confession, thereby setting up the frame of rejection he expects from his audience, as discussed in the next section. In line 9, he pursues the frame by likening himself to a Muslim suicide bomber (padded Muslim), with 'on the tube' being a reference to the London Underground. Such a reference is far from gratuitous, referring as it does to the 2008 London suicide bomb attacks, where at least one of the attackers was identified as coming from Tipton, a town in the heart of the Black Country. The West Midlands region, like many others in England, has witnessed a surge in immigration from Pakistan over the last decade or so, to which Paul also refers in his interview discussed below.

In a few lines then, Harry's policeman persona links the Black Country to London, and the globalised threat of contemporary terrorism linked to migration in ways that typify certain aspects of globalisation. Such references are met with silence on the part of his audience, acknowledged by Paul stepping out of his persona of both Harry and the policeman, with the meta comment: 'so that_s a killer' at the start of line 11, before stepping back into his persona and continuing with references to changes that have taken place in the last thirty years or so, from the local, to the national and global. These finally raise a laugh from his audience. He continues to h- and g-drop and glottal stop throughout, in addition to distinctive Birmingham and Black Country vowel pronunciations in lines 5, 9, 15 and 17. Locally, Merry Hill was the site of a former steelworks, that has been re-invented as an out of town shopping mall and thus a familiar reference to the audience; nationally *snickers* is the name of a chocolate bar that used to be called *marathon* in the UK and globally, *Jordan* refers to an international celebrity, known for her voluptuous figure. Harry acknowledges the audience's laughter with a further meta comment in line 18, evoking a frame of acceptance, moving attention away from himself to the audience. He also, through the juxtapositioning of his references, makes the audience aware of the ways in which the world has changed in living memory, and the influences both the media and globalization have had on everyone's lives. He swiftly sets up a frame of rejection followed just as swiftly with a frame of acceptance in order to gain his audience's sympathy. Harry evokes frames and references that foreground his persona as being from Dudley, aligning with a place, ethnic and social class identity familiar to his audience, and also in relation to popular culture. He then moves on to tell a series of linked jokes, that follow the set up-incongruity-resolution structure discussed in Chapter 2, framed and referenced in relation to the life of a locally based bobbie (English slang for a policeman):

(3) 1   i_m a dudley [dʊdlɛ] LAD (.) now i always[aliz] WANTed to be a
     2   poLICEman ever since i saw the SEVenties COP shows the aMERican SEVenties
     3   COP shows (-) and [an] that_s fanTAStic (.) y_know because [kʌs] it_s JUST [jʊs]
     4   like [lɔɪk] the aMERican [ɪmɛrɪkən[SEVenties COP shows DUDley [dʊdlɛ]ISN_T
     5   it [ɛnɪʔ] really ah
     6   <<audience laughter>>
     7   i mean i reMEMber their THING course it [ɪʔ] don_t [dʊn?] quite [kwɑɪʔ]
     8   SCAN (-) when you_re from DUDley [dʊdlɛ] (-) when you_re [yʌʊ]
     9   sort [sɔːd] of [a] STANDing [stændɪn]over somebody goin [ɡəʊɪn](-) I know
     10   what YOU ARE [jəwʌm] thinking [ðɪnkɪn] (-) did i FIRE [fɔɪjə] (.) FIVE [fɔɪv]
     11   or SIX BULLets (-) well don_t [dʊn] you [jəʊ] feel LUCKy [lʊki] PUNK [pʊnk]
     12   <<audience laughter>> <<audience laughter>>
     13   it don_t quite WORK does it? it don_t quite WORK
     14   <<audience laughter>> <<audience laughter>>

Dialect features are far more in evident in this stretch of the performance than in the opening lines, as Harry's policeman persona caricatures being a policeman from Dudley. He pronounces *Dudley* in lines 1, 4 and 8 with a Black Country accent as his persona changes to that of being a Black Country policeman. The distinctive Black Country [ʊ[is also evident in lines 3, 7, 9 and 11. Glottal stopping is evident in three tokens in succession in line 7 and g- dropping in lines 3 and 9, often in combination with one of the afore-mentioned features. Grammatically, the second person present tense of *be* is given as the Black Country <youam> in line 10, spoken loudly and with emphasis, and *don't* is said as *doon* [dʊn[in line 11. This sound is pronounced in quick succession four times in the incongruent punchline of lines 10 and 11 along with the distinctive second person negative of [dʊn[. As indicated by their laughter, Harry has the audience well and truly on his side by the end of this turn. The extract also shows how Paul in his Harry Pardow policeman persona builds up use of dialect to index a Black Country policeman persona throughout a comic turn, with that use featuring most prominently at a punchline.

References, frames and schemas evoked in this extract relate to concepts of policemen in British society, in ways that are heavily intertextual. They move between the burlesque and carnivalesque in creating and evoking a shared past based upon living in the Black Country at a particular moment in time. Reference is made to TV shows of the 1970s on both sides of the Atlantic, with which the audience, given their demographic, would have been familiar. Comic effect is evoked through setting up a frame of rejection in relation to American cops vis a vis British bobbies that strike a chord with his audience. The phrase *just like* [jʊs] [lɔɪk] occurs just once in the whole performance, but the combination of the [oo[sound, t-glottalling and diphthongisation in such lexical tokens that are so close together is typical of the Black Country dialect, voiced in Harry's persona of a Black Country policeman from Dudley. This leads to an incongruent comparison between Harry the Dudley policeman and Harry the American uber cop, ending with a reference to a famous scene in the Clint Eastwood film *Dirty Harry* in lines 10 and 11.

In line 10, Harry Pardow parodies the actor's lines by using Black Country not only phonological but also morphosyntacic dialect features in close proximity: *you're* becomes *youam*; g-dropping of *thinkin* and the *oo* sound in *lucky* and *punk,* swiftly followed by a meta comment on his utterance. This use serves to provide an even greater and starker contrast and incongruence between the bumbling Black Country policeman Harry is portraying and that of his suave and sophisticated American counterpart, that is the source of the audience's laughter. In this case, Harry's resolution is to recognise the incongruity that also pokes fun at established social hierarchies, and draws attention to the down to earth, self-deprecating nature of Black Country humour. Again, most of the audience would have been familiar with this film, where a young, laconic, American plain clothes cop Harry stops a bank raid by shooting at the thieves from across the road, walking over slowly to one of them lying on the ground, and questioning if he fired six shots or five. Through his double-voicing and enregistration of recognisable Black Country features, Harry thus satirises the suave sophistication of American popular culture in relation to that of the British. He contrasts it with a self-declared characteristic of Black Country people, namely that of being down to earth, coupled with an ability to laugh at themselves, as shown through the audience's laughter and discussed further below. He moves seamlessly into another comic turn on the same theme:

(4) 1   there is a FUNdamental Difference between us and [an] the Americans (.) I was
  2   up dudley [dudlɛ] high [ɹi] street last [læs] year right [raɪʔ] (.) a Lamborghini
  3   come lamborghini in Dudley [dudlɛ]
  4   <<audience laugh>>
  5   a lamborhini come past in dudley [dudlɛ] broom (.) now in AMERica (.) they go
  6   <<audience laughing>>
  7   GOOD wheels buddy good wheels (-) SEVEn blokes including [ənklu:dɪn]
  8   myself [mɪsɛlf] looked and went [wən?] TWAt
  9   <<audience laughter>> <<audience laughter>>
  10 but it_s [bʊrɪts] true seventies cop shows seventies cop shows i was brought up
  11 on the SEVenties COP shows (.) T j HOOKer and [an] all THAT [ðæʔ] lot hey
  12 because [kʌs] they_ve GOT [gʊʔ] (.) aren_t they the CAR chases that they [ðæʔ]
  13 have the police CAR chases when I joined the job these CAR chases (.)
  14 THUNderbirds and PONTiac this and FIREbird that MUScle cars (–) AUSTin
  15 alLEGro (-)
  16   <<audience laughter>>
  17 that_s [ðæʔ] what I had

18   <<audience laughter>>
19   we used to get into [gerin] to a CAR chase get in [gerin] the CAR chase i_m in
20   the alLEGro i_m think- FUCK it [ɪʔ] i_ll get out [gɛrɛrt] rand RUN it_s
21   QUICKer
22   <<audience laughter>> <<square steering wheel>>

In this sketch, Harry switches back to the persona of the British policeman he created at the start of his act, with a correspondingly less frequent use of dialect. He pronounces *Dudley* in lines 2, 3 and 5 in a standard RP way, but continues with t-glottalling. Again, Harry's comedy turns upon the incongruence between the framing and referencing of the glamourous, mediatized life of policemen in TV shows, especially in America, that are framed by him as rejection, when compared with his day to day experiences in Dudley, framed by acceptance. It is this reversal of expected framing that lies at the heart of Pardow's comedy, evoking shared experiences and feelings on his audience's part and illustrative of the ways in which not only standard language ideologies but also social stereotypes are subverted. This is crystallized firstly though his portrayal of the Black Country bobbie in the previous extract and in the one above through the stereotype of the police car chase, and the difference in the kinds of cars his screen counterparts drove compared with the actual one he drove. The British Austin Allegro was a rather prosaic, staid, family car and nowhere near as glamorous and powerful as the American Thunderbirds, Pontiacs and Firebrands to which Harry refers. From such parodying, satirical self-mockery, Harry moves on in his performance, turning his attention to his bosses, and in particular the increased bureaucracy coupled with political correctness he has seen pervade modern policing:

(5)   1   (.) i _ad a bloke right [rɔɪʔ] (.) I _ad a bloke one of these NEW [nuːw] BREED
      2   one of these NEW BREED inSPECTors (-) and [an] er at the END of this beLIEVe
            3. it or not [nɒʔ] is TRUE
      3   (.) everything [əvrɪθɪn] i_m going to [gʊnae] tell you
      4   tonight [tənaɪʔ] is GOSpel TRUE (.) right [rɔɪʔ] at [æʔ] the end of the WEEK if you
      5   did well _e gave you [yer] a mars bar
      6   <<audience laughter>>
      7   i was from the era of fuckin [fʊkɪn] jack REgan when EVerybody _ad a
      8   fucking [fʊkiŋg] bottle of SCOTCH (.) in the drawer (.) a MARS BAR (..)
      9   <<audience laughter>>
      10   and [an] i was there the ONE day i got [gʊʔ] i got [gʊʔ] called to a JOB the ONE
      11   day there was a HORSE DEAD in a POND (−) HOOVES [huːfs] (.) out the water
      12   like THAT [ðæʔ] and [an] this young TWAT (.) he must have been about
      13   thirTEEN right [raɪʔ] (.) this inSPECTor he comes up <<hyper pronunciation>>
      14   HAVE you done a STRATegy
      15   <<audience laughter>>
      16   i said well i_ve got [gʊ] some SUGar lumps

17   <<audience laughter>>
18   but [bʊʔ] i don_t [dəʊn?] think it_d [ɪʔ] quite [kwaɪʔ] WORK
19   <<audience laughter and clink of glasses>>

Again, h_ and g_ dropping and glottal stopping are evident throughout the extract above in lines 1, 2 3 and 4. the elongated *oo* [ʊ] vowel sound in line 7 is coupled with a velar nasal plus in line 8 in the token 'fucking' where in line 7 the g_ was dropped. More g_dropping and glottal stopping continues in lines 10, 12 and 13 that contrasts with the RP of line 14 and features again in lines 16 and 18. As in the preceding two extracts, dialect features are most prevalent in the punchline in line 18 that completes the comic turn. Throughout the turn, Harry continues to portray himself as down to earth and having little respect for changes in the organisation of work practices, including the fast track promotion of university graduates within the police force, as against working one's way up the ladder over time, as would have been the case when Harry first started policing. He also draws upon vernacular vocabulary in prefacing his description of the young policeman as a *twat* in line 12, a vernacular word meaning someone who has an over-inflated opinion of themselves. This in turn, positions him as a no-nonsense, down to earth kind of policeman, a trait that runs through his entire set, and one often said to be characteristic of Black Country people.

Frames and references in this extract are made in relation to 1970s television police dramas, with the reference in line 7 to Jack Regan, who was the older half of a hardboiled, whisky drinking, car chasing detective duo in the show *The Sweeney*. Harry mimics the voice of this young policeman through using RP that is more pronounced than that of the voice of his stage persona, and gains sympathy from his audience in so doing. The juxtaposition between Pardow as a Black Country policeman and all other policemen is also characterised through Bakhtin's notion of uni-directional and vari-directional voice in relation to mimicking, representing or quoting other people's voices in our speech. In uni-directional speech, the evaluative positions of the speaker and the voice being stylized are aligned, whereas in vari-directional speech they are in opposition, often in ironic or parodic ways. Having introduced the 'new breed' of policeman, Pardow then moves on to mimic the other policeman's speech in a vari-directional way and in opposition to his own stance as a policeman. In this way, Pardow constructs and reinforces stereotypes of particular 'outgroups', which he assumes are shared by his audience, an assumption affirmed by their laughter. This is re-inforced where he takes on the persona of a police inspector, where he double voices in a hypercorrected voice in line 14, followed by reverting to that of his Black Country bobbie with enregistered dialect features, as in line 18.

Jennings' evocation through his Harry Pardow persona of what might be deemed positive Black Country characteristics such as being down to earth, poking fun at pretentious behaviour and anti-establishment even as a policeman, extend to comparisons between British police and those of other nations. Just as in the *Dirty Harry* sketch Harry contrasts a Black Country policeman like himself with policemen in UK police dramas and his American counterparts, so he moves on to contrast the ways in which complaints against the police are dealt with in the UK as opposed to South Africa, namely with violent force as opposed to a verbal reprimand. In the second half of his performance, he turns to caricature a more negative stereotypical characteristic, that of male chauvinism. Harry then turns his attention to women in the police force and their carrying firearms, which in his persona of an elderly, old-fashioned policeman, is something with which he has difficulty in coming to terms. His reception of such a non-politically correct caricature though is met by frequent laughter from his audience, indicating their appreciation of such a depiction:

(6) 1   but [bur] anyway YES er political corRECTness (.) i mean (.) they_re on about
       2   FIREarms officers police FIREarms officers now they_re on about (-)
       3   recruitin_ [riːkruːtɪn] more (.) FEmale firearms officers
       4   <<audience member>> yay!
       5   yeah good on yer SISter (.) fuckin_ [fʊkɪn] YES (.) because [kʊs[YOU can do the
       6   job as good as ANy man (-)
       7   <<audience member: yep>>
       8   THREE weeks out of four (–)
       9   <<mixture of audience laughter and groans>>
      10   C_MON (.) FUCK_s sake (.) plus there_s that [ðæʔ[ONE time in a woman's
      11   LIFE [lɔɪf]   <<audience laughter>>
      12   when she_s VISited by the HORmone fairy i wouldn_t [wʊdən?] trust you with a
      13   sharp STICK
      14   <<audience laughter and <<wooh>>
      15   on about [əbaʊʔ] giving [gɪvɪn] them fuckin [fʊkɪn] GUNS (-)
      16   <<audience laughter>>
      17   we should know should KNOW they_ve been [bɪn[VISited by the HORmone fairy
      18   bye darling bye bye s- see you toNIGHT [tənaɪʔ[you come back to get you
      19   KNOW (-) fucking [fʊkɪn] BATS flying [flaɪjɪn[over (-)
      20   <<audience laughter>>
      21   lightning [laɪtnɪn] BOUNCin_ [baʊnsɪn] off the fuckin_ [fʊkɪn] ROOF

((clink of glasses))

      22   you open the HALLway an_ a chill takes [tɛks] out your SOUL
      23   she_s THERE (-) <<lower toned voice> i want your fucking [fʊkɪn] SOUL
      24   <<audience laughter>>
      25   everything [evrɪəɪn] is your FAULT> (–)
      26   <<audience laughter>>

27   so you get [gɛʔ] the CHOColate you throw it [ɪʔ] up the HALLway (.)
28   <<audience laughter>>
29   the KRAFT chocolate (.) used to be fucking [fʊkɪn] CADburys
30   <<audience laughter>>
31   on about giving [givin] them [em] GUNS (–)
32   <<audience laughter>>
33   and [an] they say things like <female voice> oh i_m feeling [fiːlin] a little TENSE
34   i_ll put   some oil of evening [iːvnin] PRIMrose behind my EARS> (–) <end of
35   female voice> try a HORSE [ors[tranquilliser (–)
36   <<audience laughter>>

As in the last extract, dialect features relate to pronunciation, particularly glottal stopping and g dropping, and the *oo* [ʊ] in *fucking* in lines 5, 15, 19 and 23. In line 10, however, where the token is given emphasis, it does not. In extract 4 above, where the token is used only once and is emphasised, the *oo* [ʊ] sound is also not articulated. Again, Pardow uses humour to mock at the idea that women would be as good at being firearms officers as men because of their unpredictability at the time of their menstrual periods. At the start of the sketch, reference to women firearm officers is met with a *yay* response from a member of the audience who is a young woman. Pardow agrees with her, engages directly with her, but then swiftly undercuts their exchange by his reference to *three weeks out of four.* The audience's response of a mixture of laughter and groans signifies that they have immediately picked up on the reference to menstruation, and the stereotypical portrayal that follows women's supposedly erratic behaviour during the menstrual period. Increasing audience laughter on the part of both men and women indicates that they recognise the almost taboo stereotype he is creating in front of them. Through such a juxtaposition of uni- and vari-directional voices, the masculinity of the persona he creates is a chauvinistic one, one that has not kept up with the times and serves to reinforce his stage persona version of a type of old-fashioned policeman who is a 'dying breed'. At the same time, the self-reflexive nature of the sketch undercuts the very persona he is creating, recognised by his audience through the way that the laughter increases in frequency throughout this turn. The globalised aspect of his performance also features here, with his aside about the fact that Cadburys chocolate, with its factory in Birmingham, had been taken over recently by the multi-national firm Kraft.

By now towards the end of his act, Harry mocks and satirises another aspect of modern life, that of automated messaging systems replacing people at the end of a phone, in which he transposes the options that are a common feature of such systems to the bulk of police work in a way that is absurd in its contrast. He locates himself back in Dudley, and reverts to his positive down to earth Dudley policeman persona:

(7) 1 but you_ve got it now i reMEMber when i first started DUDley (.) [dudlɛ]
2 DUDley [dudlɛ] poLICE station if you want [wɒnʔ] to TALK to a police officer (·)
3 you used to ring oh three eight FOUR five six nine [nɔɪn] double OH (–)
4 Harry (as Caller): hello is that [ðæʔ] the poLICE (.)
5 Harry (as Operator): yes it [ɪʔ] certainly IS (.) are you are a poLICEman (.)
6 Harry (as Caller): yes it certainly AM (.) i_ve got a [gʊda] BURglar (.)
7 Harry (as Operator): someone will be ROUND away STRAIGHT [strɛɪʔ] away
8 (whooshing sound) they_ll be there (.) FIVE minutes (·)
9 Harry: NOW (–) brr brr (·) brr bbrr (·) <<mechanical tone> you_re currently in a
10   QUEUE
11 <<audience laughter>>
12 your CALL is important to us so carry on HOLDing (·) if you_re being RAPed
13 press ONE (–)
14 <<audience laughter>>
15 MURdered press TWO (–)
16 <<audience laughter>>
17 BURgled press THREE (–) could you PLEASE obtain a dnA sample if POSSible 18
<<audience laughter>>

Even though Harry locates himself in Dudley at the start of this extract, his pronunciation of it does not include dialect specific features he has used at other times other than glottalling, using instead a hyper corrected 'telephone voice' accommodated to RP. The focus in this turn is not so much on regionality, but on an absurdity in modern British life, where increasingly, telephone systems have been automated and there is increasingly less chance of speaking to an actual person. Harry moves to and fro between the different voices of his stage persona, the telephone operator and an automated voice, making specific reference to the recent past where time and space were anchored in place – in this case a local police station, framed positively as acceptance – have in modern times, been disconnected and relocated to anywhere in the country or even the world, framed negatively as rejection. He moves on to his final turn, using the reference to DNA as a link to a chauvinist joke about women and sex, and where his use of dialect features prominently:

(8) 1 I did that [ðæʔ] (.) right [raɪʔ] I come home[aʊm] from work (·) my wife_s
2 lying [lɪm] NAKed on top of the BED (·) she said we_ve BEEN burgled (.)
3 but it_s [burits] alright [əlraɪʔ] i_ve got a [gorra] dnA sample
4 <<audience laughter>>
5 sent it away come back THIRty SUSpects
6 <<audience laughter>>
7 my name_s been [bɪn] Harry Pardow thank you very MUCH may the FORCE be with
8 you

As his performance comes to a close, and in contrast to the voices performed in the preceding extract where attention turns to a domestic setting, many of the dialect features discussed in preceding extracts are present in the one above, such as vowel pronunciations in 'that,' 'right' and 'home'; glottal stopping and h- dropping in line 1; g-dropping in line 2 and the T-R rule in line 3. In the final line, Paul signs off his performance only this time aspirates the /h/ in 'Harry' and voices a short [i] in 'been.' The word 'force' in the last line functions as a pun, a wordplay that refers both to the police and to the science fiction film series, *Star Wars*, continuing with his theme of juxtaposing British and American culture to the end. The social identity Harry performs throughout his performance is of a stereotypical, late middle-aged policeman of working class origins from a specific locality, that of the Black Country. The potential social realities evoked derive from Harry's use of uni- and vari-directional use of voice: uni-directional in relation to himself as a younger and older policeman, a chauvinistic male, sounding working class and local, but also vari-directional as a Black Country bobbie in opposition to the British police as a whole, where his use of dialect features the most. His framing and referencing throughout the sketch undercut expected ones, subverting features of modernity such as an increasingly bureaucratic and managerial approach to work through the prism of the police force, a lessening of the 'stiff upper lip' characteristic of older generations vis a vis younger ones, women being treated equally to men in occupations that require the use of firearms and an increased automation and dislocation from place of people from access to front-line services via the telephone.

Just like Johnstone's Pittsburghese radio DJs, Pardow enregisters particular linguistic forms in multiple ways that overlap with one another, with some that relate specifically to the Black Country and others that although do not, relate to vernacular spoken discourse in general such as h- and g-dropping and glottaling, thus aligning different, and sometimes juxtaposing and conflicting cultural schemata with one another. What matters, therefore, is not so much how many times Pardow says *Dudley* as *Doodleigh* [dʊdli] or [dʊdlɛ], but to what effect. In this sketch, where the enregistered features of the first vowel sound [ʊ] in *Dudley* or the second one of [i] or [ɛ] are drawn upon, they are used to create a persona that indexes a regional place, a social identity as a chauvinistic working class male, an occupational identity as a policeman, an ethnic identity as white, an age identity as middle aged, all framed within a cynical scepticism of his bosses at work, all at one and the same time. The degree to which Paul Jennings enregisters dialect features in his persona as Harry Pardow varies from turn to turn, with the most being used in Extract 6, the Dirty Harry story, where he draws upon stereotypical Black features for this representation.

3.3.1 In conversation with Paul Jennings

Paul was interviewed a few days after the performance took place, in a conversation during which he presented a vivid and complex portrait of the Black Country character. He was born in the 1950s, to parents living on a working-class social housing estate in Dudley, the Rosalind Estate, which is the same one he talked about in his act discussed above, to parents who had also been born and brought up in the same area. Although he attended Dudley Grammar School, there was no parental expectation of him moving on to higher or further education and he left school aged 16. He held a series of jobs in various occupations until he eventually joined the police force, after a factory in which he was working in Netherton closed down and manufacture transferred to China. Like many of his generation, Paul witnessed the death of manufacturing and post-industrial decline urban regions of the UK such as the West Midlands that took place from the mid-1970s onwards as discussed in Chapter 1, a period in recent history that is also the subject of the play discussed in Chapter 5. As Paul says:

(9) i saw the writin_ [raɪtɪŋ] on the WALL erm thought i_d better [bɛdə] use my [mi]
     BRAIN for a bit (·) and [an] erm (–) joined the police force

Paul explained he had always wanted to be an actor, but that had not been a profession he had felt encouraged to pursue as a young man. He recounted his attempt to break into a career in acting in his younger days, writing a letter to the local repertory theatre to ask for advice on becoming an actor, to be told that he should think of becoming an assistant stage manager since that was an easier route into working in the theatre. As he said:

(10) PEOple from MY CLASS or SOcial STANDin_ [staendɪŋ] didn_t become ACtors
      they had [aed] PROPer jobs

Seeking support from his parents, he said, would have been akin to asking to him to marry a Martian, so far apart were the two different kinds of world perceived to be. Paul had spent time as a semi-professional performer in the 1980s, and had returned to performing when he retired from the police force. He explained that he drew upon Black Country personae when performing in the Black Country and even more so when performing in Birmingham. He spoke of a difference in attitude and outlook between people in the Black Country and those of Birmingham. This difference is something he said he exploited in his performances, by creating a stereotypical Black Country persona to take his audience along an expected path, only to then undercut and undermine those same expectations:

(11) 1   i_ve worked in BIRmingham [bermiŋgʊm] (.) i worked in BIRmingham
      2   [birmiŋgʊm] with the police for for quite a number a YEARS (-) an there IS (.) a
      3   DIFFerence (.) there_s there_s an ATTitude (.) there_s a there_s a there_s a
      4   MIND [mɔɪnd] set (.) call it what you will (.) that IS different between the black
      5   country (.) and BIRmingham [bermiŋgʊm]
      6   *Interviewer*: so your comedy as to be DIFFerent when you cross the BORder then
      7   SUBTly different (.) i i i i mean i ALways err one of my BANKers is always the
      8   bla- the the west MIDlands accent (.) well i call it BIRmingham [birmiŋgʊm] when
      9   i_m OUT of the west midlands (.) erm an i PLAY on the fact that i_m this THICK
    10   black country bloke when i_m in BIRmingham [birmiŋgʊm[(.) and they
    11   LIKE [lɔɪk] that (.) the jonny HAYseed sort of [sorta[HICK (.) but then you HIT
    12   them [em] with a bit a [bidda[you JUXTapose that with a bit a [bidda[sort of (.)
    13   what i call i don_t [dunno] inTELLigent obserVATion and they go ooh
    14   HANG [aeng] on a minute is _E taking the piss out of US or are WE are taking
    15   the piss out of HIM[im]

Paul is thus aware of the self-reflexive nature of his performance, and its function as a kind of social commentary through drawing upon his own experiences, through his use in performance of double voicing, reversing assumed assumptions centred upon frames of acceptance and rejection and the effect this reversal has upon his audience, with a constant interplay between setting up particular expectations then turning them on their head. Paul went on to explain that such a way of behaving was not just about being recognised or understood. He had no interest in being typecast as, in his own words, a 'professional Black Country bloke' or a 'one-trick pony'. Rather, he claimed that his regional heritage informed his performances and he drew upon dialect features in relation to his various personae for comic effect. However, the moment he felt that his use of dialect 'got in the way' of the performance itself, he accommodated and modified his use of it. In other words, the constraints of comic efficiency 'trump' considerations of regional presentation in relation to dialect. The degree to which he enregisters features then, depends upon his audience. The more local they are, the more he draws upon them, for example 'yowm' in extract 6 in place of 'you are', which features in his performance but not in his conversation. The further away from the Black Country that he performs, the more likely it is that he enregisters fewer features.

Paul also talked about the characteristics of Black Country humour, which centre around people poking fun at themselves, not taking themselves seriously, being self-deprecating and self-effacing. When he performs beyond Birmingham and the Black Country he reported that he always draws attention to the fact that he is from the West Midlands and explains why:

(12) 1   when i take [tɜk] it (his performances) outSIDE [ɛːrtsɔɪd] birmingham [birmiŋgʊm] 2 and
        the black country i say i_m from the west MIDlands in

3   BIRmingham [bɪrmɪŋɡʊm] (.) i say i_m from the BLACK country
4   *Interviewer*: is that because NObody asSOCiates with the black country (.) so you
5   just go to the BIGger picture or (.)
6   i th- i th- well THIS is me perhaps [praeps[being [biin] a comedy COWard (.) erm
7   and and NOT (-) trustin_ the AUdience outside the west MIDlands because [kʌz]
8   HALF the buggers (.) the- they use the black COUNtry they use the word the black
9   COUNtry thinking it_s everywhere from DERByshire down [dɛːin] to SWINdon
10 (.) blokes fom wolverHAMPton [wʊlvramtʊn] will say (.) oh WE_RE from the
11 BLACK country and [an] me being [biin] a DUDley [dudlɛ] bloke
    y_know (.)
12 professional BLACK country bloke will say NO you_re not no you_re not
13 CRADley [kreɪdliː] heath [iːð] (.) TIPton maybe y_know places like that and
14 they_ve even tried to define it geoGRAPHically by that BOWL (-) if you stand on 15 top
    of rowley _ills and you LOOK (.) THAT bowl you can see is the BLACK
16 country

In addition to the various ways that the Black Country borders are imagined differently by different people in the region, Harry also talks about how the dialect in the Black Country differs within the region itself:

(13) 1   well i used to work in cradely [kreɪdliː[_EATH [iːð] (-) and [an] i worked in i use
          2   to work in cradley [kreɪdliː] _EATH [iːð] (.) by the RAILway station and [an] i
          3   lived in NETHerton (.) TWO miles two and a HALF [aef] miles [mɔɪls] up the road
          4   TOTally different (.) OLD hill [il] (–) got a DIFFerent accent to cradely [kreɪdliː]
          5   _EATH [iːð] (.) in fact when i worked in the SAWmill in cradely [kreɪdliː] _EATH
          6   [iːth[(-) the blokes from cradely [kreɪdliː] _EATH [iːð] used to take [tɛk] the
          7   piss out of the folks from old _ILL for bein_ [bɪːɪn] THICK an_ because they
          8   _AD diff- it was TOTally DIFFerent (.) TIPton (.) i lived on the ROSalind (.) a
          9   mile [mɔɪl] and [an] half [aef] DOWN the road was TIPton TOTally different again

At the same time and despite such micro-regional differences, Paul acknowledged that communities across the region were prepared to welcome and accept incomers from around the world. Like much of the West Midlands, mid-20th century migration had been the result of World War 2 and the ending of colonization that led to a wave of incomers, particularly from Europe and the Indian sub-continent, many of whom identified with being Black Country as well as their family heritage. The next chapter discusses performances by performers from an Afro-Caribbean background and the ways in which their accents and dialects cross geographic borders. Increased globalisation had led to further recent influxes of immigrants from the Indian subcontinent, particularly Pakistan, as mentioned earlier. Such immigration was coupled with maintaining links with family and communities with their home communities in unprecedented ways. Paul recalled the terrorist suicide bomb attacks that took place in London in 2008, where several of the terrorists came from the Black Country and were nicknamed by press as the Tipton Taliban:

(14) 1 you_ve got (–) er young ASian (.) kids (.) y_know THEY_re black country
2 remember the TIPton remember the TIPton TALiban an_ you got the LAD there so
3 inCONGruous an_ the ONE son the one BROTHer [buɐæ] who says he [ɪː]
4 isn_t [ai] a TERRorist he supports the BAGgies (–) now this was on NATional
5 TELevision (·) y_know an_ (.) you go anywhere ELSE in the WORLD y_know
6 especially like [lɔik] aMERica or something [sumæt] they_re deFENDing their
7 FAMily y_know they_d come [kʊm] out with something [sumæt]
8 a BIT more HIGH FLOWN than it CAN_t be a TERR- it CAN_T [kor] be a
9 TERRorist _e supports the BAGgies (.) so the bloke might have ASian PARents (.)
10 he might have ASian _ERitage stretchin_ BACK y_know he might [mɔiɪt] he
11 might [mɔiɪt](·) 11 y_know go [gʊː[to to the MOSQue an_ get the korAN an_ do
12 all this but he_s still a black country BLOKE 12 (.) because [kʌs] of the black
13 country INfluences around _im _e_s got black country _ERitage IN _im

In this extract, Paul refers to the complexities of family life for those who migrate into the region from within Asia. They are welcomed by the community whilst at the same time continue to uphold the family religion and traditions of their home country. Thus, children are brought up where it is possible to be both an Asian Muslim and a supporter of a western local football club ('the baggies' in line 9 refers to a Birmingham professional football team called West Bromwich Albion). Paul also talks about the openness and friendliness of people in the Black Country to the point of over-disclosure – he talks about how the easiest job in the world would be to be a spy in the Black Country – and also their forgiving nature. In illustration of this, he recounts a drug squad raid that took place whilst he was a policeman in the 1980s, when armed police smashed down the door of an elderly couple of what turned out to be the wrong house. Had such an event happened in London, Paul said, there would have been riots, whereas the drug squad apologised for the error by sending the couple a bunch of flowers, thereby turning a frame of rejection into one of acceptance, with the policemen aligning themselves with members of their community, as opposed to against them. Finally, Paul talked about the changing nature of language. He talked about being aware that language changed between his grandparents' generation and his own, giving the example of how his grandfather used words he himself no longer did. Even so, he was clear in his mind that there was a demarcation between the Birmingham and Black Country dialect and in turn between the Black Country one and the rest of the UK. He also recognised the ways in which dialect evokes a sense of place identity:

(15) 1 (–) i can SEE (.) where (.) YOUNG kids (·) could quite EASily _ANG on to (·) a
2 DIalect (.) y- well 2 WHAT_s [wʊris] more STREET and more easily i-

3   iDENTifiable amongst your PEER group in your AREA (.) than using DIalect
4   words like where WE come [kʊm] from it y_know KIDS (.) what better WAY
5   never mind (.) g r EIGHT on the TEXT i mean yeah great great ye- that_s their
6   OWN dialect but that_s an interNATional dialect y_know (.) what better WAY (.)
7   and they_ll TWIG this eventually what better WAY of keeping their (.) iDENTity
8   alIVE [ælɔv] an_ DIFFerent from other PARTS of BRITain or (.) just down [dɛ:rn]
9   the ROAD than _avin_ your own little DIalect it_s almost like clockwork ORange
10 type of language like y_know you got your OWN sort of LANGuage an_ your
11 own GRAMmar (.) it all boils DOWN it all boils DOWN [dɛ:rn] (.) at the end of
12 the DAY it all melts down into a usable (.) er THING y_know it_s like (.) i
13 suppose it_s like the VERBal equivalent of real ALE y_know twenty YEARS ago
14 (.) y_know real ale was dyin_ OUT in this country now LOOK at it y_know _ow
15 many _ow many independent BREWeries are there now THRIVin_[θrɔɪvɪn] and i
16 think it_s the linGUISTic equivalent of real ALE

The reference to *Clockwork Orange* in line 9 is to the novel by Anthony
Burgess where young anti-heroes construct their own dialect as part of their
anti-establishment identity construction. Paul continued with his analogy of
dialect being like the verbal equivalent of real ale, recently reinvented as craft
beer. Just as real ale was on the verge of dying out and revived as a way of
holding onto an element of the recent past that was in danger of disappearing,
so too, Paul posited, a conscious recognition and self-reflexive use of dialect may
prevent it from dying out altogether. Whether as Harry Pardow or in performance,
or as Paul Jennings in interview and the telling of stories in character therein,
dialect features occur in both types data. In his performances however, Paul
reported that he made standard English choices in preference to Black Country
ones on occasions when the Black Country choice might misdirect or obscure
the comedy. This would seem to be of a piece with his linguistic choices – comic
efficiency takes precedence over regional presentation and in this way, comic
effectiveness is prioritised over the otherwise expected linguistic choice. At the
same time, he acknowledged that he drew upon Black Country dialect features
most in punch lines towards the end or at the punchline of a joke, thereby enregistering them as indexing a place identity linked to social class and occupation.
Paul spoke of modifying or accommodating his regional presentation according
to audience and location, and manipulating his Black Country/West Midlands
persona in a variety of ways. Nevertheless, he said that he chose to paint a relatively straightforward, while still affectionate, regional portrait in performance,
focusing on facets of one broad and arguably stereotypical trait – that of being
'down-to-earth'.

This focus on creating a consistent (rather than complex) picture of character and place allows Paul Jennings in his comic persona as Harry Pardow
and through frames and references he evokes to build an increasingly familiar

imagined community that is instantly recognisable to his audience. This serves to achieve one of his comic objectives and also to portray a largely positive representation of the Black Country region and its people. Paul's grasp of the forces of modernity are evident in the way in which he talked about making connections between the past and the present, the immediate locality with the UK nation beyond it and the world beyond that in his performances, especially through references to popular culture and headline news, thereby locating or nesting the locality within today's mediatised and globalised world.

3.3.2 In conversation with members of the audience

Harry's performance was given in front of an audience of about thirty people, and it is clear from interviews that different members of the audience reacted differently to it. Performances can mean different things to different people, which interviews undertaken after the performance with members of the audience clearly indicates (Clark 2013a). People's attitudes within the UK towards the Birmingham and Black Country regions remain persistently negative as discussed previously, of which audience members interviewed were all too well aware. Two members of the audience were interviewed, Margaret and her friend Geoff, both of whom were in their forties.

Margaret told how she noticed a difference in how those around her reacted to the humour of the performance. For example, she noticed that members of the audience not from the Black Country looked uncomfortable when specific references were made to people from the Black Country particularly in self-mocking ways, whereas those from the Black Country took such humour '... in their stride'. Even though Birmingham and the Black Country neighbour one another, there is still a sense of distance between the two places that is not so much geographic, but social. Margaret lives in Stourbridge, but was brought up in neighbouring Halesowen, both of which are in the county of Worcestershire. The insular nature of the community in which she lived is illustrated by Margaret's parents's reported reaction when she got her first job after leaving school in Birmingham, which was horror at her going so far away. Halesowen is just under ten miles from Birmingham's city centre. In contrast, Geoff said that he had not taken to the humour portrayed. It transpired that he had been bullied at school earlier in his life because of the way that he spoke, and subsequently altered the way he spoke to accommodate more to an RP norm. Hearing the Black Country dialect spoken in the performance transported him back to times he would rather have forgotten about, and the humiliation he had felt. Margaret had not suffered such linguistic prejudice, but she did recall a time when she went to London:

(16) I went for a very big meeting some years ago and I virtually only said good morning or you know whatever or something about the accommodation one or two sentences...and the chairman said when we were sat down what does the lady from Dudley think about that...and you know he'd got me taped I was very proud...this is my culture and I am very very proud of it...so I'm sorry if you don't like the way I speak that's the way I speak its where I was brought up.

Margaret and Geoff's experiences encapsulate what many of those interviewed experienced. For Geoff though, locally marked speech is indicative to him of social stigmatisation, reminding him of experiences suffered in the past, either being bullied at school or being passed over for promotion or at an employment interview because of prejudice against the way he spoke. For Geoff, hearing the Black Country accent tapped into his memories of such negative experiences and he did not find its use in parody very funny. Margaret positively embraces her Black Country dialect and whilst she accommodates more towards RP nevertheless refuses to eradicate all traces of it from her day to day speech. As she said:

(17) ....the whole of society is like either a plain piece of cloth as we all speak the same would be very boring no no no deviation no erm nothing just bland everybody just the same nothing in life or we can all be threads and make a tapestry...and I think that's a lovely idea to have all these threads of all these different cultures coming together into a bigger picture...and as I say I'm very proud of it very proud of it...

As Margaret illustrates, whether or not a person embraces or rejects the regional dialect of their upbringing depends largely upon their experiences of becoming aware of it through social interaction with others from outside the immediate area of family life, in relation particularly to education and employment settings. This point re-occurred time and time again throughout the conversations held with virtually all the people interviewed: performers, members of the audience and local and nationally celebrated playwrights, actors and poets. A recurring theme throughout the interviews is the ways in which dialect use is polarised in terms of agency as either something of which to be ashamed and therefore eradicated from speech (Geoff) as much as possible or something to embrace positively as part of the rich pattern of linguistic and social life (Margaret).

Whilst Margaret and Geoff may be representative of an older generation, this feature is something that also occurs contemporaneously. For example, Liz Berry (2014) is a national award winning modern poet, who draws upon Black Country dialect in her poetry. She was born in 1980 and brought up in the Black Country, attending the local comprehensive school and gaining a place at a university away from home. She recalled how, when she first arrived at university, one of her fellow students asked her where she was from, and upon Liz replying 'the Black Country', she received the response 'poor you.'

3.4 Performance 2 *I doh like it: Comedy sketch*

This Black Country performance event was a comedy sketch by a Dudley-based women's theatre group, *Fizzog*. Like the performance by Paul Jennings, it took place at the *Holly Bush* public house, a local arts venue in Cradley Heath as part of a *Black Country Variety Show* and in front of a similarly sized audience. *Fizzog* is a colloquial shortening of the word *physiognomy,* often used in the region. The group comprises four members in their late twenties and early thirties who have been working together for over 10 years on a professional basis, building up a strong following in the Black Country and further afield. Much of their work is based on local female characters, such as the four old ladies they performed in the sketch discussed here. The performance was introduced by the compere as featuring old people abroad. The four female actors walk through the audience to come onto stage dressed in stereotypical 'old ladies' clothes, in shapeless tent like dresses which fall below the knees, baggy cardigans, white socks, sturdy shoes and hats or a handkerchief knotted on their head, with curlers peeking out of the front, walking with bent, rounded shoulders. Each spoke at least a line as they move towards the stage with its four deckchairs aligned in a row. Their double-voicing is apparent as they take on the personae of elderly Black Country working class women, in uni – and vari- directional ways. The extract below is from the start of their performance, as they walk up trhough the audience and climb onto the stage:

(18) 1   May: come [kʌm] ON RUB [ruːb] (.) wAtch [waeʧ] this stE
2   Ruby: I [ə] DON_T [dəʊ] LIKE [laeːk] IT
3   May: I know you [yer] DON_T [dəʊ] (–) I know you [yer] DON-T [dəʊ]

(Shuffles; heavy breathing as Joan tries to get onto the stage)

4   Joan: NOW [naʊw] _ow [aʊw] am I [ɑːr] supposed [səpəʊsəd] to [t][GET pASt
5   YOU [jəʊ] EH [ɛɪj]
6   Rose: i_ll [ɑːl] go [guːw] DOwn [daeːn] with [wɪ] you [jəʊ] _ere [iːjə] (.)

All four women are now on the stage, sitting on their chairs, legs splayed and facing the audience.

7   Rose: i_m [jəʊm] _OT (.) i [ə] knOW [nəʊw] _OW JOAN of Arc Felt NOW [naʊw]
8   <<audience laughter>>
9   Ruby: i don_t [dəʊ] LIKE [laeːk[IT
10 <<audience laughter>>

In contrast with Paul Jennings' performance, that of Fizzog's draws far more heavily upon dialect features, as befitting the stereotypes they portray. In a few short lines, the frames and references the women evoke centre upon stereotypical themes associated with working-class British people abroad, in this instance, working-class Black Country women. As with Paul Jennings' Harry Pardow performance in his persona as a Black Country police bobbie, dialect use in this sketch narrows down the personae represented from older working class women in general and regionalises them and their experiences as those of Black Country, older working-class women. Their dialogue, and particularly Ruby's repetition of *I don't like it,* with the ablaut negation 'doh' [dəʊ] creates the carnivalesque and incongruent spectacle of taking the women away from their familiar surroundings – in this case the landlocked Black Country – and transposing them into somewhere completely different – a seaside holiday resort on the coast of Spain. Both their appearance and dialogue evoke the 1960s and 1970s, when European holidays, particularly in Spain, became affordable to the majority of the British population for the first time and became particularly popular with middle-aged people. Until the 1960s, most British people took their holidays in seaside resorts along the British coast, with those living in the West Midlands going largely to the west of the country to the seaside town of Weston Super Mare or Wales. However, the advent of package holidays and cheaper travel abroad with guaranteed sunshine in places like Spain, broadened the social base of people who could afford such holidays to include those from working-class backgrounds. Immediately, the juxtaposition created by the women's clothing, hair styles and dialogue evokes an imagined world where the uncomfortable British abroad transport themselves from their domestic environments, in this case the urban one of the Black Country and the unpredictable British summer weather into the open and warm space of a Spanish beach holiday resort. Portraying characters of an older generation also allows for greater use of dialect features in the dialogue, which is in far greater evidence here than in Jennings' performance as Harry Pardow.

One of the characteristics of the Black Country dialect is the structure of negative uses of tense, such as the use of < doh> in place of <don't> in line 2, and repeated in lines 3 and 9 as discussed above. Use of this particular grammatical expression at the very beginning of the sketch immediately interplays with the age, dress and setting to create the scene of old ladies from the Black Country enjoying – or not – a summer holiday abroad. The image thus created draws and plays upon stereotypical images of working class Britons abroad who dress on holiday as they would back at home, but narrowing down regionally to elderly Black Country women. The cultural reference to the French Christian martyr Joan of Arc achieves its comic effect by the stark contrast between heat generated by being burnt alive and the heat of the Mediterranean sun felt by the old ladies. The audience responds to such a depiction and imagined world with hearty laughter. It then becomes clear from their dialogue that they are halfway through a two week holiday which they are each enjoying – or not – in different ways and Rose wants to go home:

(19) 1   Rose: i can_t [kɔ:r] stOp _ere [i ɛ] for another [ənʌðə] WEEK i_ve got thINgs to DO I
     2   got [goʔ] folks to see
     3   May: LIKE [lɔɪk] WHO [u:w] WHO [u:w] WANTS [waentʒ] to sEE you [jəʊw]
     4   you [jəʊw] ONly ever [ɛvæ] SEEs [siz[US
     5   Rose: OUr [ae:r] SHIRley [ʃɛ:rli] (·) it_s the BRIng an_ BUy [baɪj] down [dæ:n] the
     6   frIEndly club on FRIday i [ae] CAN_t [kɔ:r] miss that (_) they DON_T [dəʊ]
     7   LIKE [lae:rk] it when you DON_T [dəʊ] turn up (.) they DIDN_T [dɛɪj] speak [spɛɪk]
     8   to winnie ROBinson for a fortnight [fa:rtnit] after _ER DIDN_T [dɛɪj] tURn [tɛərn] up
     9   Joan: don_t [dəʊw] sOUnd [sae:nd] very friendly to ME
    10   <<audience laughter>>

The four women's speech is peppered with recognizable Black Country dialect features, far more so than Harry Pardow's, such as the pronoun exchange *her* for *she* in line 8; the ablaut negation of 'doh' in place of 'don't' in lines 2, 3 and 9 and pronunciations of diphthongs in 'like' and 'spake' for 'speak'. Their carnivalesque representation evokes the parochial nature of their life 'back home,' created by Rose who continues to pine for home, rebutted by May and undercut by Joan, with her remark about the unfriendly nature of the friendly club. The characteristic Black Country trait of being down to earth discussed by Paul Jennings also features here in Joan's response as to the unfriendly nature of the friendly club. The sketch continues with May and Joan continuing to rebut Rose's negativity towards the holiday, with the Black Country dialect heavily in evidence, and translated:

(20) 1   May: you_ve [yʊv] GOt [goʔ] this LOVley [lʊvli] sea breeze an_ an_ (.) this
     2   BEAUtiful [bju:təfʌl]weather [wɛθae] what [wot] YOU [jow] got to to back to that_s
     3   BETTer than this
     4   Rose: BinGO [bɪngəʊ] our [ae:r] PAT always [alis] TAKes [tɛks] me to
     5   BINgo [bɪngəʊ] on a THURsday AfternOON [aeftərnu:n]
     6   Joan: (.) well YOU [jae] can DO [du:] it _ERE CAN_T [kɔ:r]
     7   YOU [jae] (.) down [dae:rn] by the POOL [pu:l] on a TUESsday [tiʊsdi] with TRIcky
     8   Dicky
               <<audience laugh>>
     9   Rose: but [bur] i [ae]CAN_t [kɔ:r] understand [ʌndɜ:rstaend] what [wor] _e [ae] _s [ɪʒ]
    10 a SAYin_ [sɛɪjɪŋ] _e [ae] _s [ɪʒ] FOReign [forɪn]
    11 May: _ e _ s [i:ʒ] from NEWCastle [nu:wkaesl]
    12 Rose: but [bur]_ I can_t [kɔ:r] understand [ʌndərstaend] what [wor] _e_s sayin_ [sæɪɪm]
               <<audience laugh>>

T glottalling features throughout, and May's pronunciation of *how* in line 2 to rhyme with *bow* is typical in the Black Country as well as Birmingham, though Joan's pronunciation of the same token in line 6 is different. The Black Country negation of *can't* enregistered by Rose is evident in line 9 as *kor* that changes to standard English in line 12 where the reference is people from the Black Country not understanding those from Newcastle. T-R is also evident in line 9 where *what* is voiced as *wor*. The double voicing of young actresses playing old ladies allows for a parodic, self-reflexive caricature and stereotypical portrayal of not only old ladies, but Black Country old ladies. The Black Country traits of self-deprecation, poking fun at oneself and down to earthness that characterised Paul Jennings' sketch as Harry Pardow is again in evidence throughout the dialogue of the sketch, as May and Joan try to cheer her up Rose, against Ruby's repeated lament that 'I doh like it.' The references Rose makes to local community events such as The Friendly Club and the game of bingo in the extract above, also evoke aspects of working class social activities and self-reflexively the narrow-minded parochial aspect of her outlook on life, with both being parodied through multi-voicing. The 'things to do, people to see' motif that is indicative of busy people in today's society is also parodied by the parochial nature of Rose's activities. 'Foreignness' in the sketch is also evoked as being not of the Black Country, whether from a different English region – Newcastle in the North – or another country. The irony of Rose not being able to understand the bingo caller's Newcastle accent and dialect when her own needs translating for an audience beyond the immediate locality would also not have been lost on the audience. The heavily enregistered use of morphosyntactic variation as outlined above as well as features of pronunciation all work together to make the dialect appear as if it were a language different from English.

The dialogue evokes frames linked to television programmes such as *Embarrassing Bodies* on Channel 4, which regularly deals with Britons who have developed heatstroke in Spain wearing unsuitable clothing, and songs such Noel Coward's famous cabaret song 'Mad Dogs and Englishmen', with its refrain of 'only mad dogs and Englishmen go out in the midday sun' tying into the stereotype that Britons cannot negotiate different climates successfully. However, whereas *Embarrassing Bodies* evokes frames of rejection, those evoked here are those of simultaneous acceptance and rejection: Rose frames the holiday as one of rejection in contrast to May and Joan who frame it in terms of acceptance. Correspondingly, the audience is invited to sympathise with each perspective in turn. Through such a use of parody, the actors bring to life national stereotypes that are reconfigured regionally through both the language choices the women make and the display of identified Black Country traits. In the dialogue, Black Countryness is indexed through absence of negation (ablaut negation) and the T-R rule in line 12. Indeed, the character who indexes Black Countryness the most is Ruby, the eldest of the ladies, who says the least and whose contributions are limited to the morose 'I don_t like it' throughout. It is realised not only with the ablaut negation which is so characteristic of Black Country dialect, but with a monophthong [aː]; thus 'I don-t like it' becomes [aːdoulaːkit]. This monophthong has been identified to be characteristic only of older Black Country speakers (Clark and Asprey 2013), used here to evoke said elderly speakers through the double-voiced nature of the actors' dialogue.

The dialogue continues with Rose continuing to complain about having to stay on the holiday for another week:

(21) 1 Rose: i think ONE week_S [w ɪks]
　　　 2 QUITE sufficient ESpecially in this HEAT [ɹit] an_ ALL [ɛnɔːl] it_s enough
　　　 3 to KILL YOU [iɔ ɪ]
　　　 4 May: don_t [dʌn] YOU [jəʊw] know if it wasn_t [wɔːr] for _ER [ɛːr] moanin_[mɔʊnɪn]
　　　 5 i_d [aːrd] think _ER [ɛər] was [wʌ3] DEAD [dʒed]

May's contribution to the exchange exhibits several Black Country features in close proximity to one another: the ablaut negation of 'don't' and 'wasn't'; g-dropping in 'moanin_'; pronoun exchange of /-er/ for /she/; /s/ pronounced as /z/ in *was* and the /d/ of the word *dead* pronounced as /j/ to give *jed* [dʒed]. In this way, the carnivalesque nature of the dialogue in this performance centring upon young women parodying older ones continues, through both the content and its linguistic delivery. The dialogue moves on to talk about food:

(22) 1 Joan: oh _er CAN_T [kɔːr] be EATin_[æɪtɪn] all that FOReign [forun] muck we shall
　　　 2 ALL end up [ʌp] DEAD [dʒed]
　　　 3 Rose: you [jəʊw] CAN_T [kɔːr] go [guː] to anOTHER country an_ NOT TRY the cuisine
　　　 4 Joan: well I_M [aːrm] _avin_[aevɪŋ] (·) EGG an_ CHIPS [dʒips]
　　　 5 May:oh [əʊw]GOD presERve us
　　　 6 Rose: MAY don_t [dʌn] they DO [duːw] EGG in SPAIN [spɛːrn]
　　　 7 　　　<<audience laugh>>
　　　 8 Joan: _cause [kʌs] I _AS enough trouble with MY [maː] BOWels without shovin_ [θʌvin]
　　　 9 more of that SALmonELa down my [maː] neck well they DON_T [dəʊw] wash the
　　　10 _ANDS [ʊnds]　do [dʌn] they (.)
　　　11 they CAN_T [kɔːr] _elp it though they aren_t [bɛɪj] brITish

Dialect use pulls the women together in a uni-directional way in their personae as Black Country women but in vari-directional ways in relation to their differing experiences of being such women abroad on holiday. The same dialect features are again evident throughout this extract as in the previous ones, particularly the morphosyntactic as well as phonological ones in lines 1, 2, 6, 9, 10 and 11. The multi-voiced aspect of these features in the context of the dialogue is much in evidence here, firstly as the young women continue to portray Black Country old ladies that incorporate aspects of British culture such as suspicion of foreign food and eating habits, contrasting the foreign Spanish in suspicious opposition to the British as 'muck'. The whole sketch is redolent of enregistered features indexing not only place but also gender, age and ethnicity associated with stereotypical older middle-aged, white working-class women typical of an age gone by but remembered in living memory, brought to life in the audience's imagination through the imagined community they evoke by their representations. The dialogue about food continues, with many of the dialect features drawn upon once again:

(23) 1 Joan: no I_M [ɑːrm] goin_ to [gʌnae] _AVE [aev] EGG and CHIPS [dʒɪps]
      2 <<audience laughs>>
      3 Rose: well YOU [jəʊw] can plEASE [plɛɪʒ] yourself [jʌsɛlf] _cause [kʌʒ] I_M [ɑːrm]
      4 goin_ to [gʌnə] TRY [traɪj] some of [ə[that EH erm (2.1)
      5 I KNOWS it (-)
      6 May: _ERE [ɪar] we go [guːw]
      7   <<audience laugh>>
      8 Rose: it_s SPANish oh [əw] (-) it STARTs with a P
      9 Joan: PIZZA [piːtʒae]
      10   <<audience laugh>>
      11 Rose: IT ISN_T [tɛɪj] sPAnISH   (.) it_s FREnch
      12 May: (-) it_s itALian [ɪtali ʌn] YOU [jəʊw[just [dʒʌs] said FREnch
      13 Rose: what did I [ɑːr] just [dʒʌs] SAY
      14 May: FREnch
      15 Rose: I [ɑːr] don_t [dəʊw] think I DID
      16 May: I [ɑːr] think you [jəʊw] DID
      17 Rose: may don_t [dəʊw] think I did wELL (.) itALian FREnch
      18   <<audience laugh>>
      19 SPAnish CHINese they all looks [lʊks] the SAME [sɛərm] DON_T [dəʊw] they I
      20 CAN_T [kɔːr] tell the DIFFerence [difrens]

The pronunciation of *you* as *yow* is evident in line 3; as is g-dropping in lines 1 and 4. The exchange between lines 13 and 16 in the performance echoes pantominesque exchanges of this nature and allows for the enregistration of *don't* as *day* with *kor* for can't featuring in line 20. Though caricaturing elderly Black Country ladies, their stereotypes also evoke national English ones. The location is too hot for Rose, Joan does not wish to try Spanish food and asks instead for a typically British meal of egg and chips, and the whole of the last excerpt's humour is based on Rose's linguistic adventurousness and its subsequent backfiring as she fails not only to remember what *paella* is called, but to know the language from which the word itself comes. These three traits could be said to caricature to any Briton abroad as often portrayed in popular culture. For example, the film *Shirley*

Valentine featured a middle-aged white female protagonist who got a job at a Greek cafe helping hapless Britons to navigate Greek menus, and in one scene she offered to ask the chef to do 'double egg and chips' for an elderly British couple. As with Jennings' performance discussed above though, such traita are exemplified through a regional focus, in this instance that of the Black Country and the self-deprecating down to earth character traits that typify people from the region.

3.4.1 In conversation with *Fizzog*

The conversation interview with Fizzogg took place a few days after the performance, at The Black Country Living Museum, where the group were rehearsing a play to be performed at that venue, again in their personae as old Black Country ladies. Immediately, one of the actors, Deb, acknowledges the interviewer's introduction of them into the sound recorder as a Black Country Theatre Group with the reposte: ' we am' [aem[. It is clear from the context of this exchange that Deb enregisters the third person form of the verb *be* as indexing their Black Country identity. The conversation interview begins with the women recounting how they met, which was at a Dudley College, a College of Further Education, where they were all studying for a qualification in the performing arts.

There were not nearly as many dialect features evident in conversation as there had been in their performance, which is not surprising given the heavily enregistered nature of their performance. However, the same range is evident as in Paul Jennings' conversation. In Deb's speech, vowel dipthongization is evident in words such as *behind* [bi:aɪnd], *and* [æn], with h dropping in the middle of *behind* and d dropping at the end of *and*; in the words *like* [laɪʔ] and *working* [w3:kɪn], again with g dropping and the rounding of the *oo* [ʊ] sound typical of the pronunciation of *Dudley*, also evident in tokens such as the first syllable of *untrue* [ʊntru].

After completing their course, the women worked for a number of years in health in education, touring local schools and community groups. Although none of these plays was region specific, they wrote one more recently that was, centring upon women's experiences during World War 2, which was how the old lady characters that featured in the sketch discussed above came about. They also spoke about their use of dialect in performance, and how it has been received locally in largely negative terms, both Birmingham and the Black Country, including performing at a primary school in Wolverhampton, where the pupils had trouble understanding the Black Country dialect. Jackie gave her thoughts on this:

(24) 1   Jacquie: WHAT [wor] it IS (.)i think we_ve been [bɪn] TOLD(–) in this REGion
     2   that [ðʌ?] OUR [ae:r] accents sounds Awful and we_ve BEEN [bin[sort of LUMped
     3   ogETHer with BIRmingham [bɔɪmiŋgʌm] as well an_ there_s THAT many
     4   different DIALECTS you know TWO miles down the ROAD you can _ave a completely
     5   different WELL not a comPLETely different DIAlect but [bʌ?] er like
     6   SUbtle [sʌʔl] DIFferences i think we_ve 6 BEEN [bɪn] portRAYed in the MEDia an_
     7   sort [sʌt] of [ʌv[ERM (.) you know TOLD HOW THICK we sOUnd and _ow [aʊw]
     8   _OW [aʊw]_ow [aʊw] un (.) you [j][kNOw the the the ACCents sOUnds [sæuwnds]
     9   awful

Here, Jacquie pronounces 'sound' in line 7 in a standard RP way, but in line 8, when talking about negative perceptions of the accent, realises it with the Black Country pronunciation. Despite the negative attitudes held by the general public at large towards the Black Country accent, the theatre group believe that it is important to draw upon accent and dialect in their performances, especially those set in the present as well as the past, as a way of bringing their characters to life for their audiences. As with Paul Jennings in relation to his Harry Pardow persona, the women in their performance as Fizzog acknowledged that they draw upon regional dialect in deliberate and thus enregistered and indexical ways as a means of retaining a sense of linguistic heritage that links the present to the recent past. The women were also all too well aware of how people accommodate their speech according to the situations in which they find themselves. As Jacquie explained on the group's behalf, in the context of a situation such as the conversation during the interview in which she was taking part with a researcher, she was conscious of adjusting her accent to one that was more akin to RP in other words – accommodating towards RP – indicating their self-awareness of accommodation depending upon any given speech situation. When asked about language through which they portrayed the old ladies in their sketch, Jacquie said that this allowed them to incorporate a far greater degree of dialect than if they played women of their own age, and connects them to the working-class communities the old women represent.

3.4.2 In conversation with members of the audience and celebrities

The performance was attended by a nationally well-known producer of history documentaries, Michael Wood, who at the time was working on a series for BBC2 called *The Great British Story,* a social history of the UK that also included language change as a topic. He had come to see the performance with a view to possibly featuring Black Country dialect in one of its episodes. Michael said that the performance was not at all as he had expected. He thought that the acts would be more of the kind found in folk clubs that harked back to a nostalgic past with no real connection to today's world. Instead, he said 'he got' the Fizzog's sketch as an ironic, parodying, self-reflexive caricature of Black Country old ladies, where the audience was invited to laugh if not exactly at themselves, at people they knew who were like the elderly middle-aged ladies' portrayed in the performance. Mary, another member of the audience in her late twenties, echoed many of the observations made by Margaret and Geoff after Paul Jennings' performance: namely that the audience reaction around her seemed mixed. She had noticed that not everyone around her laughed to the same degree. In her case, she said that she throughly enjoyed the sketch, reminding her as it did of her own grandmother and grandmother's friends. She reported that she recognised many of the dialect features in the performance that her grandmother's generation in particular used but she herself nor her mother no longer did.

One of the most famous people associated with the Black Country is the actress Julie Walters, who has starred in numerous films, stage plays and television series, including the *Harry Potter* series of films, the stage play and film of *Educating Rita* and most recently, the television series *Indian Summers* set in India during colonial times. Julie began her acting career at the *Everyman Theatre* in Liverpool during the 1970s. As she recalled prior to that time it probably would not have been to an actor's advantage to have a recognisable regional accent, but she counted herself lucky to have entered the profession at a time when 'kitchen sink' drama was very popular. Like others of her generation, Julie benefitted from a grammar school education that gave her access to Drama college and subsequently her first acting role at *The Everyman* theatre in Liverpool, at a time when it was a positive advantage to have a working-class accent. She spoke of her feeling of offensiveness when people tried to get her to get rid of her accent, firstly her mother through wanting to send her to elocution lessons and secondly the standard English classes offered at drama school.

Julie attests to the issue of agency in relation to how she chooses to speak, especially her resistance to accommodate towards standard English, and that to do so would be a betrayal of who she was as a person. She spoke of her time growing up in West Bromwich, or West Brom as it is known locally, a suburb that lies between Birmingham and the Black Country, and why she has never felt the need to eradicate her accent. In the extract below, she also refers from line 6 to being given the opportunity to play the character in *Educating Rita* who was from Liverpool with a Black Country accent about which we had just been talking:

(25) 1   Julie: THAt_s why my ACcent i_ve STIll got it i_ve NEver made any EFFort to try
      2   and get rid of it i HAven_t done what some people   do is TRYand KEEP it Either (-)

3 i_ve LET it BE what what it IS (-) this is HOW it_s turned OUT you know (-) but as soon
4 as i go HOME [həʊːm] (-) of course i start or as soon as i_m with my SISter in law i
5 start sort of speaking much more like THAT because i can_t HElp it_s like it_s the way
6 it is erm the HUMour would have been different (-)   and everything (-) _cause
7 liverpools a VERY diFferent PLACE isn_t it (-) with it_s irish   influence and it_s and
8 everything HER HUmour HER turn of PHRASE (-) was NOT BIRmingham and a
9 BIRmingham girl would have (.) would have HAD a WHOle different WAY of
10 EXPRESSing it (.) i_m not saying she wouldn_t have FELT the same things but
11 WOULD have said them DIFFerently.

The only token pronounced in dialect in this extract is Julie's pronunciation of 'home' in line 4, though it is clear from our conversation that she is well aware of both how she accommodates her speech and the part dialect use plays in performance. In this particular telephone conversation, between an internationally acclaimed actor and a university professor, accommodation was towards the standard and pronouncing 'home' as she does, evokes a place where dialect use would be most prevalent: within her family. During the 1970s much TV and theatre drama was set amongst working class communities, particularly in the North of England. Willy Russell was a well-known playwright who set his plays in the North, and Julie recalled being cast as the character Rita in his play *Educating Rita*. Russell told Julie she could play the part with a Birmingham/Black Country accent, but Julie said she could not do that, since the Northern humour in the play was so different. Although she did not recall any syntactic differences in dialect whilst she was growing up, Julie did recall being called *Babs*, a Birmingham and Black Country word for a female, young or old, thinking that was her actual name until she was about 14 years old.

Other prominent actors and musicians such as the actor Mark Williams and the musician Al Atkins, a member of the well-known rock band *Judas Priest,* also testified to their refusal to bow to any pressure to accommodate the way they spoke away from their regional accents and towards standard English. Like Julie Walters, Al Atkins was born and educated in West Bromwich and still lives in the area. His parents are of Welsh and Irish descent, having migrated to the Black Country for work. Al talked of two recent occasions where he was made aware of his dialect and of how he spoke being different from standard English. The first instance was during the writing of his autobiography, his publisher insisted he changed the dialect word *glede* to standard English *small piece of coal.* The second was during interviews for American TV and radio. Al talked about the ways he felt he had to 'tone down' – in other words, accommodate away from – the Black Country dialect and more towards standard English in order to be understood by his American interviewers and audiences. He also reported that whilst in his personal life he may talk in the Black Country dialect and in contrast to Julie Walters, he recognised its limits when it came to his professional life, saying that he didn't think his records would sell as well if he sang his heavy metal songs in a Black Country accent.

3.5 Performance 3 *Any Villa fans in the room?* Stand-up comedy

The city of Birmingham borders the Black Country to the West, and despite the close geographic proximity of the two regions, has a very different demographic makeup. Whilst the Black Country is made up of a dense network of what were once in the 19th century mainly small towns and villages straddling three shire counties. By contrast, Birmingham's growth from a relatively small town occurred largely after the end of the First World War, from the early 1930s onwards, swallowing up surrounding villages in its wake, largely within the county of Warwickshire. Today the city, in common with almost all English cities, has a thriving circuit of spoken word events such as open mic nights that draw in a largely young audience of 18-to-35 year olds, a largely younger demographic than those who attended the *Black Country Variety* spoken word events at a venue such as *The Holly Bush*. The performer discussed here, Craig Deeley, is typical of young performers who can be found on any night of the week performing at the myriad performance venues based in pubs around Birmingham, both in the city centre and outlying suburbs that provide a local, grass roots circuit for new, aspiring amateur performers attempting to break into more semi-professional or professional work. These aspiring performers comprise a mixture of locally born and bred people like Craig Deeley, together with those who have moved into Birmingham from outside the region and now live and work in the city. The demographic nature of their audiences is such that they are far more ethnically and socially diverse than those that take place in the Black Country. They are also much younger, being in the main aged between 18 and early 30s.

In common with many other performers like himself and unlike Paul Jennings and the women's theatre group *Fizzog*, the Birmingham comedian Craig Deeley does not adopt stage personae but rather plays an amplified version of himself. In so doing, he is following in the tradition of contemporary comedians such as Jasper Carrot, Lenny Henry, and Miranda Hart, and earlier British comedians such as Eric Morecambe, Ernie Wise and Henry Cooper. Craig is a younger and less well established performer in comparison to Paul Jennings and the theatre group *Fizzog*, plays on the amateur circuit, in pubs and clubs around the region and is also part of a Birmingham based theatre group. At the time of the performance discussed below, Craig was in his late twenties at the time of the performance.

The performance attended took place as part of an open mic night at a pub in the Birmingham suburb of Sheldon, a predominantly white, working class area but a cut above the Rosalind Estate in Dudley referred to by Paul Jennings, which had been renamed *The Kerri Gold* since an Indian restaurant was now attached to it. The venue, although located locally in a suburban area of Birmingham, drew on a wider and more varied potential audience demographically than that of *The Holly Bush* in Cradeley Heath discussed in the sections above. As a city, Birmingham is much more culturally and ethnically diverse than the Black Country, with a large student population, and thus Craig's potential audience is drawn from a more mixed demographic than that of *The Holly Bush's* audience. As with all such venues there was no stage, and the audience comprised a mixture of people who came specifically to watch the open mic acts and those who were uninterested in it and had come in for a drink with friends. In total, there were approximately 26 people present, a mixture of men and women who were mainly young adults.

Given the Craig began his act by gauging the places from which his audience had come:

(26) 1 (.) it_s Very COsey is_nt It(-)i er NORMally do a bit [bɪʔ] of STAge DIVin_ [daɪvɪŋ]
      2 i don_t THInk i_ll do any of that TOnight(.)HOW you (jʌ) DOing [du:ɪŋ] alrIGHT
      3 cOMe fAR
      4 Audience: cheers and general noise
      5 WHERE _ave you [jʌ] cOme from (.)WOrcester [wʌstɛ] BROmsgrove nAvigation street ok
      6 AY (.)
      7 Audience put up hands and shout out. One shouts: CHINA
      8 CHINA (.) oh wEll done
      9   <<audience laugh>>
     10 TEN minutes LAte but you [jʌ] know thERE you [jʌ] go (.) no WELL WELL come
     11 we_ve gOT er (.) DOn_t DOn_t lOOk at this it_s up sTAging me a little bit DO_NT
     12 look at 12 it just look at ME (.) ERM gIve me [gɪm] a CHEER if you (jʌ) are LOCAL
     13   <<some members cheer>>
     14 give me a CHEER if you [jʌ] _re nOt Local
     15 <<other members cheer>>
     16 give me [gɪmɪ] a cheer if you [jʌ] hate audience PARticiPAtion
     17 <<audience all cheer>>
     18 NO there_ll [ðul] be NOne of THAt rubbISH (.) er I I AM LOcal I AM from
     19 BIRrmingham [birmɪŋʌm] (-)yes [jɛ] that [ðae?] Never [nɛvə] GEts a CHeer [tʃɪəjae]
         <<laughing>>
     20 never gets a cheer [tʃɪəjae]EVen whEN i do local gigs

Dialect features are far less prevalent in Craig's act, with glottal stopping in line 1 and the velar nasal plus sound in line 19 when he says 'Birmingham.' Craig begins his act by engaging in dialogue with his audience lines 1 to 9 to both gain a sense of form where they are drawn and to establish a rapport, interrupted by someone walking to the bar in front of him in line 10. Indexing place occurs more through reference to local streets and other places rather than through enregistering features of the dialect itself. The first two places he mentions in line 5 are nearby towns in Worcestershire, and Navigation Street is a street in the centre of Birmingham. The cheers emanating from his question as to whether or not people self-report themselves as local is equal. Having engaged the audience in participation, he undercuts this by inviting their response to such participation. He then draws attention to himself in line 19 as being local and from Birmingham as a frame of rejection, acknowledging the negative perceptions associated with the city ahead of his audience. Craig moves onto a turn about Birmingham City Football Club, which was owned at the time by a Hong Kong businessman:

(27) 1   I was goin_ [gɛʊɪn] to a costume party for Halloween the other week and I put [pʊʔ]
2   this bid on this Mickey Mouse outfit [ɛʊʔfiʔ] (...) I ended up owning birmingham city
3   football club what the fuck [fʊk] am I goin_ to [gʊnæ] do with that [ðaʔ]
4   <<audience laugh>>
5   Birmingham City [sɪʔl] are a bit-of-a [bɪrəvə] strange club
6   <<audience laugh>>
7   YES (.) big lookalike agreein_ [əgɹiːɪn] with me (.) thank you Gary
8   they've just been bought [bɔːt] out [ɛʊt] by [baɪ] the Hong Kong hairdresser Carson
9   Yeung and he's told [tɒʊɫd] Alex McLeish he needs to start [staːʔ]
10   deliverin_ [dɪlɪvəɹɪn] so that's [ðaʔs] two chicken fried rice two curry sauce and some
11   prawn crackers to the Keri Gold I take it
<<audience laugh>>

In this extract, the 'oo' [ʊ] sound is also evident in lines 2, 3, 8 and 9, indicating that Craig probably comes from the west side of Birmingham that borders the Black Country, which turns out to be the case when he was interviewed. He frames Birmingham City Football Club as one of rejection, that of an underperforming one through juxtaposing it with the American cartoon character of Micky Mouse. He intersperses his performance with interjections directly related to the audience in order to retain their interest, as in line 7. The globalised nature of popular culture in relation to both football and food is crystallised in lines 9 to 11 through his pun on the word 'deliver', linking Hong Kong to Chinese food and the performance venue with its Indian restaurant. In much the same way as Paul Jennings in his persona of Harry Pardow, Craig contemporises his comedy by referring to imaginative spaces and associated people across the globe and linking them back to Birmingham and the specific place in which the comedy venue is situated. Craig then moves on to a turn centred around two Birmingham football clubs, that of Aston Villa known locally as 'the villa' and Birmingham City known locally as 'the blues.'

(28) 1 any Villa Fans in the room Villa fans
2 <<audience cheer>>
3 Blues fans
4 <<audience cheers louder>>
5 fucking [fʊkin] hell [ɛʊ] (.) start [stɑ:ʔ] the car [kɑ:] love [lʏv] (.) quick
6 <<audience laugh>>

The pattern identified in Paul Jennings' and Fizzog's performances is repeated here in Craig's, namely his use of features associated with the Brummie accent are at their highest level at a punch line, when he seeks to elicit laughter. Craig avoids glottalling when discussing how Yeung 'bought out Birmingham City' yet can be seen to return to heavy levels of glottalling when he delivers the punchline at the end of the excerpt in line 5 in which he appears to feign fright and horror that the room is full of more Birmingham City football fans than Aston Villa ones.

In the extracts given above, Craig begins his act by references to the immediate locality which requires local knowledge on the part of the audience, linking local referents to a broader shared cultural understanding of Birmingham as a city and England as a nation. These in turn give way to a more general cultural understanding of well-known icons of the Western world, such as *Mickey Mouse* and *Hallowe'en*, interspersed and intertwined amongst references to football and Chinese take away food. Through his parody, Craig draws upon a range of stereotypes to create a world of Brummies in opposition not only to the rest of the UK but also to wealthy people from Hong Kong and not so wealthy people from India, who appear to be encroaching upon British Birmingham culture through the proliferation of Asian restaurants and the purchase of local football clubs. The imagined community centring upon Birmingham in Craig's performance is bound by reference to immediate localities, with parody taking the form of puns on place and people's names. His audience is much younger and more demographically varied than those that attended *The Hollybush* events in the Black Country, with all references made throughout and frame evoked of contemporary events with none of the harking back to a past drawn upon by Paul Jennings and Fizzog in their performances. Craig's performance given here is an example of the ways comedy at this local level exposes and plays on people's prejudices and insecurities in a rapidly changing cultural and social world, characterised by increased globalisation. Being Brummie in this sketch is defined more by the content of the sketch – football and takeaway food in this instance – and its references to local people and places, and not so much through drawing upon dialect features to the extent identified in the speech of Black Country performers.

3.5.1 In conversation with Craig Deeley

Craig was born and brought up in west Birmingham in the early 1980s, and like other performers and actors such as Paul Jennings and Julie Walters, went to grammar school and also onto higher education, the first of his family to so do. Whilst at university, he ran his own radio show, spending time in France and Germany before undertaking a teaching qualification. In common with almost all of the performers who took part in the project, Craig self-reported as working class but with a middle-class lifestyle.

His current occupation is as a lecturer at a college of further education. He began performing comedy in 2003, and he reported that the main source of his material is, as discussed in Chapter 2 part of a process whereby conversations he hears between people around Birmingham that he finds funny (contextualised), which he jots down (decontextualizes), adapts and embellishes (encontextualises) before weaving them into his comedy act. When asked about his use of dialect, Craig reported that he had not thought consciously about his speech until he went away to university, where he said in relation to his Brummie accent, that he 'had to tone down a bit' and thus accommodated more towards standard English. Previously in his teens, he had worked in the outdoor market in West Bromwich, a town whose inhabitants believe lies on the Birmingham and Black Country border, and as a result of mixing with market traders his accent became noticeably more Brummie, something of which he was not aware until he attended university. Whilst he had accommodated his speech more towards that of standard English and RP since attending university, like other performers who took part in the research, he said that when he comes home and talks to his family, he reverts to his Brummie accent and accommodates back towards it. In terms of dialect use in his acts, Craig talked about striking a 'middle ground' between RP and Brummie. He said he invariably started his performances by saying he was from Birmingham followed swiftly by acknowledging that this never gets him a cheer. This is because of his experience of having identified himself as Brummie being met either with silence from the audience or from some of its members saying 'never mind' or 'poor you.' Craig puts this down to the nature of the Brummie character:

(29) 1 we we can SLAG BIRmingham [bɜ:mɪŋɡəm] off an_ the BLACK country off no one
  2 ELSE can
  3 Interviewer: _OW do you READ your AUDiences then WHEN you (.)

4   erm (–) (-) OFten [ofʌn] OFten [ofʌn] you can just JUSt have a LOOK at the demoGRAPHic
5   of the AUDience you knOW you can TELL often [ofʌn[by(-) the AGE 6 (-) what [wʊʔ[
6   you GAUGe the AGE to be you can TELL by the surrOUNDin_ [səraundɪŋ] areas as
7   WELL (.) you know but [bʌʔ]   you CAN't always get [gɛʔ] it RIGHT you know i_ve
8   sometimes TONed DO WHAT i _m goin_ to [gʌnnae] SAY (-) because i think it_s a
9   MORE (-) sophisticated AUDience (.) when in FACt they_re not [nʊʔ] so sometimes
10 you get it [gɜrɪt] wRONG
11 Interviewer: would you START to tone DOWN and then (.)
12 Craig: YES (jɛ) (.) if if i i_m erm i_ll OFten [ofʌn] (.) WATCH the comPERE because
13 see which way they GO and [an[if the audience reLATEs in a certain way to
     HIM (-) or
14 HER I_LL [aɪ] (–) know HOW to adapt my (-) my SET

Like Paul Jennings in relation to the Black County then, Craig gauges the extent to which he draws upon his Brummie accent and dialect in relation to his audience and the extent of their familiarity with Birmingham. The further away from the locality he performs and the more mixed his audience is demographically, the more he accommodates towards standard English and dialect switches in increasingly metaphoric ways. This indicates then, that the extent to which people enregister dialect use in their performances relates directly to the perceived demographic of their audiences. The more local the venue, the greater the degree of features that are enregistered, the further away, the degree is lesser.

3.5.2 In conversation with Rob Hazel, local librarian

Alongside performance venues that give space to locally based performances and audiences, local libraries have also come to play an increasingly important role as both social spaces and local history archives and museums alongside their function of lending books. One such library is in Tipton, in the heart of the Black Country. Robert Hazel is the chief librarian, who was born in the neighbouring town of Wednesbury but has family in Tipton, and he has lived in the region all his life, spending his working life as a librarian, the last ten of which have been at Tipton. He recalls:

(30) the first day i started (.) one member of staff came up to me and asked are *yow ouer manager do yer spake proper* (.) i remember having to think before i answered as that depends that_s a very leading question when she said *cos I spake Black Country* and i said *well that_s good because I do as well so youw OK* i thought that was interesting (.) since she thought I couldn_t speak in dialect because i was a professional

Robert recalled how he had always been interested in dialect, a curiosity that increased when he came to work at Tipton Library. One of the first customers he came across on his first day in the library, an elderly gentleman, said to him: *ower you me mon?* (how are you my man) which Robert found a very welcoming term of endearment, *me mon*. He also organises open mic nights in the library and recalled overhearing a member of the audience say in the library the next day in regards to a female performer: *it were a top night what a wench*. Robert also talked about how the loss of industry in the region had affected people's social identity centred upon work as discussed earlier in the chapter, pointing out that was once the power-house of the country, with dialect being spoken as a matter of course in the factories and the banter that would have existed between large groups of men working in close proximity with one another, in often sweltering heat. Older people in the region who may have left school at age 14 and who had never gone beyond it might still speak in dialect as a first order indexicality, as given in the example of the audience member above. Robert also talked about giving talks in schools where some of the parents in their 30s had been born in the region and never moved beyond it, citing one male parent who had never left Tipton in his life.

He also talked about hearing dialect words spoken that he had forgotten about, such as *clarnet* (idiot), and how he made a point of deliberately incorporating them into his own speech: in other words, using them in an enregistered way to index affiliation with the Black Country region. He also testified, like many, that he was well aware of the various ways in which he accommodated his speech:

(31) everyone does it really you modify your accent (.) cos I can go out with a group of friends and be as broad as I like it just depends (.) one of my best mates from school moved to oxford and he_ll come down for the weekend visiting and his wife will phone me and say *I know he's been out with you*and I_ll say *what_s he done* and she says *the first night he comes home he_ll say tarra a bit*

Tarra a bit is Birmingham and Black Country dialect for *goodbye* or *see you*. Robert was also aware that he accommodated his voice to that of the library's customers. If they spoke in dialect so did he, but if they did not, he didn't either. The extent to which people engage in accommodation then, varies from person to person and situation to situation. Reflexivity about language use on behalf of the general public at large however, provides the conditions whereby performers, particularly when performing in local venues to highly localised audiences and in a region such as the Black Country, can exploit their linguistic awareness for both comic effect and in relation to identity construction simultaneously.

3.6 Conclusion

Discussion of performances and related conversation interviews undertaken in this chapter, provides a contemporary snapshot of sociolinguistic reality and represents a moment of temporal and spatial mobility. It also allows that snapshot to be extended out and panned beyond the moment of temporal and spatial mobility in which the performance occurred, to the wider social and cultural contexts in which they took place. All of the performers self–reported themselves as coming from working class backgrounds and by virtue of their education and occupation had become middle class. Rather than bowing to hegemonic pressures to eradicate dialect features from their speech in a centripetal way, individuals may, centrifugally, choose to retain some of them. Dialect use vis a vis standard English, particularly as used by performers in performance contexts, is thus in constant dialogic tension that both constitute and reflect differing ideologies upon which world views are predicated. All were well aware of the stigma accorded to the region's dialect yet steadfastly retained aspects of their accent and dialect, particularly when talking to family members and accommodating to other speech contexts accordingly. In general, people are all too well aware of the social attitudes and prejudices towards dialect use that permeate British society and the negative perceptions held towards those of Birmingham and the Black Country.

It is also clear from discussion in conversation interview with performers and celebrities that the features identified in this chapter are drawn upon indexically to mark an identity linked to place, in this case one linked to the Birmingham or the Black Country, that is in turn linked to working class personae. The localised nature of performance venues means that performers are able to evoke a working-class past that is shared collectively by the majority of their audience in self-reflexive ways, bringing time and space together through a sense of a specific place. It also allows for performers to relocate social institutions and day to day activities that have become increasingly dislocated from local communities – such as the police, holidays and football – in ways that embed them back into the community. What all performers have in common, is the ways in which they construct imagined communities that are conjured up in relation to Birmingham or the Black Country that relate the local place in which the performance is performed to spaces outside of it across the whole world, whether that be a European location such as a beach in Spain, or further afield as in the United States or China.

Clearly, in terms of confronting social and economic change, performers draw on dialect use and localised references in carnivalesque and self-reflexive ways to evoke imagined communities centred upon the region in which they live and the performances take place, and through such use subvert or mock contemporary cultural norms, including linguistic ones. They do so in ways that are also received differently by members of their localised audiences. Either they find them amusing or uncomfortable, depending upon individuals' past experiences. The performances also exemplify the underlying sociocultural contexts within which they occur as a means of juxtaposing the norms and values of those 'within' the community from those 'outside' or 'beyond' it, in ways that subvert traditional notions of linguistic and social hierarchy, and particularly by poking fun at them.

The analysis above indicates that dialect use in Birmingham and the Black Country can indeed be an active resource in creating identity for performance effect and on a personal identity level (performer versus individual). Above all, the discussion shows that situational use can transcend traditional social categories; that is, speakers of middle-class origins and working-class origins can project the same linguistic norms in a performance situation, and a mixed-class audience can evaluate the linguistic variation in the same way because of situational context. Performers index their affinity with working-class origins, even though they themselves have moved, through education and employment, into the middle class. The extent to which performers enregister features associated with the dialects of their region also depends upon the performance locality and the demographic makeup of their audiences. Discussion with performers verified that the further away from their locality, the more likely it is that they use dialect less frequently and in a more enregistered way. Performers thus consciously interweave a specific set of dialect features in ways that relate, connote or signify specific geographic places and the speech communities that inhabit them. Such conscious choice is indicative of an understanding on the part of both performers and their audiences of the underlying hegemonic cultural and social forces associated with the use of a sociolect such as standard English and regional dialects. Discussion with members of the audience though, revealed that individuals related to the use of dialect in oppositional ways. Upon realising that they spoke with a recognizable regional dialect, they either embraced it or eradicated its traces from their day to day speech. Their motivation for either position depended upon their own personal experiences and their reactions to them.

4 Staging language in performance: Comedy and parody in contemporary Afro Caribbean performances

4.1 Introduction

The performances discussed in this chapter were performed by young minority ethnic performers in Birmingham of Afro Caribbean origin. Also discussed is a conversation interview with Benjamin Zephaniah, a well-known poet of Afro Caribbean origin. It highlights the complexity of youth identities and language forms in contemporary super-diverse settings. Analysis of performance recordings, performer and audience member interviews also identifies the ways in which performers draw upon a range of identified dialects from a designated 'linguistic or feature pool' to create a new urban multiethnolect of English that I call 'Black Brum'.

As discussed in Chapter 1, the concepts of the 'linguistic or feature pool' and 'mulitethnolects' have arisen in the context of contemporary mainland Europe and the ways in which people interweave features of their differing home languages into the host one, thereby transcending geographic anchorage to one place and instead draw upon several. The performers also draw upon a range of contemporary music genres for their influences including Rap poetry, incorporating Jamaican Creole lexis into their vocabularies, alongside phonological systems which are redolent of Birmingham. Others drawn from American English alongside Jamaican Creole and varieties of British English, most notably Multicultural London English (MLE) (Kerswill et al 2012) or *Jafaican* as identified by Kerswill (2014), who also draws upon the concept of a multiethnolect.

The discussion that follows centres upon the ways in which features of both regional dialects associated with Birmingham and to a certain extent London in England and global varieties of English such as Jamaican Creole and patwa are drawn upon to index a range of localities that crosse different places and spaces from within England – Birmingham and London – and beyond the UK – the Caribbean – bringing them together within the situational contexts and place of contemporary Birmingham. Situational use not only transcends traditional social categories but also problematizes the construction of localness as a matter of using a single local code or evoking a single local place, through drawing together different local codes associated with a range of places into the recontextualisation of a new, hybrid dialect of English. The range identified draws from four different dialects, namely those of: Birmingham English (BE), Black British English (BBE), Jamaican Creole (JC) and Multicultural London English (MLE).

https://doi.org/10.1515/9781501506796-004

With regard to the nature of the relationship between performers and the communities they purport to represent, the performers are from the same region or locality as their audiences and thus, as interview data shows, share common experiences in relation to social and cultural changes. They share similar histories and heritage and the performances acknowledge these, acting as vehicles for expressions of cultural and social identities. In this way, the two performers discussed in this chapter, Andre Soul Hesson (ASH) and Deci4Life (DFL), and the poets Rob McFarlane and Benjamin Zephaniah, can be described as mixing linguistic forms of both the past and the present, and across place and space, in giving rise to new linguistic forms that cannot be categorised straightforwardly as 'Black'. I also consider what the performers have to say about the language they use in their performances, and the degree to which they themselves are aware of enresgitering certain linguistic features as a way of indexing a sense of place and sociocultural identity.

4.2 Birmingham and superdiversity

Birmingham is the UK's second city in terms of population (Manchester is larger in area). Landmark places in the city such as Digbeth, Handsworth and Sparkbrook carry the imprint of post 19th century Famine Irish migration and post-World War 2 African Caribbean and Asian migration, respectively. To this can also be added post World War 2 migration from Eastern Europe together with more recent migrations of second wave Eastern European migration and migration from Asia, particularly from Pakistan and Bangladesh. Birmingham then, is characterised by its multiculturalism, which has been understood largely in relation to post-war immigration to the city. Today, the abovementioned areas to which others such Aston and Alum Rock among others can also be added, are celebrated as spaces of multicultural community along with the more predicable enclaves of ethnic business that characterize large cities. This recent migration has added new layers of diversity to the city, along with the emergence of second and third generation minority ethnic youth, which work to disrupt settled notions of the way multiculture exists in the city. It is a bustling metropolis, and its size, demographics and increasing international feel are some of the factors that have helped put the city on the global map. Figures from the 2011 census show that although the largest ethnic group in Birmingham remains White British, the percentage has decreased since 2001 to 53.1%, and far lower than the average in England as a whole (79.8%). The city's current demographic profile is such that it is well on its way to becoming a majority black city. At the same time, the number of people defining themselves as Black Caribbean has declined over the past decade.

As discussed in Chapter 1, commentators such as Vertovec (2007) use the term *superdiversity* over *multiculturalism* or *diversity* to capture some of the new dynamics resulting from such globalized movements of people and the impact this has on communities and identities. It is in this context that language use among young 'black' performers in the city was analyzed, to uncover what it reflects and constructs about their identity in an increasingly globalised age (Blommaert 2010). A bird's eye view of the city's demography resembles the patchwork of an ideal type multicultural mosaic, since the spatial segregation of different ethnic groups patterns the city into areas of predominantly white settlement, with clusters of black and Asian neighborhoods around the city centre. Many of these areas (Sparkbrook, Balsall Heath) have been early attractors for immigrants since the 1940's. In recent decades, new waves of migration have brought newer nationalities to these areas such as refugees fleeing conflict in the Balkans and the Horn of Africa in the 1990's. As well as this, the emergence of second and third generation black and Asian youth has altered the way multiculturalism exists or plays out as it results in 'transruptions' (Hesse 2000) of old orders of society, particularly as being layered in terms of ethnic groups alone. Thus life in these areas could be read in terms of dynamism and relationality between groups and processes such as globalization, migration and economic development rather than merely on the basis of which ethnicities inhabit certain places.

Demographic and spatial settlement patterns thus emerge out of specific histories and trajectories (of immigration) giving a certain texture to black life in the city. Patterns of difference/diversity lend themselves to particular impressions of minority ethnic 'community' and identity. Superdiversity sees diversification in terms of national, ethnic, religious and linguistic categories. Globalisation – flows of culture, capital and people; changing communities, conditions and contexts of diversity; new complexities of diversity – thus gives rise to an interplay of origin, religion, regional and local identity, cultural values and practices. Within this paradigm, black (and other) youth cultures find themselves working through these legacies and beyond them. As Blommaert (2010: 196–7) has pointed out, "... sociolinguistics is traditionally more at ease while studying a village than while studying the world...we need to understand the sociolinguistic world as one in which language gets dislodged and its traditional functions distorted by processes of mobility". The performers under discussion in this paper provide an example of such dislodgement.

The performances given by the performers discussed in this chapter were performed by professional, highly talented linguistic players who making their living from their performances, in which they draw upon the various influences that circulate within and beyond Birmingham's minority ethnic communities and the musical cultures associated with them. The section below provides a brief overview of Black popular culture by way of further background before moving on discussing the linguistic aspects of their speech styles in more detail.

4.3 Black popular culture

Superdiversity unsettles the idea that people – in this case second generation African Caribbean youth – might have a simple reference point toward which their cultures are oriented. Black popular cultures (and even Asian) in the UK have long been viewed in mainstream analysis as oriented toward homelands that were linked to the migratory journey of the first generation. In the case of African Caribbean people, these popularly became known in the UK as the *Windrush* generation, following iconic images of people stepping off a ship with the same name that transported them from the Caribbean. Instead, scholars such as Gilroy (1993) who in his seminal work *The Black Atlantic*, uncovers the multiple trajectories that link black popular cultures in the UK to influences such as Hip Hop in the USA as well as reggae from the Carribean and African folk and Rastafarian from Africa, all at one and the same time. As Gilroy (1991) says: "It ain't where you're from, its where you're at..."

Since the 1990s, scholars in the field of ethnic and racial studies and cultural studies have been concerned with reconceptualising minority ethnic cultures and identities in the UK in light of young peoples' complicated engagements with various different influences within and beyond their ethnicity and homelands. In the case of the performers we discuss, their performances and linguistic styles are made up of complex musical processes and cultural exchanges that are not effectively captured by classificatory schemes such as reggae, rap, hip-hop, garage or grime. DFL and ASH are engaged in a much more unstable and multifarious form of cultural production, that is not only musical but also involves performance and spoken word, influences that are global and not linear in the sense of being only 'black British'. In their cases, I suggest that ethnicity or race is not a determinant of their style but a temporary position that offers a strategic space from which they speak, similar to the *intermezzo* culture described by Back (2003 [1995]) in his study of Birmingham based bhangra artist Apache Indian, akin to Rampton's (1995) notion of linguistic 'crossing' and Clyne's (2000) notion of 'multiethnolect' and developed in a UK setting by Kerswill (2014).

All three concepts refer to the use of a language which is not generally thought to 'belong' to the speaker, but rather involves a sense of movement across sharply felt social or ethnic boundaries in ways that raise issues of legitimacy that participants need to reckon with in the course of their encounter. Thus ethnicity and race are not determinants of the two performers' style but temporary positions that offer a strategic space from which to speak (Hall 1992). Modernity and the postmodern turn (Lyotard 1979 [1984]) has brought about cultural globalisation, in that main-stream popular culture is infused with difference of all sorts (sexual, cultural, ethnic and racial), thereby bringing about stylistic shifts in the dominant culture as well. Global culture is also played out in new sites. For Hall (1992) popular culture is the dominant site and its terrain is the street, everyday practice and local narratives:

> However deformed, incorporated, and unauthentic are the forms in which black people and black communities and traditions appear and are represented in popular culture, we continue to see, in the figures and the repertoires on which popular culture draws, the expe-riences that stand behind them. In its expressivity, its musicality, its orality, in its rich, deep, and varied attention to speech, in its inflections toward the vernacular and the local, in its rich production of counternarratives, and above all, in its metaphorical use of the musical vocabulary, black popular culture has enabled the surfacing, inside the mixed and contra-dictory modes even of some mainstream popular culture, of elements of a discourse that is different – other forms of life, other traditions of representation
>
> (Hall 1992: 27)

These are diasporic traditions that enregister historical experiences and memo-ries (Gilroy 1993). For example, in black popular culture the body is a source of cultural capital. One of the performers talks about his *swagger,* and how when he is in London, one of the ways in which other performers identify him as being from Brum is by the distinctive way in which he walks. This recounts complex relations between African origins and diaspora movement of peoples from con-tinent to continent, most notably encapsulated in the slave trade. Black popular cultures involve a selective appropriation of local and global influences alongside an African heritage that lead to '…linguistic innovations in rhetorical stylization of the body, forms of occupying an alien social space, heightened expressions, hair-styles, ways of walking, standing, and talking, and a means of constituting and sustaining camaraderie and community' (Hall 1992: 28). Such an anti-essentialist idea is propounded by cultural critics such as Hall and Gilroy. Both argue for moving the signifier black into a "…new kind of cultural positionality, a different logic of difference" (Hall 1992: 2), thus opening up possibilities for interpreting black identity and cultural production beyond essentialist ideas that valorise *only* influences from the Caribbean or from particular musical genres or linguistic styles such as reggae or patois. Such a possibility can be shown to have opened up amongst performers of Afro Caribbean origin in Birmingham.

4.4 The emergence of *Black Brum*

As discussed previously, *Brum* is the localised lexical item for *Birmingham* (based on a parallel local form of the place name which contains metatharsis and renders the name as Brummagem) and *Brummie*, the demonym for a native of the city. This label captures the fact that the linguistic features observed in performers' speech, at phonological, morphosyntactic and lexical levels, are drawn from varieties that at one and at the same time, have clear links not only to Birmingham and the wider West Midlands, but also to some kind of British Black ethnic identity, and equally, other global (i.e. 'non-British') Englishes from the Caribbean and USA. This section and the tables within it give an overview of the linguistic characteristics of this new, urban dialect of English.

The data from which the variables discussed in this section are drawn comprises a subset of the data as discussed in Chapter 1, namely 310 minutes of recorded audio data, broken down as follows:

Performances	163 minutes
Conversation interview(s) with performers	96 minutes
Conversation Interview(s) with members of the audience and celebreties	121 minutes

As with the data discussed in the previous chapter and the next, linguistic variables across the spoken data of performances and interviews were identified and classified in terms of phonology, morphology and syntax. Identification of linguistic variables was undertaken by firstly, identifying tokens across the performance and interview data and secondly, identifying the potential sociolinguistic provenance of each token. This identification allowed for further analysis to be undertaken in relation to the function and role of variability in terms of the nature of the relationship between the performers and the communities they purport to represent. The extent to which any member of the audience has an affinity with the linguistic variation shown by a performer and the ideology produced and reinforced by both performer and audience is also considered.

The analysis that follows in the next sections of this chapter discusses the ways in which different linguistic variants become rationalised differently by different speaker groups, in this case those of *Black Brum*, in ways that can at one and the same time carry different ideological meanings for different groups. For example, characteristic of West Midlands pronunciation generally is use of velar nasal plus as discussed in Chapter 3. Similarly, the lexical item *fing* may index 'limited education' or 'Cockney' pronunciation of the word *thing* in the standard language ideology of the UK, but in relation to people of Afro Caribbean descent, can index authenticity. Examples of aspects of *Black Brum* given below are taken from an overall inventory of the spoken data.

4.4.1 Phonology

Across the data set, a broad set of features relating to consonantal variation that is common across the speech of both white Birmingham and Black Country performers discussed in Chapter 3 and that of Black performers of Afro Carribean heritage can be identified. These relate to *velar nasal plus, g-dropping* and *glottal stopping*. In addition four further features are evident that are found only in this particular data set. Firstly, the two known as *'TH' stopping and 'TH' fronting* distinctive of British Creole (Dray and Sebba 2011); secondly *post stop gliding* identified in Black British English(es) and thirdly *kiss teeth,* a feature found in Black British English(es) and Jamaican Creole.

The same consonant feature 'TH' has two non-standard variants in the data. 'TH' actually relates to two allophones as it can be voiceless and stopped as in *thing* to make *ting* or voiced and stopped as in *brother* to give *brudder* (Dray and Sebba 2011). In many dialects of British English, the phoneme represented orthographically as *th* is realised consistently by /f/ and /v/ instead, to give *fing* and *bruvver*. This TH feature then, is a site for identity building in the speakers' dialect and a repertoire of sounds upon which to draw. Sometimes they will say *ting* and sometimes *fing*, depending on where they align themselves at a particular point in the discourse. *Post stop gliding* is another feature of Caribbean Englishes that is present to some extent in Black British English(es). It only happens after velar stops /g/ and /k/ in tokens such as *girl* to give *gyal*. The phenomenon known as *Kiss teeth* as identified by Figueroa & Patrick (2002) is phonetically an ingressive sound similar to clicks found in South African languages and the sound often represented by *tsk* or "tut tut" in written English, although there is no cognate apparent outside Black Britith English(es) and Jamain Creole social networks. Pragmatically and semantically this feature has complex patterns of usage. It is not only used for disapproval although this is one of its primary linguistic functions and the one that most non-specialists would recognise.

In relation to *rhoticity,* one of the audience members' interviewed was also the mother of one of the performers, Andre Soul Hesson, that has allowed for a cross-generational comparison. She is one generation older than her son, was born and had lived in Jamaica, hence her variety is closer to Jamaican Creole than than his. Her pronunciation of the /r/ sound in *girl* is rhotic, meaning that the /r/ is pronounced after a vowel in words such as *ha̲r̲d, co̲r̲n* and *nu̲r̲se*. However, at the end of a token such as *trusting*, she uses the alveolar (formed by putting the tongue against the hard palate behind the front teeth) nasal /n/, realised as *trustin'*. This feature appears in Birmingham English cross-ethnically (Clark and Asprey 2013, Khan 2006) and is also a feature of Caribbean English. as noted above, younger speakers do not evidence as much rhoticity as the older generation and are more likely to pronounce *girl* as *gyal*.

In relation to the *velar nasal plus*, as Chapter 3 has already discussed, [ŋg] happens more frequently in the West Midlands traditional dialect in monosyllables such as <sing>, <ring>, <long>. In the present participle <-ing> form, bare nasal [ɪn] is often found. The RP variant [ŋ] can also be found throughout the speech community in both mono- and polysyllabic items. In polysyllables, bare nasal [n] appears in many varieties of English, including Black British English, Jamain Creole and West Midlands English. *Consonant cluster reduction* is where strings of consonants are often simplified by deleting the final sound as found in *g-dropping* but also in tokens such as *best* that becomes *bes*. Within the data, this is most likely to be found in specific 'iconic' words such as *vexed* for angry, though among older Jamaican Creole speakers and in some Black British English(es) speakers it is more widespread and not undergoing attrition as it would appear to

Table 4.1: Consonantal variation.

Dialect indexed	Feature	Example
Black British English	TH-stopping /θ/ or /ð/ [t] or [d]	*you know when you do karate you get like a white belt or a black belt like one of them **things** [tɪŋgz] there* (DFL, performance)
Jamaican Creole	Rhoticity-r-colouring	*and he said how one **girl** [gɝˡl] was so trusting* (ASH, audience member)
Jamaican Creole	Word final consonant cluster simplification	*vexed* is a salient word used to mean annoyed or angry. It can be pronounced [vɛks] losing the final [t].
Black British English & Jamaican Creole	KST (kiss teeth) Ingressive dental click [ǀ]	Performer A: *what you chat about* Performer B: *KST*[ǀ] Performer A: *times are changin_*
Multicultural London English	TH-fronting /θ/ or /ð/ [f] or [v]	Performer: ***Everything*** [ɛvɹɪfɪn] *I say I do...* *I'm the realist*
All	t-glottalisation (intervocalic and syllable final) [t~ʔ]	*changin_* *everythin_* *wha_ever*
All	Velar nasal plus variation in -ing [n~ŋ~ŋg]	*so you're think**ing** I either don't eat this...*

be in our performers. It can be pronounced [vɛks] losing the final [t]. *Glottalling* of sounds such as /p/, /t/, /k/ glottalisation where the sounds are not pronounced can occur intervocalically in tokens such as *butter* and *matter* to give [buʔa] and [maʔa] and is not lexically restricted. Final glottalling can occur as cluster-final *tent* or *cat*. These features are summarised in Table 4.1.

The vowel sounds chosen for consideration shown in Table 4.2 are those already identified in Chapter 3. This is because Birmingham is on the dividing line (isogloss) that separates the North from the South and the vowels chosen are distinctive for Birmingham and the Black Country as well as throughout the English West Midlands regardless of ethnicity. To summarise, these are: the difference between southern from northern vowel sounds [ʌ] and [ʊ] in tokens such as *colour* to give *coola* [kʊla] and and *London* to give loondn [lʊndn̩]; the Northern shortening of vowel sounds in words such as *bath* and *grass* to rhyme with *hat;* the diphthong in tokens such as *like, price* and *quite* realised as /aɪ/ is often pronounced as [ɔɪ] and realised as *liyek* [lɔɪk] and *quiyet* [kwɔɪt] (se also Chapter 3). In a token such as *face* the [aɪ] sound is pronounced more like *fayce* [æɪ]. The token *you* is often realised as *yow* [jəʊ]. *h-dropping* in words such as *how* give [aʊ].

In addition, features specific to Jamaican Creole are also considered, in relation to the pronunciation of *a* as a broad /aa/ sound given in IPA as [ɑ:] so that a token such as *card* becomes [kyaad] (Patrick 2014: 132). A further feature is in relation to a feature known as *r-colouring* which is in between rhotic and non-rhotic r as commonly found in the US/AAVE pronunciation of a token such as *bird* that has been included in the consonant section above.

Table 4.2: Vowel variation.

Dialect indexed	Feature	Example
Birmingham and Black Country	[ʌ] to [ʊ]	*no matter what* **colour** [kʊla] *you are if I'm in* **london** [lʊndn̩] *I might just drag my words a little bit*
Birmingham and Black Country	[o] to [[ʊ]	**Looky** /lʊki/ **poot** /pʊt/
Birmingham and Black Country	[i] to [ɪ]	**Everything** [evrɪfɪn]
Birmingham and Black Country	[ʌɪ] to [ɑɪ]	*bad boys we* **RIDE** [raɪd] *together* *like* [laɪk] or *like* [laɪ̈k]
Jamain Creole	Broad *aa* (Unrounded low back vowel):	***can't*** becomes [kyaan]

4.4.2 Morphology and syntax

From the data, a small set of grammatical features that are associated with Birmingham and Black British speech can also be identified. The speakers are in fact relying mainly on phonological variation to index stance, since they do not use non-standard West Midlands forms that are found in older Birmingham varieties nor the basilectal morphological forms such as zero third person marker, zero past tense marker and pronoun variation which can occur at the basilectal end of the Creole continuum.

In Table 4.3, the first row of table is from Maria Hesson again, Andre Hesson's mother. She has the occasional feature that seems to align itself with British or Jamaican Creole. Sebba (2004) mentions that person and number (and sometimes tense) agreement are often absent in creole Englishes. She uses *bring* where standard British English require – s inflection. However, this feature has also been identified in the Black Country. In the second row in *I'm gonna*, the *(gonn)* part is much less articulated than it could be. This sounds like the US/AAVE future intentional *Imma*. In the third row, there is a feature of contemporary urban British English that Cheshire et al (2011) have identified as a feature of *Multicultural London English* (MLE). There are also non-standard forms of past tense of *to be* in both directions, i.e. things like *you was* and *they was*, but also things like *I were* and *she were*. In fact, what we really get is *I weren't* and *he/she weren't*. The move in British English is that *was* is used in positive polarity and *weren't* is used in negative polarity. Cheshire and Fox (2009) call it the *was-weren't* split.

Table 4.3: Morphosyntatic variation.

Dialect indexed	Feature details	Example
Jamaican Creole	lack of – **s** verb agreement for 3rd person singular present tense.	*he bring_ things as well to his performances*
Jamaican Creole	(a_an) use of article *a* even when following noun begins with a vowel	*I'm **a** artist*
ALL	(was_weren't) non-standard past form of *BE* we/you they **was** I/he/she/it **weren't**	*it **weren't** just me it was a few of us imagine you **was** in the Matrix*

In Andre 'Soul' Hesson's performance, he uses a negative *weren't* where standard English would have *it wasn't* and a positive *was* where standard English would have *you were*. Finally, there is an example that is on the interface of morphology and phonology. Standard varieties have an alternation between *a* and *an* for the article, depending on whether the following noun begins with a vowel or not. BE does not use *an* much, preferring *a* even when following word is vowel initial. In interview, Andre says *a artist*. What actually happens here is that he inserts a very quickly released glottal stop between the two words to separate them, a feature also associated with MLE.

4.4.3 Lexis

The lexical items present in the data as given in Table 4.4 are all in relation to Black English (BE). This starts with a couple of nouns: *garms*, which is very BE and also found in MLE (note also *fam* clipping for family), and using the American term *homicide* for the British term *murder* highlights the globalised/superdiversity aspect of linguistic usage With phonology and grammar, there has not been as much American influence, but with lexis and particularly with nouns (even specific semantic domains like here, crime and "perceived toughness": *feds, homicide*) there is conscious evocation of Black/US varieties. The verb *ramp* and the adjective *vexed* are highly indexical of British Creole. *Ramp* is the kind of word that linguistic outsiders might not immediately get the meaning of, especially out of context. *Vexed* has fallen out of (high frequency or unmarked) usage in standard British English. These lexical choices then, are making a strong statement: our word is *ramp/vexed*. Using *ramp* or *vex(ed)* is as indexical as the TH-stopping in *ting*. Also interesting is to consider whether *ting* a separate lexical item or a productive phonological process applied to *thing*? The last two lexical items are high frequency tags for the three younger speakers, but not the older. Tags like these are on the borders of lexis and grammar, but have been included as lexical. *You get me* is found in BE as well as MLE.

Table 4.4: Lexical variation.

Item	Meaning	Additional notes
Garms	Clothes	Clippings of lexical items are ubiquitous in Black British English. Here we have an example of a back-clip of 'garments.' Also found in Multicultural London English.
Ramp	to fight	Typical of Black British English
Vexed	Angry	Jamaican Creole term from Old English, widely used in Black British English and wider youth vernacular

(Continued)

Table 4.4 (continued)

Item	Meaning	Additional notes
you get me	'you understand?'	Very popular tag question in Black Britiash English and also found in Multicultural London English
Wagwan	'what's going on' or 'what's happening'	Popular Jamaican Creole term, often used as greeting. Now prevalent in Black British English and wider vernacular
Homicide	Murder	This Americanism is used in place of the British usage
enit?	isn't it?	Birmingham pronunciation of the tag question

The analysis above identifies the range of linguistic features drawn upon by young minority ethnic performers of Caribbean heritage that are associated with a range of regional dialects. This range encompasses differing geographic spaces and places to index identities linked to a globalised, rather than regionalised, senses of place and ethnic identity as expressed through English. Rather than operating as separate regional and spatial dimensions then, the analysis shows how new linguistic forms mix the past and the present, drawing from across place, time and space, thereby giving rise to the fact that they cannot be categorised straightforwardly as indicative of 'Black' or 'Black English/British' performers. Deci 4 Life and Andre 'Soul' Hesson are anchored in the present within a defined geographic region, that of Birmingham in the English West Midlands and to a certain extent, London. At the same time, they perceive themselves as historically rooted in their Afro Caribbean past as their conversation interviews show. As such, they conceive themselves as being members of a global, as well as a national and local community, in ways that take account of their contemporary locality, in this case Birmingham and nationally with London and their Afro Caribbean heritage as manifested across the world, especially in the USA. Added to this, is a further dimension of influences drawn from popular culture as summarised in the section above. As Khan (2006: 322) points out, as with other social categories, there is a need to "... go beyond the description of ethnically-based variation and identify the social mechanisms underlying linguistic variation/change within the local context". To this can be added the mechanisms underlying the global and national, as well as local, context.

4.5 Performance 1: Andre 'Soul' Hesson (ASH)

Andre 'Soul' Hesson is of Afro Caribbean heritage, born in Birmingham in 1987 and where he has lived all his life and was in his mid twenties at the time the recording was made. He is a versatile actor, comedian and performance poet, acting in stage plays as well as comering and hosting the event discussed below in addition to performing by himself. In this respect as in many others, he was very similar to Craig Deeley discussed in Chapter 3. The performance by Andre Hesson in his persona as Soul was recorded at *The Bluu Bar,* in Birmingham's city centre, in Summer Row just outside Birmingham's main Brindley Place and Broad Street complex that houses bars, restaurants and night clubs as well as businesses and hotels. It is situated between these two areas and St Pauls Square nearer to the Jewellery Quarter which hosts other well known national night spots such as the *Jam House.* All the bars in the area including the *Bluu Bar* cater for a sophisticated and up market clientele, and its entertainment evenings are held in a basement area away from the main bars. The audience for such performances then, is a cosmopolitan one, made up of a combination of people who may be visiting Birmingham from outside either from the UK or elsewhere in the world or local people out for a night out with friends. Unlike the amateur open mic events in Birmingham discussed in Chapter 3 in pubs in suburbs of the city, the one at *The Bluu Bar* is a professional venue and charges an entrance fee.

Under the title of *Artistic fusion,* the performance recorded was as part of a regular weekly spoken word performance. Andre was one of the performers at the performance as well as being the host for the night. He was born in Birmingham, has lived in Smethwick, Edgbaston and Great Barr areas of the city and self-identifies as a Brummie. The persona Andre adopts on stage is that of *Soul,* a young, heterosexual male. About half of the audience at the performance, who numbered about 40, were regular attendees at the *Artistic fusion* performances. Andre opens the performance by explaining the purpose of *Artistic fusion* to be that of breaking cultural barriers between people. He moves on to the performances's slogan with which many of the audinec are clearly familiar as he says:

(32) 1   it [ɪʔ] goes like this REPEAT /ripi:ʔ/ after me We_RE ARTISTIC LIFE_S POETIC
     2   Audience: LIFE_S POETIC
     3   WE ALL HAVE SOULS [sæʊs]
     4   Audience: WE ALL HAVE SOULS
     5   so don_t neglect it
     6   Audience: So don_t neglect it
     7   ok BASICALLY that slogan (.) was formed it weren_t just [dʒʌʔ] me it
     8   was [wʌz] a few of us (.) an_ it [ɪʔ] was [wʌz] talking [tɔːkɪŋ] about (.) an_ we was
     9   [wʌz] watching [wʊtʃɪŋ] three [frɪː] hundred an_ the whole Spartans thing [fɪŋ] an_
    10   a lot [lʊʔ] of things [fɪŋs/ throughout the movies they_ve always [ɔːlɪs] got [gʊʔ]
    11   one thing [fɪŋ] they say an_ it_s kind of [æ] like (.) bad boys we RIDE [raɪd]
    12   together [tʌgɛvɛaː] we DIE [daɪ] together [tʌgɛvɛaː] (.) BAD BOYS FOR LIFE
    13   [aɪf]
        <audience laughter>

15 an_ everybody_s got [go?] that [ðæ?] kind of [æ] thing /fing/ so we thought [ðɔ:?]
16 you know what we have to have a little [likl] slogan to where it_s like no
17 matter [mæ?æ] everybody has a soul most people just [dʒʌs] believe that [ðæ?] you
18 jump on a mic get [gɛ?] a beat say some stuff an_ there_s [dɛ:rs] no value but (.)
19 it_s a lot [lo?] of hard work (.) to it and to kind of come up with the [dʌ] end result

In this extract, t-glottalling is evident throughout in lines 1, 7, 8, 10, 15, 17, 18 and 19 although not in line 5, where Andre invites his audience to repeat a key theme as a slogan within his performance. Here, three items out of the four in the utterance feature /t/ which is vocalised in each case. /th/ is also vocalised as /f/ in lines 9, 10 and 11. The prounication of the vowel in *ride* in line 11 and *die* in line 12 is that associated with Birmingham; /th/ is given as /v/ in line 12 and /d/ in line 19. In line 10, the vowel sound in *lot* and *got* is also that associated with Birmingham and the Black Country but not in the *lot* of line 19. Reference to the Spartans in line 9 (and also made in a play discussed in Chpater 5) is to the 2006 film *300* based upon the 1998 comic series of the same name based upon the battle between 300 Spartans and 300,000 Persian soldiers in Ancient Greek times. Andre refers to it in the context of the importance of a slogan for creating a sense of common purpose amongst a minority group, chanted first by a leader then their followers, in this case, the performer and his audience. Such a device also features in Roy McFarlane's performance, discussed below. Andre then goes immediately into a Rap:

(33) 1 WHY yes [yɛ] WHY that_s all I want to [wʊnæ] ask ONE question WHY if you can
  2 answer that [ðæ?] (.) then [dɛn] maybe so (.) we could both [bauf] understand (.)
  3 why WHY IS IT [i?] (.) that [ðæ?] we sleep at [a?] nighttime an_ wake up in the
  4 DAY why do we open our eyes (.) for those [dəʊz] that [ðæ?] can why do we EXIST
  5 in a realm [ɹɛlm] (.) where we judge so much of each other [ovæ] (.) imagine you
  6 was in the matrix imagine if we was in an [æ] animated [ænimeɪ?id] cartoon (.)
  7 imagine if somebody else was actually [æktli:] putting [pʌ?in] the storyboard behind
  8 our lifestyle to reveal the direction they want us to go but [bʌ?] then yet we_re
  9 standin_ here contemplating [kʊtnmpleɪtin] WHY (.) why do I exist (.) why am I
 10 constantly LIVin_ (-) but [bʌ] I feel PARTS of me are DYin_ why do lights
 11 turn OFF <laughs>
     <audience laughs>

The influence of Jamaican Creole and patois is evident in Andre's speech here, with /d/ for /th/ in *then* in line 2 and *those* in line 4 but not for *that* in line 4; rhotic /r/ in *realm*; /v/ for /th/ in *other*. In his persona as Soul, Andre intersperses his rapping with audience participation on the topic of absent fathers as a frame of rejection, inviting members of the audience to share their experiences. The frames he evokes are nearly all from a masculine perspective, which reflects the gender make up of the audience, who are also nearly all male. The extract below is typical of the short sketches he tells, centred around a recount of his encounter with a girlfriend:

(34) 1   because [bɪkʌz] the [vɪ] other [ʊvæ] part [pæʔ] is some WOmen can_t COOK
      2   properly (.) but [bʌʔ] then every man likes a good home [hoʊm] meal from a
      3   WOman [wʌmæn] (.) so if you go to a GIRL-s house an_ you_re like babes I_ve
      4   cooked for you [yæ] in your head I should have [æv]ordered Chinese (.) YOU know
      5   I should have [æv] WENT KFC (-)
      6   <<audience laughter>>
      7   but [bʌʔ] i_m just [jʌs] going to [ɡʊnæ] CHill an_ appRECIiate this meal an_ have
      8   you ever wanted to (-) I know that [ðæʔ] certain people is in the room so I_m not
      9   [nʊʔ] going to [ɡʊnæ] say but [bʌʔ] (.) have you EVER wanted a girl SO bad an_
      10 she looks good [ɡuː/] but [bʌʔ] you [yʌ] go to the YArd an_ you_re like rah you_re
      11 <<audience laughter>>
      12 like rah you (.) [yʌ] get [ɡɛʔ] me an_ THEN as you COOK it yeah you_re [yʌ]
      13 cutting [kʌtɪn] into the meat because being [bi: ɪn] at girl_s house you [yʌ/] don_t
      14 just use your hands because [kʌz] I_m a wild child (.) mean I_m a part [pæʔ]
      15 ANImal (.) chickEN
      14 <<audience laughter>>
      16 me an_ chickEN have a commUNICation where chicken could COME on my plate
      17 an_ just [dʒʌs] say TAKE me SACrifice like as if it_s religion [rilɪɡʌn] but [bʌʔ]
      18 when you_re at [æʔ] a girl_s house [æus] you can_t EAT like that beCAUSE [kʌz]
      19 then she starts to get [ɡɛʔ] ideas an_ then TINGS A GWAAN you get [ɡɛʔ] me
      20 <<audience laughter>>
      21 GET [ɡɛʔ] me nah it_s TRUE an_ then you cut [kʌʔ] into it an_ you realise she
      22 has_nt /aint/ COOKed it properly so you're thinking [θinkin] I either don_t EAT
      23 this an_ offEND her an_ don_t get [ɡɛʔ] no nookie
      24 <<audience laughter>>
      25 or eat this an_ clench my butt [bʌʔ] cheeks so I don_t go toilet
      26 <<audience laughter>>
      27 or I end up doing [dʊ:in] somethin_ [sʌʔɪn] halfWAY through an_
      28 <<audience laughter>>
      29 I get [ɡɛʔ] kicked out of the room you get me like big tings can_t GWAAN
      30 <<audience laughter>>

In Afro Caribbean culture, chicken is viewed not simply as sustenance for the body but also as a food for the soul. KFC is a reference to a global chain of fast food take away restaurants, *Kentucky Fried Chicken.*While the white performers discussed in the preceding chapter make both local and international references as part of their peformances, Andre draws upon mainly international rather local, cultural references, in ways that illustrate the different geographic spaces upon which they draw. KFC is a global restuant takeaway and restaurant outlet, prefaced in Line 4 by the simple past *went* used in place of past participle *gone*.

This is prevalent in many vernacular dialects of British English. In Line 7 *yard* is used in place of *home*, a word used in both American vernacular and Jamaican Creole, and now common in British Black English. Also in Line 7, *rah*, a Jamaican Creole interjection expressing shock/surprise is repeated, followed by the *you get me* tag, both features associated with younger speakers of Black British English. Andre also drops 'g's and glottals, but sounds 'h'. In this way, features from British English, American vernacular and Jamaican Creole are drawn upon in creating or constructing an identity of *Black Brum*. The frame evoked in the performance, inviging one of acceptance on the part of male members of the audience, is that of heterosexual dating in the western hemisphere and of a girl cooking a meal for her boyfriend. In the performance, it is given cultural specificity in relation to being both Black and British, both in terms of cultural references specific to food and home and through the speech itself.

In Lines 19 and 29, arguably *tingz* can be treated as separate lexical item as well as an instance of th-stopping (common in Caribbean English). Equally *gwan*, a shortening of *wagwan* meaning *what's going on* is also lexicalised in Andre's speech although clearly phonologically derived from *going* in Caribbean varieties. In Line 23, Andre uses the non-standard negated form of *have*; *ain't* and the double negative *don't get no nookie* (slang term for sex) common in many UK and US Englishes. In Line 5 there is deletion of *to* in places habitually visited (*shall we go school, just wanna go MacD's* etc) and *went* in place of *gone*. Phonologically, in Line *home*, as well as *going* in lines 7 and 9 is sounded as a very round back vowel [oʊ] closer to the British Creole monophthong vowel [o] in /home/ and different from Brummie [haʊm]. In Line 4 *you* has a very pronounced Brummie [jɐ] sound. In lines 19 and 29, *things/tings* are typical examples of th-stopping.

There is a sense then, in which such encounters between young men and women trigger frames of acceptance that cut across racial, social and cultural divisions. At the same time, specific instances of such occasions are racially, socially and culturally bound, which in the case of Andre both as himself and in his stage persona as Soul, are bound by him being a Black Brum of Afro Caribbean heritage.

4.5.1 In conversation with Andre Hesson

When asked about himself and his background, Andre said first of all he was from Birmingham [b ɛrm ɪ ŋgum], talked about his mother who hd been a singer [sing æ] and how he used to travel around to watch her performances. In both the tokens given in IPA he raelises the Birmingham verlar nasal plus. Unlike Benjamin Zephaniah discussed below, Andre was not aware of any racim while he was growing up, even though he was the only black kid in his class. Many of the linguistic featuers present in his performance were evident in his speech since like Craig Deeley discussed in Chapter 3, his performance style is close to his own conversation speech style, even when performing in the persona of Soul which he describes as his alter ego. Also like Craig, Andre reported that he makes it clear from the outset at performances that he is from Birmingham. When asked why, he said:

(35) 1 I do it [ɪʔ] as an icebreaker to take the piss but [bʌʔ] but other [ovə] times I actually
2 do it [ɪʔ] because its like [laɪk] something [səmðən] will happen in that gig to
3 make me go oh ok first [fɜrst] of all I let them know who I am so before I even
4 [iivn] go on stage, half the crowd will know who I am (–) I make a loud random
4 stuff (.) make a loud sound i_ll be walking [wɔ:kŋ] like an_ i_ll go 'yo' just [jʌs]
5 randomly an_ everyone look back and i_d say 'who was that you looking [lu:kɪn]
6 at me that [ðæʔ] wasn_t me hi i_m soul i_m the performer from Birmingham
7 [bɜmɪŋʌm] nice to meet you

Andre went on to say that when a performer plays out of town in other towns and cities he has no-one who is in his corner, rely on comperes and hosts to 'warm up' the audience before the performer comes on stage. When that does not happen then as a performer he said he feels 'crap' as it's not his fault. At times like these, he preempts further potential hostility from his audience by letting them know he is from Birmingham.

(36) 1 spoken word poetry [pʌʊtri:] in the dialect to me (.) inspires people more because
2 people seem to forget everything [evrɪfɪn] is words singers (.) rappers [evrɪfɪn]
3 breaks it [ɪʔ] down (.) the other [ʊðæ] thing [fɪŋ] as well is being [bɪ:ɪŋ] able to
4 make it [iʔ] strong by itself its like[laɪk] there_s so much different [dɪfrent] things
5 [fɪŋs] that [θæʔ] break barriers down able to make it [iʔ] stand on its own an_ also
6 like yeah i_m standin_ i_m not going [gʌʊɪn] nowhere i_m here the way I speak is
7 the way I want to come to meet you when I walk i_ll still be here talking [tɔ:kɪŋ] so
8 ten years from now you_ll still remember the conversation we_ve had

Andre was well aware of the stigma accorded to Birmingham and its dialect, but in terms of how that affects him, he stated that he considerd himself an artist first and foremost before being a Brummie. Like the performers discussed in Chapter 3, being understood by the majority of his audience is a key consideration in his performances. Thus, whilst he believes that performing spoken word poetry in dialect seems to inspire people, it has to be intelligible to as many of his audience as possible. When asked if he ever drew on Jamaican patwa in his performances Andre said:

(37) 1 OK yes and no (.) i_m not going to [gʌnæ] lie [laɪ] if I could do it [ɪʔ] a hundred
2 percent and be able to do it would be great (.) but i_ve seen white [wiit] people do

3   it [ɪʔ] i_ve seen Asian people do it [ɪʔ] i_m in stitches it_s a shock a guy come up
4   /ʊp/ leather boots trousers t shirt white long hair glasses an_ he_ll [iː] be [biː] like
5   [lɪək] *(moving into patwa)* 'you know what [wʊʔ] you see them [dem] girl [gairl]
6   upon a corner [kɔːɪnæ] me say 'yo' me ask [ass] me brethren [bredrin]' *(out of*
7   *patwas)* an_ you_re like 'what [wʊʔ] an_ say just [jʌs] like you_re engaged because
8   you get [geʔ] that [ðæʔ] but [bʌʔ] they [deɪ] expect that [ðæʔ] from me I don_t have
9   to I don_t have to and as I said to you before it_s contingency it_s being [biːŋ] able
10   to do it throughout the whole thing [fɪŋg] I can_t usually when I perform sometimes
11   it will come [kʌm] out other [ovæ] times i_ll do like [lɪək] I just [jʌs] did that [ðæʔ]
12   i_ll do it as a joke it_s like [lɪək] I go to a different [difrent] city [cɪʔ/iː] an_ i_ll
13   purposely have a string vest on an_ shorts an_ sandals an_ go on stage like [liik]
14   I i_ll go there like [liik] in my normal clothes backstage i_ll change off in my string
15   vest (.) it [ɪʔ] was amazin_ [ʌmæɪzɪn] I remember I did it one time I did it [ɪʔ] once
16   I did it [ɪʔ] I got pissed off an_ the thing [fɪŋg] is everybody was askin_ me what
17   [wʊʔ] because I had singles in I had long hair I had singles in my hair plaited an_
18   everybody thought it [ɪʔ] was dreadlocks an_ [ɪʔ] was like [laɪk]
19   'the rasta man_s goin_ [gʊɪn] to perform some poetry' (..) I didn_t say nothing
20   [nʊðɪn] I would hear people talkin_ [tɔːkɪn] so I say 'yeah man i_m moqapi selassie
21   I love each an_ all of you [ya] that_s why i_ve come [kʌm] with [wɪ] my [miː]
22   poem this poem i_ve called the [dæ] mango (.) the [dæ]mango tree the [diː] mango
23   likes [liiks] to drop on everything [evrytin] else (..) yeah let me start again
24   basically my name_s andre i_m from Birmingham [bɜmɪŋgʌm] <laughs>

The Moqapi Selassie Andre refers to in line 20 is another performer who also took part in the project, discussed further below, and is older then Andre. In the extract above, Andre doubl-voices as Selassie in conforming to his audience's stereotypical expectations of an Afro-Caribbean perfomer in lines 20 to 23, of speaking in patwas as part of his performance. He undercuts this swiftly at the end of line 23 and moves into his own performance voice. For Andre, his ethnicity was not a central or crucial aspect of his identity, and he viewed himself more as a multicultural performer rather than as an Afro Caribbean one. He embraced the diverse venues in which he has performed and the audiences therein, using humour to draw attention to the colour of people's skin without being inherently racist. As he goes on to say, in relation to skin colour:

(38) 1   i love [lʌv] cartoons superheros are all different colours green purple orange yellow
      2   an_ all them come together [togevæ] an_ create the justice league an _avengers an_
      3   like [liik] an_ the mutants [myuːʔants] an_ that_s why it [iʔ] doesn_t bother [bʊvæ]
      4   me because i_ve always watched the xmen (.) an_ I used to always say ok
      5   mutants [myuːʔants] are racist like that [ðæʔ] that_s what [wuʔ] it [iʔ] is when
      6   people say mutants [myuːʔants] black people asian people the beast is a
      7   black man (..) i used to say i used to break stuff it_s never
      8   bothered [bʊvæd] me it_s a cartoon it-s never bothered [bʊvæd] me i_ve loved lots
      9   of different [difrent] stuff that_s why I think [tɪnk] when it comes to my performance

10   an_ how i am i_m just [dʒʌs] me there_s no point in me tryin_ to black up yeah
11   man when i perform certain places people think that [ðæʔ] I have to be like [liik]
12   this [ðɪsse] (.) an_ then so I perform angry an_ i_m like [liik] yeah I can perform
13   to a white audience an_ get [gɛʔ] some white jokes get some jokes like [liik] 'Hey
14   have some coffee milk an_ no sugar [ʒʊgæ]' an_ it was OK... i just mess about
16   [æbaʊʔ] i love comedians I watch a lot [loʔ] of lenny henry lee evans my good
17   friend i love a lot [loʔ] of different comedians they take the piss out [æuʔ] of all
18   cultures [kʌltʃæs]

Unlike some other black performers, Andre made it clear that he has never allowed being black to differentiate him or distinguish him in any way from performers of other ethnicities. He attributed this to the way he had been brought up, where the colour of his skin was not anything to which he could recall attention being drawn to either in relation to himself or members of his family. Creative performers such as Andre Hesson are thus well aware of the socially constructed nature of race in society, as discussion of the next performance also shows, and subvert the ideologies underlying racial politics through their performances by drawing attention to it. As Markus and Moya (2010: x) say:

> Race is not something that peole have or are, but rather a set of actons people do...Doing race always involves creating groups based on perceived physical and behavioural characteristics, associating differential power and privilege with these characteristics, and then justifying the resulting inequalities.

Language is one of the actions by which people 'do' race, and performers overtly 'do' race in their performances in relation to themselves, the characters they perform and their audience's expectations. Howver, as a second generation Afro-Caribbean born in England, Andre was also very well aware of his own limitations when it came to enregistering Jamaican Creole or Patwas in his performances since, as he said, and like others such as Deci4Life and Roy Mcfarlane discussed below, this did not come to him 'naturally' as it did to older performers. Where he did draw upon features from this dialect, it was by way of undercutting or subverting his audience's expectations, in ways that bear a similarity to the Black Country performers discussed in Chapter 3.

4.6 Performance 2: Deci4Life and Moqpal Selassie in *The Spiral*

The performance discussed in this section took place at a performance venue called *The Drum*. *The Drum* is Birmingham's premier black arts venue and sits on the outskirts of the expanding city centre in Aston, an area with almost 80 per cent minority ethnic inhabitants. It serves to further the artistic creativity of Black Asian British African and Caribbean performers for the betterment of local communities, and celebrates black art through performance. The venue also offers training in all aspects of performance, music . drama poetry in the form of workshops and courses to coach interested parties. The two perormers in this performance are from different generations: Moqpal Selassie was born in 1956 and Deci4Life, a contemporary of Andre Hesson, in 1987. The performance took the form of a dialogue between an up and coming young grime artist called Glitzy (Deci4Life) who has been offered a grant to study under an older dub poet and radical activist Leroy Steppin Razor Ujima (Moqpal Selassie). Their dialogue sets out to challenge each performer's stance towards the world. Like Andre Hesson, they draw upon the various influences that circulate within and beyond Birmingham's minority ethnic communities and the musical cultures associated with them. In the performance, Selassie as Leroy dresses in a stereotypically older Jamaican 'Rasta' way, complete with a beard, dreadlocks and a beehive hat. This contrasts with Deci4Life as Glitzy, who is much younger, with a more urban, dya old stubble and cropped, short hair reminiscent of Wil Smith in the 1990s American sitcom *The Fresh Prince of Bel-Air*. Their performance exemplified their generational clash:

(39) 1 D: you know what [wʊʔ] you know what [wʊʔ] Eugina
      2 S: Eugina
      3 D: you_re [jʌ] IGnorant you [jʌ] know
      4 S: what [wʊʔ] you chat [tʃæʔ] about [bæʊʔ]
      5 D: an_ arrogant
      6 S: an_ you [jæ] a drink out of [o] the JUG
      7 D: ignorant arrogant an_ STUCK in a time zone Rasta man
      8 S: what [wʊʔ] you chat[tʃæʔ] about [bæʊʔ]
      9 D: KST[l]
     10 D: times are changin_
     11 S: me never tell you [jʌ] somethin_ [sʌmtɪn] up to the [dʌ] time
     12 D: NAH times are changin_
         <<<audience laughter>>>>
     13 D: changin_ is rearrangin_ (-) you see me (.) I_m evolvin_
     14   EVolution is the Revolution (.) you're part [paːɹʔ] of the   problem
     15   if you_re not [noʔ] part [paːɹʔ]of the solUtion (-) you [jʌ] see people
     16   like you (.)
     17 S: yeah (.)
     18 D: people like you get [ge ʔ] left behind (-)
     19 S: found with backward you never heard that [ð æ ʔ] youth [juː]/
     20 D: shut your mouth
     21 S: about shut up man come up in _ere

22   halfway through and <<audience laughter>>> I get kicked out of the
23   room you get me like big things [t ɪngs] can_t go on [gwan]
          <<<audience laughter>>>>

The interplay here is the age old clash between older and younger generations, made more poignant here by the older generation, as represented by Selassie in his character as Leroy, being 'stuck in a time zone' of a specific social and cultural point in time, that of the post war migration from Jamaica to England in the 1950s. By contrast, Deci's chacater Glitzy represents British born youth of Afro Caribbean heritage whose future does not lie in the past, and for whom Jamaica is not the land of their birth. The repetition of *tings can't gwan*, given in Andre Hesson's performance as well as here, appears to act as an enregistration of African Caribbean heritage, as does the KST in line 9. T-glotalling is prevalent throught . In the next extract, DFL and S continue the theme of generational dissonance by seguing into a rap:

40) 1   D: i_m a new an_ improved model an_ you (.) you_re just out [a ʊ ʔ] of [o]
2   date [deɪ ʔ] design let me give [gɪ] you some advice (·) you should resign
3   DON_t BITCH and whine because technology is improvin_ an_ you ain_t up to the
4   time
5   S: what you chat [tʃæʔ] about [bæʊʔ]you hear me you know (.) an_ you
6   know something_ [sʌmɪn] youth [ju:ʔ] i _ave a LAPtop
7   D: you don't know about [æbæʊʔ] Facebook though (·)
8   <<<audience laughter >>>>
9   D: there_s unity in this new community (·) things [fings] ain_t what [wʊʔ] they
10   used to be (.) it_s not that [ðæʔ] you_re blind (.) it's just you don_t choose to see
11   (·) take a look (.) read a few pages out my [mɪ] Facebook (–) before you make
12   assumptions [æsʌmʃʌns] an_ judgements about MY ways against your frequency to
13   my way (.) take a step into my space (.) stop twitterin_ an_ get [geʔ] your head up
14   out [aʊʔ] the sound cloud (·) yo the revolution will be televised (·) because [kʌz]
15   we_ll record it on our phones an_ upload it [ɪʔ] to you tube it_s major
16   you_re [jʌ] MINiscule (–)
17   <<<audience laughter>>>>
18   D: you_re [jʌ] analogue I_m digital (.) adapt because if you can_t connect you_ll
19   NEver reach a PINnacle (.) you_re [jʌ] CYnical look man if you DON-T [dunʔ]
20   like [laɪk] it (.) don_t [dʊnʔ] FIGht [faɪʔ] it (.) because there_s nothin_ you can do
21   (.) stay STuck in the past an_ nothin_ will EVER be new to you (.) an_ you will
22   watch life [la:f] go PAST you like [la:k] a ZUlu (–) you know what /wʊʔ/ you
23   ain_t no different to me (–) you can_t challenge me (.) don_t take your [jʌ] ISSues
24   ou_ on me yo (.) DON_t get [geʔ] mad at [æʔ] ME (·) unity in this lifetime [la:ftaɪm]
25   (.) it_s all a FALLacy (·) an_ all that truth you stand for (–) it_s ALL a fantasy
26   theoretical doctrines ideologies it_s ALL a parody (.) i_m stuck in this REALity
27   (–) an_ if i don_t survIVE [sʌvaɪv] (.) if i don_t stay alIVE [ælaɪv] (·) then i_ll be
28   just ANother fuckin_ fatAlity (·)
29   S: what [wʊʔ] i TELL you about [æbæʊʔ] your [jʌ] TONgue

The generational clash between the two characters continues as the performance unfolds, with Deci framing the older Selassie in terms of rejection, particularly in his impassioned speech in lines 18 to 28. This is immediately undercut by Selassie's remonstration with Deci over his swearing rather than the verbal beating he has just been given, that raises a laugh from the audience. Selassie's use of patwas lexis as in line 5 *what you chat about* that references or evokes older Afro Caribbeans such as Leroyand contrasts with Deci's use of technological lexis that references or evokes the new, technological age. Leroy may as he says in line 6 own a laptop, but his ignorance of social media that in turn is acknowledged through the audience's laughter in Line 8 is followed by Deci as Glitzy mocking Selassie as Leroy for his ignorance. T-glottalling is evident throughout, and the West Midlands vowel sounds evident in tokens 'alive' and 'survive' in Line 27.

4.6.1 In conversation with Deci4Life, Moqpal Selassie and the audience

Deci4Life took part in a conversation interview a few days after the performance, held in Birmingham's city centre at a McDonalds restaurant, at his During it, DEci4Life illuminated many aspects of his childhood, both in terms of growing up and his entry into performance poetry. During the interview he also shared with us media clips of some of his other performances. He was born in Solihull, a town to the south of Birmingham, to parents were of Jamaican origin. His father was a DJ as well as being a lay preacher and his mother a poet. They moved extensively both in this country and in America where they had relatives. From an early age, Deci said he was involved in all kinds of performances, either in church choirs or learning the poems his mother wrote. She would explain to him the notion of performance and what that meant in terms of bringing words to life. He recollected his first performance at Hollyhead School, aged eight or nine, reciting a poem his mother had composed for African Liberation Day about black on black violence. It was this moment, he reported, that he wanted to be a performer himself. He had always immersed himself in all forms of creative performance and has worked in both the theatre and within the community, although he had no desire for commercial success, rather seeing the value of his work in taking people on journeys so they can make decisions about their own lives. It was clear from talking to Deci that he is well aware that his accent is influenced by a range of different dialects. As he explains:

(41) 1   i_ve got [goʔ] a strong Brummie accent yes but [bʌʔ] it_s also very erm inter-like-
     2   national it's more of a national accent (.) because [kʌz] like [laɪk] if i_m in the way
     3   i_ve designed my accent is if i_m in london [lʌndən] I might jus_ drag my words a

4   little [lɪʔl] bit [bɪʔ] (.) but [buʔ] it [ɪʔ] still will be very much [mʌtʃ] from brum (.)
5   but [buʔ] the way that [ðæʔ] i say it [ɪʔ] (.) like [laɪk] you [juː] know what [wʊʔ] i
6   mean i think that_s a birmingham [bɜmɪŋʌm] thing [fiŋg] because i don_t [dʊnʔ]
7   really see when londoners are in america or jamaica they_re londoners [lʌndənɛs]
8   you get [geʔ] me (.) but with my friends especially if I_m in america my accent starts
9   starts to go american (.) like [laɪk] it starts to happen they can tell you_re from
10 England but [buʔ] it [ɪʔ] will influence wherever I am if I_m in Manchester it [ɪʔ]
11   will influence it [ɪʔ] (.) i_ve been in america an_ a man walks to me like [laɪk]
12 'what's gwarning' i_m like [laɪk] that [ðæʔ] means like [laɪk] 'what's up dog'
13 like [laɪk] like [laɪk] 'what's up man what_s cracking [krækɪn] blood' 'what_s
14 popping [papɪn] it_s still brum [brʌm] but [buʔ] I_ve jus_ dragged the words out
15 (.) an_ he_s [iːs] like [laɪk] 'where you from you from you from England' an_ I_m
16 like 'yeah yeah yeah I_m from England still' like [laɪk] (.) so depending [dɪpɛndɪn]
17 on who i_m talking [tɔːkɪn] to i switch it [ɪʔ]

Here, various features can be identified such as in Line 1, L-vocalisation in 'inter-
like-national' and 'national' that is very typical of younger standard English
speakers, spreading fast through England and Scotland. Also in Line 3 (and twice
in line 7) Deci very consciously makes the /o/ sound more open [lʌndən] or even
[landənə] as a Cockney would do, where the Brummie accent often has the /oo/
sound [ʊ]. TH-fronting is also evident in the token *fing* [fɪn] in place of *thing* with
'ng' as [n] and *go* is realised as 'goo' [oʊ]. In the last line, he pronounces the 'i'
vowel in *switch* and *it* in a typically unregistered Brummie way, which typically is
much tenser and closer to [i] where RP would have [ɪ]. Deci is well aware of how he
changes his voice or the degree to which he multi-voices – or as he says, 'designs
his accent' in line 3 depending upon his audience and where in the country he is
performing. He is also well aware of the degree to which many dialect speakers
are bi-dialectical:

(42) 1   there_s always two accents ennit [ɛnɪʔ] my Mum she ever spoken to you or if you
      3   spoke to my mum right now she_d go like 'hello good morning' like 'how are you'
      3   very intellectual very softly spoken very nice that_s how she speaks to the majority
      4   of people even me in the day time (.) make _er angry yes (.) piss _er off or just [jʌs](.)
      5   something [sʌmɪn] getting [gɛʔɪn] on _er [ɔr] mind (.) THEN the patwas would come
      6   out [æʊʔ] (.) an_ it [ɪʔ] would come out [æʊʔ] strong it would come out [æʊʔ] hard
      7   [haˈd] (laughs) you wouldn_t even YOU YOU LOT wouldn_t even think that [ðæʔ]
      8   it_s the same person you know what [wʊʔ] I mean
      9   *Interviewer:* So do you use Patwas language in your stuff?
      10 well you know what [wʊʔ] I say funnily enough yeah (.) that erm the
      11 Birmingham [bɜmɪŋgəm] accent especially amongst Caribbean people is very
      12 influenced by Jamaican dialect more so than anywhere else in the UK I think like
      13 London anywhere because [kʌz] people in Birmingham [bɜmɪŋgəm] say like
      14 whagwan blood you cool blood what_s [wɒʔs] cracking fam d_you [jʌ] get [gəʔ]
      15 me what_s [wæs] popping [papɪn] what [waʔ] you [jə] saying [sein]

16 you [jʌ] get [gə?] me blood right that_s [dats] _ow they talk but [bʌ?] like [laɪk] in
17 Jamaica they're like [wawagwanbludwejasei] same thing[fing] (.) highly
18 influenced because [kʌz] a lot [lo?] of Jamaicans came to birmingham [bɜmɪnŋgəm]

Deci draws upon many identifiable Jamaican Creole or Patwas features in this extract as he talked about the ways in which the Birmingham accent has influenced the way people from his kind of background spoke and his awareness of not only himself but others like his mother dialect-switching according to the inercational situation. In line 1, the tag 'ennit'; r-colouring in 'hard' in line 7; 'whagwan blood you cool clood what's crackin_' in line 15 followd by 'you get me' in line 16; and 'dat' for 'that' in line 16; 'fing' for 'thing' in line 17. At the same time, Birmingham features are also present in the voicing of 'birmingham' in lines 11 and 18 with the velar nasal plus evident; 'like' as [laɪk] in line 16 and the elongated 'oo' in place of 'o' in line 7.

Deci's upbringing, like that of the performers discussed above and again below. typifies and exemplifies the movement of British Afro Caribbean families and communities between Jamaica, London and a city such as Birmingham. Deci was born to the west of Birmingham, on the border with the Black Country, into a working-class area. The family then moved to Jamaica via London, before returning to Birmingham and settling to the south of the city, into one of its leafier, more middle-class suburbs, (which is also the home of Warwickshire cricket). For example, the audience member interviewed about the performance of *The Spiral*, himself a performer in his early 20s called Evoke, said of DFL's performance character:

(43) 1   the character [kæræktæ] is universal (.) could be anywhere in England (.)
      2   youths [juːvs] like _im like that all over england in every other borough but [bʌ?]
      3   there was particular things about [æbou?] his character [kæræktæ] that you could
      4   tell he [ɪː] was from birmingham [bɜmingʌm] because there was certain like [laːk]
      5   slang that /ðæ?/ he would use (.) certain body posture an_ like [laːk] the way he [ɪː]
      6   would dress (.) his demeanour you know what I mean (.) like [laːk] you [jʌ] know i
      7   remember one time i went to manchester [mæntʃestæ] yeah (.) and someone said
      8   to me 'you're from birmingham [bɜmingʌm] aren_t you [jʌ] I can tell by your
      9   character [kæræktæ]' and it_s true you [jʌ] know you [jʌ] can tell distinctive traits
      10 that [ðæ?] look birmingham [bɜmingʌm] Manchester [mæntʃestæ] liverpool
      11 London (.) the way they carry themselves (.) this swagger (.) [swægæ] yeah that_s
      12 what it is (.) everyone has it you know (.) even though [dau] he [ɪː] was a universal
      12 character [kæræktæ] (.) the swagger you [jʌ] could tell was from
      13 birmingham [bɜmingʌm]

Birmingham was pronounced as /bɜmingʌm/ throughout with the /r/ sound r-coloured. Thus, indexing being a Black Brummie is through an interrelated set of 'markers' or 'indexes' that include a mix of skin colour, dress and posture as well as linguistic characteristics of expression. The concept of a Black Brummie is further complicated by the fact that the geographic place and space to which it links are, at one and the same time, Birmingham in the West Midlands, England's capital London, Jamaica in the Caribbean and African Americans in the USA. For example, Evoke goes on to say:

(44) 1 home (-) home is one of two places (-) home is either your initial abode where you
       2 live an_ area that [ðæʔ] you_re in you know the people that [ðæʔ] you congregate
       3 with [wɪv] which for example are people like [laɪk] you [jʌ] or then you_ve [jʌ]
       4 got [gʊʔ] home in say a natural state would be back in the Caribbean but [bʊʔ] they
       5 would say BACK A YARD home is a community (.) not [nʊʔ] necessarily an area
       6 like [laɪk] it_s about [æbæʔ] the people what tend to happen is that [ðæʔ] people
       7 afixiate themselves afixiate their community (.) it_s a struggle (-) community is the
       8 struggle us an_ them understandin_ is understandin_ the struggle you can tell a man
       9 the way he [ɪː] talks the way he [ɪː] expresses himself [ɪːself] the way he [ɪː] carries
      10 _is swagger you can tell if he_s [ɪːs] experienced the same struggle as you an_
      11 that_s [dæts] how you relate you can tell by the [dæ] way they speak (.) you can tell
      12 by the [dæ] way they look at you you can tell by the way they [dæ] act you know
      13 what [wʊʔ] I mean it_s all in their body language

'Home' then, for members of a community such as the one with which Evoke aligns himself, has two dimensions or meanings: the immediate, geographically anchored community in Birmingham, and at the same time, his ancestral geographic space and historic past of Jamaica. Evoke goes on to say that unlike Deci4Life, he does not perceive himself as having a distinctive Brummie accent because he has travelled around a great deal, although he reported that sometimes his interlocuters would recognise he was from Birmingham because of the way he sounded a particular word:

(45) it_s sometimes hard to place me but [bʌʔ] hear a particular word I might say an_ people say you sound like [laɪk] a brummie when you say you_re from Birmingham [bɜmiŋʌm] aren_t you [enɪt]

He also spoke of two opposing reactions he got when he travelled around, when people asked him where he was from and he replied 'Birmingham.' Either they reacted negatively and said 'you're from gun village' or positively and said 'Oh Brummies are really friendly.' The negativity, he reported, did not affect the way he spoke. Rather, he interpreted it as having more to do with the perceptions his interlocuters showed towards his accent, and the degree to which they perceived his speech either negatively or positively in relation to their own experiences and backgrounds.

The conversation interview with Selassie was carried out at Aston University, and included finding out about Selassie's background growing up in Birmingham. He was born in a suburb of Birmingham called Small Heath, to Jamiacan parents and his older siblings had also been born in Jamaica and attended the George Dixon Grammar School for Boys. He attributed his interest in performance and poetry to his local Baptist church when he was growing up, recalling an elocution competition held in Birmingham where children would recite poetry and be judged on their recital. At grammar school, he wrote poems that contributed to the school magazine. In terms of ethnicity and nationality, Selassie said:

(46) 1 because my parents wise well we were english because [kʌs] we were born in
      2 England yet we_re black so we were_nt english english because [kʌs] it was like
      3 you _ad to be white to be english so we were like [la:k/] i don_t know _ow we
      4 would describe ourselves (.) black british

As with other performers, Selassie was well aware of code or dialect switching between Jamaican patois and English and also how the younger generation were drawing less upon Jamaican patois than his own. Well educated, he quoted the work of the black cultural theorist Paul Gilroy (1993), his identification of the black Antlantic and people of Selassie's generation being a transitional one, between the old, colonial and postcolonial world to modern times. Selassie said he had been aware of having two dialects from an early age, and his parents switiching from Jamaican to English. The first time he became aware of the Brummie way he spoke English, was when he went to Bradford, a city in the north of England, and people would say to him 'you're from Birmingham aren't you?' He also spoke of the way his parents would discourage home from talking Jamaican, whilst at the same time talking in Jamaican themselves:

(49) 1 strange thing was that_s what they spoke so they would tell us they wouldn_t say for
      2 example 'you must speak proper english' they_d say 'don_t [tʊk] talk [tʊk] bad'
      3 you know what i mean an_ not [nʊʔ] only that our parents would switch as well so
      4 we could realise we were like [la:k] in the _ouse when they spoke to us they_d speak
      5 in like [la:k] jamaican language or patwas an_ then [den] for example if they went
      6 to the [dʌ] door or telephone rang then the voice would change you [jʌ] know
      7 what [wʊr] i mean an_ so obviously at school it_s the same kind of thing we would
      8 just [dʒʌs] speak like [la:k] english at school or amongst our friends we would drop
      9 in the usual Jamaican words or whatever [wʊʔevæ] so yeah we did that [dæʔ] all the
      10 time

He also recalled that he or his siblings knew when they were at trouble at home through the evident use of Jamiacan patois in utterances such as 'cum ya' in place of 'come here.' When he was growing up the Jamiacan Selassie spoke was called |patois and only later on in life did he become aware of its negative connotations and its use as a perjorative term. This happened when he attended a course at Birmingham City college, a college of further education, on Jamiacna language. At first, he was resitant to the notion of Patois being called Jamaican language. However, after discovering the work of cultural theorists such as Paul Gilroy and Frantz Fanon and realising the cultural and sociopolictical dimensions of language use, he has called it Jamaican language, not Patois. He was also well aware of the hierarchy into which people placed language in public and social life, with European languages at the top, creoles in the middle and indigenous languages at the bottom.

Selassie cited the Doctor Seuss children's books he would read from the public library and Louise Bennett's poetry, written in patois, as having influenced and shaped the way he wrote poetry. When he first read her poetry, Selassie said that this was the first time he had seen patois written down and when he read her poems, recognised them as being how his mum, dad, brothers and siters spoke. Later on in his teens in the 1970s, he was also influenced by the dub poet Lyton Kwasi Johnson. To Selassie, writing dub poetry he said, came naturally. Asked if he felt he was expressing his Brummie or Jamaican identity in his writing, his reply indicates that it is both:

(48) i_m a brummmie ennit because [k ɒs] I was born in birmingham [bɜmiŋɡʌm]
      you [jʌ] know what [wʊʔ] i mean so um i_m not [nʊʔ] jamaican right so (.) yea i_m a
      jamaican brummie eh small heath [ɪːð] (.) whatever

Selassie stressed that he drew upon Jamaican language in his poetry because his roots were in Jamaica even though he was born and had lived in England most of his life. He has performed in venues across the world and to a wide variety of audiences, and reported that he accommodated his language use towards his audiences in the interaction he had with them between poems. He also stressed that his use of patois was not as broad as someone who came from rural Jamaica and it was more akin to 'Jamenglish' than Jamaican. Likewise his son, who writes and performs rap poetry, does not draw upon any aspects of Jamaican language in his poems and performances. Selasie attributed this to the fact that he was closer generationally to the source of Jamiacan language than his son. Selassie also recounted an interview he gave on BBC radio with another Jamaican poet, Simon Swanson. The interviewer asked both poets where they were from and Selassie said he was born in England and Simon Swanson that he was born in Jamaica. After both had read their poetry, the interviewer remarked that Selassie, although born in England sounded Jamaican, and Simon, born in Jamaica sounded more English. How anyone sounds, said Selassie, is attributable to a number of factors:

(49) 1 you know it depends on _ow you come up the influence of your parents an_ those
2 around you pertaining to the language so some would say well you [jʌ] know like
3 'stop speed man oh top people' you [jʌ] know [næ] what [wʊʔ] i mean(.) ok for me
4 to get [geʔ] through I need to speak proper english because speaking jamaican
5 language is bad (..) I know some people who were born here /ejæ/ of jamaican parents
6 who can_t speak jamaican language because their parents just beat it [ɪʔ] out
7 of them /em/

Selassie, though, felt he has a responsibility to use Jamaican language in his poetry and performances as a way of acknowledging his Jamaican heritage that for his generation, is closer to postcolonial times than his children and grandchildren are. At the same time, he acknowledged that the range of features he drew upon is more restricted than that of his forefathers and incorporated features of his Brummie upbringing in his speech.

4.7 Performance 3: *Where are you from? From Birmingham*

The performance discussed here was given by the poet Roy McFarlane, performed in the foyer of Aston University, in front of an audience of university students from local, national and international backgrounds, called *where are you from?* Every year, Birmingham appoints a poet laureate and in 2010, Roy was given the title which helped to raise the profile for Black poets in the region and also poetry as a form of social comment. Hua and Wei (2016) discuss the significance of a question such as this in everyday conversational intercations, and particularly when voiced as 'where are you really from?' as an example of nationality and ethnicity talk (NET). NET, they say, '...is essentially an act of identity calibration and involves categorisation and positioning of self and others and stance-making (2016: 450). Although they acknowledge that the question "where are you really from" itself does not of itself contest immigrants' entitlement. "...what makes difference to the perception of whether one is an "interloper" – someone who is not wanted – is the 'tangled' history, memory and expectation imbued and fuelled by power inequality" (2016: 449). Mcfarlane's poem exemplifies such an entanglement, and the complex socio-cultural and historical complexities of what counts as 'home' as discussed already above when an immigrant is asked the question: 'where are you from?' He prefaced his reading a poem given below with a short anecdote that included the audience participating as follows:

(50) 1 As a black going on holiday in Europe or America and this is something my Asian
2 brothers an_ sisters will probably share now when we go over there and we sit

3   making up [ʊp] on my suntan [sʊntan] sunning on the beach and somebody say
4   'where you from' and then I'd say ' I say I'm from England, Birmingham
5   [bɜɪŋgʊm]' and they say 'no mate where are you REALLY from' I say 'I'm from
6   Birmingham [bɜɪŋgʊm] England' they'll say 'but where your parents from' 'they're
7   from Birmingham [bɜɪŋgʊm] in England so this I dedicate this this is what this is
8   about right and actually you're going to [gonæ] have to join in right I'm going to get
9   them to join in yeh all the students   when I say where you from you say
10   Birmingham [bɜɪŋgʊm] (-) where are you from
11   Audience: Birmingham [bɜɪŋgʊm]
12   Roy: how many people here are from Birmingham [bɜɪŋgʊm]
     < a few members of the audience put up their hands>
13   Roy: put [pʊʔ] on a Brummie accent then so one more time where you from
14   Audience: Birmingham [bɜɪŋgʊm]
15   Roy: where you from
16   Audience: Birmingham [bɜɪŋgʊm]
17   Roy: what do you mean where are my parents do I come from my geneology,
18   generation (.) gene pool (.) my family tree my next of kin or simply going back to
19   my roots (.) where you from
20   Audience: Birmingham [bɜɪŋgʊm]
21   Roy: why because we have been blessed with all the colours god has given us our
22   cocoa butter [bʊʔɜ] caramel flavoured milk milk chocolate black coffee black
23   turmeric gold spice flavours of the world where you from
24   Audience: Birmingham [bɜɪŋgʊm]
25   Roy: where you from
26   Audience: Birmingham [bɜɪŋgʊm]
27   Roy: Why as we can speak other languages as well as the queen_s English mix
28   you [y] want to [wʊnæ] to with Punjabi with Gujerati throw the lyrical with the
29   patwa from the Caribbean sing my mother_s tongue from my father_s land where
30   are you from
31   Audience: Birmingham [bɜɪŋgʊm]
32   Roy: where spaghetti junction mixes with the Balti mile where carnival vaults
33   with Irish celebrations where Chinese year begin and German markets mark the
34   end of the year where heavy metal was forged in the workshop of the world from
35   the gun [gʊn] quarter to the jewellery quarter and that's only half the story so i_ll
36   tell you what [wʊʔ] I'll stop going [gʊm] around the Wrekin in a manner [mænæ]
37   of speaking [spiːkɪn] Birmingham [bɜɪŋgʊm] is where i_m from and that_s my
38   home

As with the two performers discussed above, Andres Hesson and Deci4Life, Roy Mcfarlane's concept of 'home' includes his parental homeland of Jamaica and England, especially the city of Birmingham where he was born and lives. His sense of place includes an intricate imaginative weaving of the two countries' histories. 'Around the wrekin' in line 36 is a local expression. The Wrekin are a set of Shropshire hills that provide a popular ramble for local walkers, and 'going around the wrekin' has become a local idiom for someoe who talks in armbling fashion, taking a long time to get to the point. He also evokes the multicultural aspect of contemporary life in a city such as Birmingham in lines 32 to 35, with his references to the Irish and Chinese quarters and the Frankfurt Christmas market that takes place in the city centre every year. His pronunciation at the start of his performance is unmarked with dialect features apart from the enregistered pronunciation of Birmingham as [bɜɪŋɡʊm]. In line 13, Roy voices *put* with both the closed Brummie 'o' sound and t glottalling as he asks his audience to 'put on' a Birmingham accent, repeated throughout. Portraying being black, of Jamaican heritage and from Birmingham in Roy's performance is framed in terms of accept-ance, as in lines 22 and 23 where he talks about shades of skin colour in a posi-tive way. In lines 27 to 29 he refers to the various linguistic or feature pools upon which people from the Caribbean and Asian subcontinents have to draw upon in addition to English in creating multiethnolects.

4.7.1 In conversation with Roy Mcfarlane

Roy's performance took place as part of an event organised by the German Department at Aston University, which in turn was part of a project called *Crossing Boundaries* that took place across the university in 2010/11. We were able to talk to Roy briefly after his performance, about himself and what had influ-enced the nature and conent of his performances. Roy was born in England, had spent much of his life in Wolverhampton although much of his work is based in Birmingham and the Midlands and he currently lives in the Black Country. His parents are from Trinityville, St Thomas, Jamaica and came over to Britain in the 1960s. His father was a deacon, a minister of the Gospel and it was from watching his father preach that Roy said he got his love of performance. He first became aware of issues related to race and identity when he attended Bilston college, a college of further education. He started to take part in arts community projects, learning about aspects of performance from other performers who taught him about interaction, rhythms of rap and so on. He also reported that he had been influenced by meetings with several prominent people while working within race organisations and feeling constrained by the politics of how issues relating to ethnicity and race can be spoken about. One of the most notable of these was a meeting with Roi Kwabena, a Trinidadian cultural anthropologist. Meeting Roi, Roy said, gave him the confidence to speak about his own experiences of ethnic-ity and race in ways that cut through what he saw as racial politics.

He also cited Langston Hughe's *The Negro speaks of rivers* that inspired him to write "words that spoke of my worlds". He has performed at venues in Birmingham such as *The Crescent Theatre* and *The Drum*, as well as taking part in a *City Voices* project in Wolverhampton. His poetry has been published in an anthology *Out of Bounds* and his debut collection called *Beginning with your last breath* was published in 2016 by Nine Arches Press. For Roy, his poetry and his performance of it provide a vehicle for reflecting upon life, and the ways in which an individual's experiences such as his own relate to the wider socio-cultural world within which his life is lived. He reported that race is part of life so the preconception that Black poetry is confrontational he felt was, like Andre Hesson, a misconception. Roy said he wrote and performed poems about all aspects of life, including his experience of being a black man in a predominatly white society whilst at the same time being fiercely proud of both Birmingham and Black Country regions. It would seem then, that for performers and poets discussed in this chapter, identifying with a specific English region transcends ethnic and racial boundaries and histories, in complex and multifaceted ways, and discussed further in the next section.

4.8 In conversation with Benjamin Zephaniah

Benjamin Zephaniah is a well-known English writer and dub poet born in Birmingham in 1958. His father worked as a postman and originally came from Barbados and his mother worked as a nurse and came from Jamaica. He was born in the Birmingham suburb of Handsworth, which at the time had a majority Jamiacan community, which today is mainly Asian. He was interviewed in a well established and well known vegetarian restaurant in the city centre, situated on the first floor of a converted warehouse between the newly refurbished Moor Street Station and Bullring shopping centre and the older, more industrialarea of Digbeth, and so is part of both new and old Birmingham.

Benjamin recounted how, in looking back on his childhood, he had felt himself to be more Jamiacan than English, since the food, the sounds, the culture around him, was all Jamaican. Jamiaca was the world in which he lived at that time, with his parents coming from Jamaica which he thought 'was just there'. to illustrate this, he told of a time when his mother told him that an uncle was coming to visit the family from Jamaica, he went to the local park, expecting to see uncle walk over the horizon. To Benjamin, Jamaica was 'next door' and Handsworth an outpost of it. Like the mothers of other celebrities interviewed such as Julie Walters, Benjamin's mother was very class conscious and sent Benjamin to an all-white primary school which he hated, and where he first came across overt racism on the part of his peers. He recalled one of the first incidents at this time, which was a boy riding past him with a brick in his hand that eh threw at Benjamin's head, shouting 'you black bastard!" he said that when he and his mother recall the incident now they laugh, since when he came home he asked his mum, 'mum, what's a bastard?' Benjamin began writing and speaking poetry from an early age, but hated school, became increasingly aware of the racism with which he was surrounded at the time and was a rebellious adolescent.

The big change in his life, he said, was when he decided to 'go straight' in his late teens and wanted to perform his poetry. There were at the time only one or two places where he could do this in Birmingham, so he moved to London. Since that move to London, Benjamin conceives of Birmingham as his home. He recalled becoming more aware of himself as coming from Birmingham and defending the city in response to people's negative perceptions of it and the way he spoke changing as a result, "soundin_ more English and toning down my accent". As he has grown older, and especially through contact with the media on the radio and television, Benjamin reported that his accent had become noticibly less Jamaican and more Brummie and English sounding. For example, he recalled a time he was interviewed on the radio before the Brixton riots in the late 70s and early 1980s, when he said:

(51) i an_ i er suffer i an_ i er feel the pain [pæiyn] and if something_s [sʌmθɪŋs] not [nɒʔ] done i go CHANT [ʧaːnʔ] babylon we_re going to [gʌna] deal with [wid] babylon (.) babylon burns

The /r/ in *suffer* and *burn* is rhotic. Anyone who understands Jamaican talk, said Benjamin, would know that what he said was: "we're suffering and we're gonna rise up". Babylon refers to the passage in the in the Book of Revelations in the Bible where Jews were captured and endured hardships in the city of Babylon. Jamaicans, and Rastafarians in particular, draw a parallel between the suffering experienced by the Jews in Babylon and the transatlantic slave trade. His comment though, was reported in the press as tantamount to him inciting a riot which took him aback. The way in which what he said was reported, made Benjamin realise that when he spoke publicly, what he said was taken not only as an expression of his own views but on behalf of a whole community. As a consequence of this, he changed the way he spoke when participating in the media. At the time, he said, black people had such a small voice in media and Benjamin realised that every time he spoke it mattered. Whilst living in London, in the 1980s the news channel Channel 4 began broadcasting, the fourth TV channel of the time which billed itself as a radical tv station and Benjamin often appeared on it at the time. As a result of such public exposure, he said he made a delibarate effort to accommodate his speech more towards that of standard English, in the interests of being understood by as many people as possible. As he said:

(52) 1   the other [əvə] thing [fɪŋ] i started erm doin_ [du:ɪn] was soundin_ [saʊndɪn] more
      2   english understanding [ʊndəstændɪn] more ye understanding [ʊndəstændɪn]
      3   more english you know (.) kind of toning [təʊnɪŋ] down my accent [æksən?]   i
      4   DIdn_t [dɪdən?] THInk of it [ɪ?]   as TOning [təʊnɪŋ] down my Accent i
      5   thought of it as i_m presentin_ [prəzəntɪn] a programme on radio four you know
      6   (.) i want to [wʊnæ] be undersSTOOD (-) at the same time (.) you_re very aware
      7   (.) that [ðæ?] as I said (-) black and Asian people they didn_t [dɪdən?] have a voice
      8   in the media then [dɛn] no black mps all the black people were from america so we
      9   wanted to (.) well I certainly [sɜ:?ənli:] want to voice myself (.) rather than have
     10   somebody be a spokesperson for me so I erm I you know it [ɪ?] was that kind of
     11   duty to speak for our community beCAUSE it_s it_s KIND of /a/ HARd for a lot
     12   of [lʊ?ə] younger people to understand I mean there was sus laws you you you
     13   (.) if you were black or <laughing> asian it was difficult to walk the streets at [æ]
     14   night [naɪ?]. we (.) were in the media we were aware that [ðæ?] there were
     15   people DESPARATE for all of us to speak about [əbaʊ?] about [əbaʊ?] our
     16   housing [haʊzɪɪn] conditions if i_m speaking [spi:kɪn] on about [əbaʊ?] i_m not
     17   [no?] a politician but [bʊ?] if i_m talking / tɔ:kɪn/ to the mainstream media
     18   about [əbaʊ?] the way we are policed the way we are housed our lack of work
     19   etcetera I don_t [dəʊn?] want to [wʊnæ] be doing [du:ɪn] it [ɪ?] in a accent the
     20   media who doesn_t [dʊzən?] understand you know i be understood by the
     21   majority of people so I don_t think it was constantly let me get rid of my
     22   Birmingham accent it was like (.) i_m speakin_ to the nation here I have a
     23   privileged position where if you say to me you_re interviewin_ me you say right
     24   ok Benjamin have you got [go?] a poem on that subject I can do poetry and can be
     25   myself again oddly enough I really don_t [dəʊn?] like the way I sound i_m or i_m
     26   like the way I sound in poetry don_t [dəʊn?] get [gɛ?] me wrong when i_m
     27   talking [tɔ:kɪn] i just [dʒʊs?] think [fink] my accent [æksən?] now is so mixed
     28   up it_s not [nʊ?] brummie not [nʊ?] London it_s kind of sometimes I wish I was
     29   more one or the other [əvə] but this is me i_m a product my Accent is a
     30   product of my upbringing [ʊpbrɪŋgɪn]

T-glottalling and g-dropping is prevalent thoughout Benjamin's speech as is the Birmingham and Black Country pronunciation of /o/ but also [f] for /th/ in line 27. When he talks about the way in which he accommodates his speech when interviewed by the media in lines 19 to 25 he pronounces *Birmingham* in RP within the specific intercational conext and its subject matter. Benjamin also recalled white rebels of his youth who were of Irish origin, at the time when the 'Irish troubles' were at their height, including the bombing of Birmingham city centre pubs, going to evening and night classes to get rid of their Birmingham accents and speak with an Irish one as an overtly political act. He also shows his awareness of the indexical nature of language use through distinguishing a non academic distinction between a Birmingham and a Brummie accent, with the latter typical of poor, white working class people who do not ever venture out of their immediate area or if they do stay within their own little group, much like the characters caracatured in in the Fizzog sketch discussed in Chapter 3. He spoke of communities living in the outer suburbs of Birmingham who are fightened to venture into the city centre. In recent years, Birmingham's city centre has been transformed into a modern, gloablised shopping and eating space and, the outdoor and indoor food and retail markets apart,many local people do not recognise it as a place for them but for foreigners, and describe the city centre as a different country. However, he also observed the difference between older and younger generations in terms of the relationship between dialect and social class, as older generations from a working class background may have prospered financially and their children's accents differed from their own as a result of their education, or younger generations from working-class parents whose accent and dialect is far less regionally oriented, again through education and employment.Benjamin speculated that as poorer people from Birmingham and the Blck Country began to stay later in education and gain better employment, thendifference between dialects would level out.

At the same time, whilst perceiving Birmingham as home never changes for him, and he consciously accommodates his speech towards standard English when talking on the radio or the television; for example, in a 2017 documentary immigration for BBC Radio 4, when he goes on stage and peforms his poetry, in his imagination he goes back to Jamiaca, playing in a character but in his own poetic voice. At the same time, Benjamin also recognises the multi-voiced nature of that voice and its multicultural nature:

(53) 1   An_ even though (.) when i_m doing [duːɪn] my poetry also the brummie comes
2   out a lot [lɒʔ] an_there_s a poem that [ðæʔ] I do called what_s that [ðæʔ] got to
3   [goræ] do with me i just [dʒʊsʔ] want to [wʊnæ] live my life mate [mɛɪʔ]
4   so just [dʒʊsʔ] leave me alone why should I fight [faɪʔ] the state when i_m
5   trying [ʧɹaɪɪn] to buy my home i just [dʒʊsʔ] want to [wʊnæ] earn my bread
6   guy an_ feed my family you may starve you may DIE
7   but [bʊʔ] what [wɒʔ] _as that [ðæʔ] got to [gʊdæ] do with me
8   poets are dying [daɪjɪ] in nigeria or forced to leave the area [ɪəriːæ]
9   multinationals are superior [suːpɪɹɪæ]
10 but [bʊʔ] what [wɒʔ] has that [ðæʔ] got to [gʊdæ] do with me
11 and in some wasteland i_ve heard [hɜrd] that [ðæʔ] she can_t [kaːnʔ] say a word
12 an_ he [ɪ] must [mʊsʔ] grow a beard
13 what [wɒʔ] has that got to do with me
14 WHAT [wɒʔ] HAS that [ðæʔ] got to [gʊʔæ] do with me
15 i_m just [dʒʊsʔ] this guy from Birmingham [bɜːmɪŋhæm]
16 an_ all I want [wɑnʔ] to do was live good in the hood
17 it_s got [gʊʔ] nothing [nʌθɪn] to do with me
18 i_m just [dʒʊsʔ] your average football [fʊʔbɔːl] fan
19 there_s some foreign teams are VERY VERY good you know
20 I will change the accent [æksənʔ] <laughing> to make it sound like a

21 bigot [bɪgʊ]/ saying [sɛɪjɪn] oh I HATE [hɛɪʔ] black people but [bʊʔ] those
22 FOREIGN teams are very you know very good so within one poem there are
23 different voices that [ðæʔ] are going [gʊɪŋ] on

In this extract, Benjamin shows his awareness of the mulit-voiced nature of his performances, the different peronas he evokes that include drawing upon features of Birmingham dialect. He exemplifies this by going on to recite a poem from lines 3 to 18 where he juxtaposes a persona from a background of his own, mixing references to the locality of Birmingham with Jamaican ans American influences in lines 15 and 16 as the "guy from Birmingham who just wants to live good in the hood". 'Living good in the hood' is contrasted with the various influences of globalisation that are framed as rejection in having nothing to do with him. It is clear then, that the ways in which black performers of Afro Caribbean heritage construct their identities in relation to dialect and region is in polyphonic ways that draw upon a linguistic or feature pool associated with a range of dialects – Birmingham, Jamaican Creole or Patwas and London.

4.9 Conclusion

The discussion in this chapter shows how regional communities are not necessarily geographically, linguistically or socially homogenous. Indeed, it demonstrates that they can be multi layered and in the case of Black Brum, not fixed by geographically defined national or regional borders. This urban dialect or multiethnolect draws upon the linguistic or feature pool of several others in its creation in ways that correlate with the life histories of the performers and their ancestral heritage. The performances and interviews discussed also present a contemporary snapshot of sociolingustic reality, representing a moment of temporal and spatial mobility. As well as demonstrating the fact that regional communities are not necessarily linguistically or socially homogenous, this chapter, like the one before it, has shown that not only do speakers have choices, but they are aware of choice, particularly in performative contexts. Regionally based performers and audiences, regardless of ethnic background, may shift between positive and negative attitudes to their home area and linguistic use situationally. All of the performers and people interviewed attested to their self-awareness of how they spoke and the degree to which – or not – they drew upon the various linguistic resources at their disposal. They were well aware of the degree to which people modify their speech and accommodate it according to the intercational context, something they expoloit to comic effect. They are also all too keenly aware of the social construction of race, constructions to which they draw attention and undercut in their performances.

Urban dialects in particular, it seems, serve a sociocultural purpose that is also partly historical. For those of an Afro Caribbean heritage, their use of patwas, Jamaican Creole or Jamaican language is indicative of a link with the past as as well as with the country of their forefathers that lives on in collective imagination. For many poets and peformers, it is also a way of keeping alive the memory of past injustices and struggles, and in this way features associated with the dialects from which they draw can be said to be metaphorical in nature. At the same time, a linguistic or contact pool that comprises features of Jamaican dialect with features drawn from Brummie, American or London dialects anchors them in the present.

5 Staging language in performance: Performance poetry and drama

5.1 Introduction

This chapter turns to consider creative, live performances which have been more scripted than those discussed in the previous two chapters, namely performance poetry and dramatic plays. Firstly, performance poetry discussed is taken from an amateur open mic event in the centre of Stoke on Trent, a town in the Staffordshire Potteries region, and similar to those that take place in Birmingham and the Black Country as discussed in Chapter 3. This is followed by a consideration of the performance of three plays is discussed. The first is *Riot* by Richard Green, set in Birmingham at the time of the riots in 2011, performed in a small semi-professional theatre attached to a public house in the centre of Birmingham. The second is *Too Much Pressure* by Allan Pollock, a play set in 1970s Coventry, performed by professional actors at its professional repertory theatre *The Belgrade* in the centre of the city. Coventry is the second largest city in the West Midlands after Birmingham some 12 miles south of Birmingham and like Birmingham, is located historically in Warwickshire but now forms part of the metropolitan borough of the West Midlands. The third is a performance of a medieval Mummers' play traditionally performed by amateurs and performed consecutively in public houses at around the time of Christmas and New Year. The particular performance discussed was performed in a public house in the town of Leamington Spa, which, since the creation of a West Midlands metropolitan area that lifted both Birmingham and Coventry out of Warwickshire in the 1970s, is the shire's largest town.

The dialect variables identified in Chapter 3 are considered again here as they pertain to the data taken from the performances in Staffordshire and Warwickshire, followed by analysis of their context of use in both performance and interview data. As with the performances and conversation interviews discussed in Chapters 3 and 4, this chapter discusses the extent to which identified variables are present in the data; the part they play in terms of indexing place and enregistering social identities; their role in live performances in creating, maintaining and challenging imagined communities; the ideological implications of such use and the extent to which any identified, underlying ideologies implicit in the performances were shared by members of the audiences.

https://doi.org/10.1515/9781501506796-005

5.2 Features of Staffordshire and Warwickshire dialect in performance

Both morphologically and phonologically and like Birmingham and The Black Country, the counties of Staffordshire and Warwickshire also lie in a Midlands transitional zone between the so-called North-South divide in England, as discussed in Chapter 3. Staffordshire is the most northern county of the West Midlands, reflected in some aspects of its dialect features, and especially in relation to vowel sounds. The northernmost boundary of Warwickshire adjoins the southern boundary of Staffordshire. Parts of the Black Country fall within the Staffordshire border, and until the 1970s, a large part of Birmingham and all of Coventry were both part of Warwickshire. As one would expect then, some features are shared across the region, whilst others are more locally bound. Overall, far fewer dialect features were identified across the performances in these two counties than those found in the Birmingham and Black Country ones.

5.2.1 Phonology

Consonantal features identified in Chapter 3 and some in Chapter 4, as shown in Table 5.1, also appear in the data for Staffordshire and Warwickshire. This are consonant cluster deletion or h- and g-dropping; t-glottaling and the T-R rule discussed in Chapter 3 where /t/ is replaced with /r/, is also evident, as in *matter* pronounced *marrer*. The velar nasal sound in final position words such as *sing* and *ring*, where a velar nasal plosive is pronounced, placing the consonantal /g/ after /n/, are all present in the data. However, the velar nasal plus characteristic of Birmingham and the Black Country discussed in Chapter 3 does not feature here at all.

Table 5.1: Consonant features.

Dialect indexed	Feature	Example
Staffs and Warks	h-dropping	*Merry Hill* as *Merry _ill* *had* as _ad
Staffs and Warks	g-dropping	giving [gɪvɪn] and [æn]
Staffs and Warks	Glottal stop	alright [əlrɑɪʔ] put [pʊʔ]
Staffs and Warks	T to R	*matter* to *mara*
Staffs	Th to f	*three* to *free*

In relation to vowels, and in common with the rest of the region, the short [a] in words such as *bath* and *trap* heard in these counties indicates that it is a northern variety. Also in common with Birmingham and the Black Country, the single vowel *o* or *u* [ʌ] in words such as *but, bus* or *come*, sounds instead more like *oo* in word such as *foot* [ʊ]. Another shared characteristic is the shortening of vowel sounds in a word such as *been* to *bin* and *my* to *me* [i:]. The sound [u] becomes a long [u:] in words like *book* [bu:k] and *cook* [cu:k]. The long /i/ vowel in words such as *time* is pronounced as *tiome* [aɪ]. The vowel sound in the token *like* is pronounced as *liake* giving an extra vowel sound and thus a triphthong to give /laɪak/. The token *Stoke* is also realised to rhyme more with *goat* than *poke*.

A distinctive feature that marks the Staffordshire potteries dialect out from the rest of the West Midlands relates to the phenomenon known as the Great Vowel Shift (GVS). The GVS that affected the pronunciation of long vowels of English from the 15th to 18th century mainly did so in the south of the Country and did not reach this far north in the west Midlands. Where diphthongs are found in RP then a monophthong is heard instead. For example, tokens such as *pay day, down* are realized as monophthongs as in *pee dee, dine*. In Warwickshire and elsewhere throughout the region, such monophthongisation is limited largely to the pronunciation of *my* / maj/ as *me* /mi:/. Levitt (1968) identified other features such as the orthographic representation /oa/ of the [oʊ] sound in tokens such as *boat, throat, coal* is realized as [ʊ] *boot, throot, cool*; the long /e/ sound [i:] in *meat, key, seem, piece* is realized more as a long /a/ sound [ei] giving *mate, kaye, same, pace*; the orthographic representation of /ou/ in tokens such as *about, shout, cloud* is a long /i/ sound realized as [ai]

Table 5.2: Vowel features.

Dialect indexed	Feature	Example
Staffs and Warks	*but* and *come* as *boot or coom*	*boot* [bʊt] *coom* [kʊm]
Staffs and Warks	*been* as *bin*	*bin* [bɪn]
Staffs and Warks	*book* as *book*	*book* [bu:k]
Staffs and Warks	*my* or *myself* as *me* or *meself*	*my* [mɪ:] *myself* [mɪsɛlf]
Staffs	*take* as *tek*	take [tek]
Staffs	Transposition of vowel sound	*mom* for *mum*; *mon* for *man*
Staffs	*time* as *tiome*	*time* [taɪm]
Staffs and Warks	*like* as *like* to rhyme with *quiet*	*Like* [lɪake]
Staffs	*stoke* as *stoak* to rhyme with *goat*	*Stoke* [stʊak]

abite, shite, clide. Conversely, tokens such as *there* or *where* may be pronounced as *theyere* or *weyer* and *door* and *floor* as *dooer* and *flooer.* Such features indicates that this dialect is further north in character than that found in other, further south West Midlands regions. This is not surprising given that Staffordshire is the most Northern region of the West Midlands, although it does indicate the likely boundary of this feature. A further feature also identified by Levitt is the absence of the replacement of the sound *l* in tokens such as *ball* with a long /o/ sound to give *bow,* and *oud* in place of *old.* With the Black Country but not with Warwickshire, the Staffordshire Potteries also dialect shares the features of /o/ and /a/ vowel transposition in words such as *mon* for *man,* and *hond* for *hand,* often with the h dropped to give_*ond.* Table 5.2 summarises the features found in the data set.

5.2.2 Morphosyntax and lexis

Grammatically, the pronoun exchange of *her* for *she* is also found in the two counties, though did not occur in the performance data under consideration here. *Were* is also used instead of *was* in the past, first person singular declension of the verb *be: I were born. Done* is also used in place of *did* in the past tense: *I done it; don't it. As* is used in place of *who* in an utterance such as *it were _im as towd me* (*it was him who told me*). Omission of *to* also occurs as in *I'm going Leek* in place of *I'm going to Leek.* The past tense is used in place of the past continuous in utterances such as *she was/ were sat* in place of *she was sitting; he was/were stood* in place of *he was standing.* A distinctive feature commented upon by Mark Bailey the Staffordshire performance poet is the tendency to reduce a string of sounds to a single one, so that *what's up* becomes *sup* in an utterance such as *what's up with you?* He also used the archaic form *thee* of the second person singular pronoun *you* at the end of his conversation interview. These features are summarised in Table 5.3. The only lexical variation found in the data was the reduction of the word *Coventry* to *Cov; Staffordshire* to *Staffy Cher;* in Coventry, women are often called *luv* and in Staffordshire *duck.*

Table 5.3: Morphosyntactic features.

Dialect indexed	Feature	Example
Staffs	2nd person singular past tense in place of 1st of 'be' and 'do'	*I were* in place of *I was* *I done* in place of *I did*
Staffs		*Sup* in place of *what's up*

(continued)

Table 5.3 (continued)

Dialect indexed	Feature	Example
Staffs		*Thee* for *you*
Staffs and Warks	Past tense in place of past continuous 'sit' and 'stood'	*I was sat day* in place of *I was sitting; I was stood* in place of *I was standing.*
Birmingham and Black Country	-s endings added -s endings absent	*I knows; a couple of year ago*
Black Country	Pronoun exchange	*Her* for *she*

5.3 Performance 1: Staffordshire Potteries and the Trent Vale poet

The county of Staffordshire to the north of Warwickshire and the West Midlands metropolitan country comprises a mixture of densely populated urban areas centred upon towns and cities that, like many in the region and also throughout England, were once villages and towns, interspersed with rural areas that include farmland, woodland and ancient common ground. It includes within its boundaries some of both the poorest and most affluent areas of the country. Its industrial heartland lies to the north of the country and centres upon the city of Stoke on Trent, known locally as *Stokey*. It is the largest Staffordshire city in the north of the county, and known by the locals as *North Staffy Cher*. The major industries of the area up until the early 20th century included mining, with plentiful local supplies of coal; steelworks for railways and the manufacture of bricks and tiles. The creation of the canal network in the 19th century enabled china clay to be imported from Cornwall for the production of pottery and fine *creamware*, from which The Staffordshire Potteries derive their name. The region comprised six towns: Hanley, Fenton, Longton, Burslem, Tunstall and Stoke on Trent. In 1910 the towns were merged together to form the single county borough Stoke on Trent, with the town being awarded city status in 1925. However, as the performance discussed below shows, people living in the region primarily identify with the town in which they live, particularly when it comes to media reporting of events that happen in the region. Late 20th century decline in these industries have led to a high unemployment rate in the region, which peaked in 2007 at just over 33%, since when there has been a small decline.

The performance discussed in this section was given by Mark Bailey, who self-styles himself as The Trent Vale poet, Trent Vale being the name of the village in which he lives. Mark was born in 1960 and was in his mid 40s at the time of the recordings undertaken of his performance and conversation interview. He was born and has lived in the region all his life, as have his parents before him. Until their retirement, his father worked as a digger driver, driving excavators on building sites and roadworks and his mother as a cleaner. Mark left school at 16 years of age, and self-identified his current social position as working class, the only performer to so do. He has worked in various jobs but considers his main occupation to be that of a poet. He had written poetry all through his education and continued to write after he left school. He performs all across the Stoke region, occasionally in Cannock, a town in south Staffordshire and at other slam or open mic events in Staffordshire. Mark organises and hosts the open mic night at *The White Hart* pub which is in the centre of Stoke on Trent, where local writers and musicians can perform their own work to a local audience. As with Craig Deeley's performance in Chapter 3, the clientele ranges from regular customers who frequent the venue and are not necessarily there for the performance to those who come especially to either take part in or watch the performance.

On the night in question, Mark's act opened the evening's performance, with an audience of around twenty people and similar to other events of this kind, his turn lasts just under 15 minutes. His poetry comes in the form of rhyming couplets covering a range of topics, from reflective pieces about his own life; about couples, families and married life to general, contemporary issues, of which the ones discussed below are typical. Mark's recited turns are interspersed with talking directly to his audience about a topic on which the forthcoming poem centres. In the extract below, he recites a poem he wrote in protest of the neighbouring area of Burnley, whose residents are known for their racist attitudes and where in 2002, the British National Party had its first electoral breakthrough by winning three seats on the local council. Just before the recitation, he talks about Stoke on Trent being in the news 'for all things bad':

(54) 1   WELL AS you know STOKE [stʊək] ON TRENT at the moment HAS been [bɪŋ]
2   in the NEWS for all things BAD (-) ba BASically (.) ERM we_re a bit [bɪʔ] LIKE
3   BURNley [bɜːrnliː] we vote [vɔːt] for the british NATional PARTY well some [sʊm]
4   of DO [duː] (.) and SHAME on you (.) IF YOU DO [duː] (.) I WROTE this POEM and [ʌn] I
5   I WRITE it [ɪʔ] in response to [t] (.) STOKE [stʊək] on TRENT bein_ [biːjɳ] you [yʌ]
6   know (-) BASically TWINned with BURNley [bɜːrnliː] <<laughs>>
7   GOD (.) if anybody_s twinned with BURNley [bɜːrnliː] I don_t [dəʊ] want it be MY own
8   TOWN (.) erm (.) YE_ [jɛ] exactly ye_ SO We_re no_ [no?] ALL RACIST in
9   STOKE [stʊək] SO (.) I WROTE this an_ it_s CALLed aSYLum seeker [sikʌ] on PAGE
10   three [friː] THERE_S ASYLUM SEEKER [sikʌ] on PAGE three [friː] POSING TOPLESS
11   Illegally [ɪliːgʌliː]
12   a NATION DROOL over AMPLE BREASTS(.) SHE   can STAY (.) SOD the REST
13   (.) an ECONOMIC MIGRANT with curVACious CURVes an_ LEGS the LENgth of

14 the DOLE queue to MAN RIGHT WING RACIST PERVE we_d CHANGE our views
15 If they LOOKED [lʊkəd] like YOU [jʊ] (.) from the BACK of a lorry with a fake
16 PASSPORT are The stars the SUN the DAILy SPORT a WELcome addition to the
17 BREAKfast TABLE that BAStion of the full English <<short breath>> ASYLUM
18 SEEKER [sikʌ] on PAGE THREE [fri:] a DARK an_ sultry REFUGEE POSING
19 TOPLESS ilLEGALLY [ɪli:gʌli:]
20 <<audience laugh>>
21 Open BORders <<whistles>>> sounds good to ME <<applause>> <<applause>>
     <<applause>>

The dialect features evident in this recitation are ones previously identified in Chapter 3 and are mainly phonological, such as in the word *illegally* with the sounding of /i/ as /e/ and /y/ as /ee/ in lines 12 and 20; d-dropping throughout in the token *and* to give [ʌn] in line 4; the elongated *o* [ʊ] in *Stoke* throughout and *some* and *looked* in lines 3 and 15. Consonantly, /th/ in *three* becomes [fri:] in line 11. G-dropping is also evident throughout as is t-glotalling. One of the distinctive features of Mark's performance is his declamatory style, as can be seen through the significant amount of emphasis he places on topic content words in his speech and in his recitation. As with other performances discussed in Chapter 3, Mark's focusses on contemporary issues related to increased globalisation, such as that in the extract above of his neighbouring town's attitudes towards immigration, framed as rejection, unless such immigrants pose as topless models, when they are accepted. Such undercutting of racial prejudice is acknowledged by the audience in its copious laughter at the end of this poem.

Just as people living in the Black Country take exception to being portrayed as from Birmingham in the media, so too do people in Stoke on Trent take exception to being included in the reporting of events that happen in one of the other neighbouring towns such as Hanley and he mocks of his neighbouring town's attitudes towards asylum seekers. Reference in the first line to *page three* evokes reference to a daily national, right wing tabloid newspaper, *The Sun,* and an intended working-class readership which until very recently, featured a topless women on page 3 every day. His audience would have been familiar with this publication and Mark lampoons the widespread racism of the Burnley area through drawing attention to male *Sun* readers' chauvinistic attitudes towards women, juxtaposing this frame of rejection towards asylum seekers against that of acceptance of them on *The Sun* readers' part if they happen to be female and willing to pose as topless models. This poem, in common with other sketches given by performers in the region, illustrates how performers draw attention to economic and social change wrought about by mediatization and globalization such as illegal immigration whilst also drawing upon stereotypical aspects of British male chauvinism through the prism of the immediate or neighbouring locality – in this case

Stoke on Trent and Burnley, anchoring or tying attitudes and events to everyday activities such as reading a newspaper and eating breakfast. The audience's laughter at the end shows their recognition of the sentiments Mark expresses in his poem. Mark moves on to recite a poem about himself:

(55) 1 I WERE BORN IN FENTON (–) THERE I_LL GE_ [gɛ?] my PENSION
      2 <<applause>>
      3 i_ll ALways STAY i were BORN in FENTON I WENT to SCHOOL [skʊːl] in FENTON
      4 I _AD the CANE i got deTENTion (.) I_LL not [noʔ] LEAVE I_LL live i_ll breathe
      5 that GIDDY AIR of FENTON (·) I were WED in FENTON to a GIRL [gɔrl] from FENTON
      6 WE _AD a KID we NAMED _im [ɪm] SID the BAStard moved to LONGton
      7 <<audience laugh>> <<applause>>

H- and g-dropping are evident in this extract, as is second person use of the verb *be* in line 1, *were* in place of *was*. Diphongisation is also present in the word *had* in line 4, where h-dropping is evident and also in line 6. The persona Mark evokes in this poem is that based on stereotypical notions of a British working class male, parodying the parochial and narrow horizons often associated with the working class, regionalised locally in his performance as Fenton, characterised by not getting on in school, marrying a local girl and having a family, all framed as acceptance with the comic disruption in the final line of his son moving out of Fenton to Longton as if this were some way distant geographically, when it is in fact a neighbouring area still within the Stoke on Trent region. The two extracts given above are characteristic of his performance, where he switches between poetry that comments upon contemporary social issues with that which relate to himself as a local lad. Mark ends his act with a poem about one of Stoke on Trent's other neighbouring towns, Hanley:

(56) 1 HANLEY BUS STATION (.) at DUSK
      2 <<<audience laughs>>>
      3 EVERY WIERDO known to MAN can be found THERE swiggin_ from a CAN (..)
      4 SLURRIN_ [slɜːrɪŋ] SPEECH in POTTERY TWANG their oatCAKE [ɔʊtkæik] filled with
      5 MISERY FERAL GANGS of PIMPLED YOUTH [yuːθ] (.) SPIT (.) SNARL (.) SCREAM
      6 ABUSE TRACKsuit TRAINED (.) HOODED CHAPS the MOOD [muːd] is Always UGLY
      7 WADING THROUGH CIGARETTE BUTTS FOREVER SPENT WAITING for a BUS
      8 EYE CONTACT at ALL TIMES must be STUDIOUSLY AVOIDED (.) I DON_T _AVE
      9 TEN pee I DON_T DO DRUGS I don_t SMOKE (.) I don_t KNOW your BROTHER I don_t
      10 NEED NEITHER [nɪðɛ] TROUBLE or FUSS (.) going to [gʌn] CRY upon MY shoulder
      11 (..) IT-S _ELL on EARTH up HANLEY [aenlj] DUCK DOWN and [ən] OUTS DOWN
      12 on their LUCK HEADBUTTIN_ [hɛdbʌtɪŋ] WALLS even the BLOODY PIGEONS GIVE
      13 YOU [jae] BOTHER but [bʌʔ] FIRST IMPRESSIONS of STOKE [stʊək] on TRENT is
      14 it_s VILE it_s FILTH an_ STENCH from across the globe they CAME they SAW they
      15 WENT (.) our tourist trade in TATTERS (..) HANLEY bus station (.) at DUSK thank YOU
      16 for your aTTENTion THANK YOU
      17 <<<audience applaud>>>

Pronunciation features of Pottery dialect in this extract is exemplified through the pronunciation of *oatcake* in line 4, *neither* in line 10 as *nithe* [nɪðɛ] and the pronunciation of *Stoke* in Line 13. G-and h-dropping is also evident throughout as in lines 4 and 8. In this poem, Mark's portrayal of the type of characters who fraternise Hanley bus station is given as one of rejection, bemoaning the impression it would give to putative visitors from around the world to the area, and again dwelling on the negative characteristics of people from low socio-economic classes. His intertextual allusion to the words popularly attributed to Julius Caesar 'I came, I saw, I conquered' changes the last word to *went* to further emphasis the unwelcoming nature of the bus station as an entrance point into the region. This also satirises the town's unlikely status as a tourist destination on the global travellers' list of places to visit in the first place.

As with the performers discussed in the preceding two chapters, during the course of his conversation interview discussed below, Mark revealed that he was well aware of his use of dialect in his performances and its relationship with constructing the identity of a place as well as a social class identity.

5.3.1 In conversation with the Trent Vale poet and members of the audience

Mark was recorded in the *White Hart* pub along with two members of his audience Ben and John, on the same evening that the performance discussed above was recorded, and who were also performers or writers themselves. Mark began his conversation interview by saying that he was proud to be from Stoke on Trent (Stokey) and that, unlike Paul Jennings from the Black Country, he makes no attempt to accommodate his accent when he performs depending upon location, explaining that this marks him out as different from other performers and thus encourages audience members to ask him where he is from. At the same time, Mark thinks of himself as distinct from other locally well-known performers associated with the region such as Grandad Piggot and Club Paper Jack who perform and speak in dialect all the time. He reported that he does not say his poems in dialect for the sake of it, but because he does not want his audience to think that he is just from Stoke and that his poems only refer to Stoke. In contrast to other performers discussed in Chapter 3, Mark reported that the further away from Stoke he performed, the more he drew upon features of the dialect in deliberate and conscious ways rather than less. His motivation for so doing was to mark himself out as different from other performers:

(57) 1   THAT_s the THING you SEE when i_m DOWN london OR (.) bloody up PORTSmouth

2   or bloody (.) SCOTland or somewhere like that [θæʔ] I i just (.) DO [du:] the STOKE [stʊək]

3   ACCent because I find in PUBS PEOple come up to you an_ say OH YES you know (.)

4   WHERE you from like you know an_ [ən] they they_ll TAKE more interest otherwise you

5   can be just MIDDLY you just _ave a [aevə] NONdescript ACCent an_ PEOple just say to

6   you (.) oh that_s a good POEm like [laɪk] (.) but you DO [du:] it ACCENT

7   an_ they they (.) they_re [ðə] more interested WHERE you from (.) STOKE [stʊək] on

8   TRENT where_s STOKE [stʊək] on TRENT between MANchester an_ [ən] BIRmingham

9   (.) WHO-se from STOKE [stʊək] well (.) ROBbie Williams don_t like Robbie Williams (.)

10   WELL never mind <<laughs>> get [gɛd] on with it an_ they say like erm (-) OH

11   YOU you_re parochial you_re very parochial poet an_ stuff like that I says i_m not [no]

12   (.) but [bʌr] i_m not /no/ going to [gʌnae] change my ACCent I_m not [ɛɪnt] going to

13   [gʌnae] put no WORDS into my [mɪː] bloody GOB as CAN-T be put [pʌʔ] in so YES (.)

14   SUP [sʌp] with you know NOT WHAT IS UP with you (.) SUP [sʌp] with you

Mark's last comment draws attention to a specific feature of dialect, in compressing more words than one into a single lexical item, in addition to other features already discussed. When asked, Mark thought that the dialect was heard much less than it had previously had been. Ben, one of the other performers taking part in the conversation, said that he thought the dialect was disappearing and attributed this to jobs disappearing. What he called the 'hot bed' of dialect had been the pot banks and coal pits where men routinely spoke in the local dialect before going home and speaking in one that accommodated more towards standard English with their family. A consequence of the pits and potteries closing down was that the dialect associated with them was being lost in the region in ways similar to what had happened in the Black Country. Ben also said that he thought his education had eradicated the local dialect from his speech, together with the fact that he had also worked away from the region before returning. A combination of these factors he reported, had had an impact upon how he spoke, with dialect use not being evident in his speech all. John, another performer, also spoke of the impact of the pit and potteries closures had had upon families who had lived and worked together, with many young people leaving the area and moving away to find work. John had been born and brought up in Bromsgrove in Worcestershire to parents who originally came from Liverpool, moving to Newcastle in the north and going to school in that city, but now lives in Dorset. He spoke of how his dialect has been affected by all the places he had lived and said he was like a beachcomber, picking up different accents and dialects. In common with other performers, John also reported that the degree to which he drew upon dialect features depended upon the situational context he was in. he gave as an example the fact that when he and Mark talked on their own, then their dialect use was greater than when others were around, and he switched to such use as an example:

(58) onnə   GOin_ [guːɪŋ] down [daeːrn] there
    I am not going   down   there

John also agreed with Ben's observation sees that the decline of manufacturing in the region has led to a corresponding decline in dialect use. When asked if he made changes to his poems by taking his intended audience into account, Mark replied that since he was too old to become famous, and so he did not make any allowances. He also spoke of how he wrote his poems:

(59) 1   I don_t like say OH this must _ave this in (.) because (-) the POTTeries people might [maɪt]
     2   like [laɪk] THIS or this must _ave this in because NATIONWIDE people might [maɪt] like
     3   [laɪk] this I just [jʌs] WRITE [raːt] the POEM an_ I do it in dialect an_ ACCent an_ I cannot
     4   [kaːna] change the way I SPEAK [spɛɪk] so you [yʌ] know I won_ just [jʌs] DO a poem
     5   just [jʌs] say LIKE [laɪk] you know don_t do [dʌnæ] this don_t do [dʌnæ] that I I do a lot
     6   of political STUFF an_ but [bʌʔ] with er (-) a DARK sense of humour BLACK humour
     7   TYPE [taɪp] stuff (-) so I write [raɪt] STUFF like [laɪk] REALLY ABOUT REAL livings
     8   an_ the (.) CURSE they are upon our lives [laɪvs] but i i want to do it in an entertaining
     9   FASHion (.) not just BLOODY PREACH say like [laɪk] wheely bins are CRAP we know
   10 they_re CRAP so you know what I mean so (.) YES then just [jʌs] do it in an
   11 entertaining FASHion.

Mark is very clear then, that the subject matter of his poems is of the kind that is of wider interest and not confined to his immediate locality in ways that are reminiscent of the content of Paul Jennings' and Craig Deeley's performance discussed in Chapter 3, where the locality serves as a prism through which to filter matters that are of wider interest. He is well aware of his own Potteries dialect in his speech which he reinforces or enregisters in his performances rather than accommodating away from it. When the group were asked about what dialect features they thought were specific to the region, they pointed to the potters' slang associated with the Staffordshire Potteries is the negative past tense forms *don't, can't, won't* to *dunna/er, conna/er, wunna/er*. Of the three, only *dunna* featured in their conversation and in Mark's performance of his poetry. Mark ended the conversation by saying in – and enregistering – the Stokey dialect: 'see [sɪ] thee duck, see [sɪ] thee again.'

Mark, like other performers from the region, enregister features of Staffy Cher dialect into their performances and poetry and makes no attempt to accommodate his speech wherever he performs. The persona he creates in performance is an amplified version of himself, in much the same way as Harry Jennings' various personae are amplifications of a white, working class, heterosexual male linked to a specific region.

5.4 Performance 2: The play *Riot*

Performances performed in urban regions of the West Midlands of the kind discussed so far have been of the grass roots kind, with pubs like *The White Hart* often providing an informal venue for their activities and some, like *The Holly Bush* in Cradeley Heath discussed in Chapter 3, acting more formally in the sense of providing a local arts venue. In addition, performance venues such as *The Drum* discussed in Chapter 4 provide a space for a specific black ethnic section of the community, in this case performers of Jamaican heritage. in many cities in the UK, some pubs have a theatre on their premises, often located upstairs and above the main bars. One such pub in Birmingham is *The Joint Old Stock,* located in St Phillips Square in the centre of Birmingham. It has a purpose-built small theatre which holds between 40 and 50 people. It varies its performance from comedy to plays and spoken word performances given mainly by local companies and performers or by having local performers supporting touring headline acts.

Riot is a play based on a collaboration between Richard Green, a playwright from Walsall Wood, a suburb of the town Walsall on the Birmingham/Black Country border, and a recently formed theatre company called *Studio Three*. During a heatwave in August 2011 riots broke out in English cities, including London and Birmingham, which inspired Green who had witnessed riots in Birmingham to write this play about that experience. At that time, students from the *Birmingham School of Acting* had just formed the theatre company *Studio Three* and together with Richard Green scripted the play. The play revolves around three stereotypical couples who get caught up in the riots: an Indian shopkeeper and his wife; a married man who is drawn into the riot on his way to visit his female lover and a couple of young people characterised as *chavs*, young people from lower class backgrounds who wear real or fake designer clothes and engage in loutish behavior, who go out specifically to take part in the riot. Two other characters are interwoven into the play who provide a commentary throughout from their differing perspectives; *white suit* who represents the establishment perspective and *black suit* who represents a riot instigator, the white suit's frame of acceptance is the black suit's frame of rejection and vice versa. The play thus explores the portrayal by the media and politicians of bored youth who engage in opportunistic violence and crime to considering the possibility of rioting as a political protest against structured inequality (Akram 2014), including its impact upon local businesses struggling to make a living. The black suit's commentary portrays the riot as a victory for the underprivileged whilst the white suit champions more peaceful ways of supporting them. At the end of the play, neither side triumphs.

The background of the theatre company's members provides a snapshot of the various demographic backgrounds of people who currently live in a culturally diverse city such as Birmingham: of the five men, Damien is of mixed race, born in a West Midlands county to a father from Yorkshire and a mother from Seoul, North Korea. Abhishek was born in India to Indian parents and where he still lives officially, currently living in the UK on a student visa; Christopher was born in Newcastle Upon Tyne to a father from Portsmouth and a mother from Surrey; Guiseppe is Italian with Italian parents but he has lived in the UK since he was sixteen and Harry was born in Nottingham to parents from the same city. Of the three women, Rachel was born in a West Midlands county to parents from London and Liverpool; Bushra was born in Newcastle Upon Tyne to parents who came to live in England from Pakistan when she was 16 years old. Jayne is from Walsall a town on the Black Country borders, and her parents are also local to the area. Richard Green, the playwright and producer, was born in Northfield, Birmingham in 1958. He moved to Walsall Wood, to the north of Walsall bordering Staffordshire, when he was very young and has lived there ever since. Both his parents came from Birmingham, his mother has been a housewife all her life and his father worked as a stock controller. Richard stayed at school until he was 16 finding work in journalism and is currently freelance.

Thus, whilst the play is set in Birmingham and features characters living in the city, the performers' speech reflects that of the characters in the play who like themselves, come from a range of different backgrounds, both from within and beyond the UK. Of all the performers in the play, only Jayne's character Tracey speaks with a noticeable accent, which is that of Brummie rather than Black Country. Whilst the play is set in Birmingham and all characters live in the city, only one character has any trace of a Brummie accent, and that is Tracey Turvey, who plays the character of a young hoodie who is part of the couple who decide to go into the city specifically to join in the riot. Hoodie in the UK refers to young people who wear zip up sweatshirts with hoods, and associated with criminal activity, because of the face-shielding anonymity they provide. They are also synonymous with the youth group called Chavs. Etymologically the word is derived from the Romany word 'chavi' meaning a child, but has been borrowed into English and falsely etymolygised as a class-related acronym for 'Council House and Violent' (Jones 2012) as part of an ideologised discourse that demonizes the working class. In 2010, the word entered the Oxford English Dictionary and defined as: In the United Kingdom (originally the south of England): a young person of a type characterized by brash and loutish behaviour, the wearing of designer-style clothes (esp. sportswear); usually with connotations of a low social status (OED *Online* 2010).

As Bennett (2012) points out, '...discourse on *chavs* not only draws on well-established stereotypes of poorer groups of poorer social groups but intensifies the ideological force of these representations by suggesting *chavs* are a distinct kind of person, marked off from a perceived mainstream of British society by virtue of their own faults.' The word thus polarizes people, especially the young, into an underclass or underserving poor of 'chavs' and distinct from 'non-chavs.' Though socially based in the working class, the concept is not regionally bound but rather cuts across the whole country. Chav culture – antisocial, anti-authoritarian – was also held responsible in the media for the riots that took place in Birmingham. Such a representation of chavs has entered mainstream media representation in recent years, through the comedian Catherine Tate's character Lauren and Armstrong and Miller on BBC. *Chavspeak,* the language of Chavs, is characterised as an 'antilanguage' (Halliday 1978) in that it is the langage of an anti-society, defined by Halliday as: '..a society that is set up within another society as a conscious alternative to it' (1978: 164).

The play begins immediately after the first night of riots has come to end. It is structured like an Ancient Greek tragedy with three acts, each comprising a set of scenes played by each of the three sets of characters, interspersed with the two suits who provide a commentary on the action from their two opposing sides. The scenes of the play in the first act are set at the end of the first night of the riots, alternating between the three couples, who first appear on stage one scene after the other: the shopkeeper couple, the lovers and the chavs respectfully, all appearing to be initially independent of one another. The last scene of the first Act introduces the two suits with their differing perspectives on the night's events. The suits then remain either on stage to a darkened side or in the audience throughout the remainder of the play. Although set in Birmingham, the only character who has a distinctive Brummie accent is Tracey, the female half of the chav couple. The extracts below are taken from the script of the play and the IPA from its recording.

(60) Act 1 Scene 3
  YOUNG WOMAN and YOUNG MAN, wearing trainers, trackies/hoods, rush on carrying
  arms full of goods – golf club, box of roll up tobacco, clothes, booze, DVD, CD, ipods etc
  FX: *Murmer of rioting in background, subtle but constant*
  FX: *lights are dim with red hue – focus central stage, both wings darker*
  Young woman: That was sick, well wicked
  Young man: I'm buzzing
  Young man: It's better [bɛʔæ] than Christmas << *flops down with all the goods and hugs*
  herself like a child with new toys on Christmas Day>>
  Young man: Best high ever. I'm tingling all over, heart's pounding (·) i feel (·) i feel
  (·)so fuckin_ alive you know

> Young woman: got some cool gear [gi:yæ] (laughs)
> Young man: <<*lies down spreads arms and legs and stares at ceiling*>> man what a rush never seen anything like that have you seen anything like that
> Young woman: No [næ] except on the tele maybe
> Young man: Everybody going for everything, anything
> Young woman: like in the sales
> Young man: grabbing and grabbing
> Young woman: like in house clearance (laughing)

The two continue talking about people they have just seen during the riots, including an old man who chastises the young couple saying: *I fought for people like you.* The young man then launches into a long speech about how he squared up to the old man and his negative feelings towards him, ending with how he hates old people and they should die at 60, or even better, 50. The young woman says, as she's trying on clothes:

(61) Young woman: My mum_s [moms] nearly 50
      Young man: she's a right cow an_ all
      Young woman: Yeah

She immediately turns the conversation to the clothes she is trying on, and how they will take part in more rioting the next day, before arguing about the young woman's appearance that ends with her hitting the young man. Only one dialect feature is evident in this extract, which is the vowel transposition in the token represented orthographically as *mum* to *mom*.

The scenes of the second act centre on the fall out of the previous evening's riot on the shopkeeper couple struggling to make ends meet with a failing business; the young chavs drug taking and involvement with local drug pushers and the disintegration of the lovers' relationship, all interspersed with the suits' commentary. In the first scene between the young couple, the woman talks of meeting a girlfriend at 'the clinic', which triggers a subsequent argument about what the young woman was doing there:

(62) 1   YOUNG WOMAN: Saw kelly down the clinic (.) you _ear about Dylan getting_ [gɛʔɪn]
      2   jumped the other night (.) Kelly told me they was walking [wɔ:k ɪn] _ome from chippy
      3   when a car pulls up an_ three of them [ɛm] piles out of it [ɪʔ] an_ laid right [raɪʔ] into _im
      4   chips went everywhere (.) she said she was screamin_ and cryin_ callin_ for _elp but no one
      5   come or did nothing_ <<*Enters with two cans and packet of crisps*>> said she was shit scared
      6   couldn't move (-) strange how different people react to stuff (.) maybe i_d freeze (.) don_t
      7   think i would <<*holds can out to* YOUNG MAN *who keeps her waiting taking time in*
      8   *accepting it*>> I think if it be me and you i_d _ave a go at them [ɛm] nobody goin_ to attack
      9   my man an_ get [gɛʔ] away with it [ɪʔ] don't care _ow many there are (*Sits on floor back*
      10 *against sofa as continues*) anyway they battered dylan (.) broke _is arm an_ slashed _im

11   on the back (.) mashed _im up bad (–) kelly said he [ɪː] was in a right [raɪʔ] state (-)
12   nineteen stitches in _is back (-) cracked ribs (-) lost three teeth (-) split lip (-) both eyes
13   closed up

In this stretch of dialogue, the Chav female character voices several distinctive features associated with the Birmingham accent as identified in Chapter 3: h- and g-dropping, t-glottalling, *was* for *were* in Line 2 and the vowel pronunciation in *right* in line 11. In a later scene, the chav couple appear with the young man walking with a pushchair, angry because money he has been expecting has not appeared in their bank account. The young woman calls the relevant department:

(63)   1   YOUNG WOMAN: <<*Cover mouthpiece, rolls eyes as makes aside to* YOUNG MAN>>
         2   fuck-sake <<*Back into phone*>> got no baby food what [wʊʔ] am I going [gʊna] feed my
         3   baby on not [nɒʔ] right [raɪt] this (-) me an_ my baby got to [gʊda] suffer cos someone
         4   there aren_t [aint] doing [duːɪŋ] their job right (-) it_s meant to be in there (2.5) *irri-*
              tated <big
         5   *sigh>* I suppose [spauz] it_ll _ave [av] to be won_t it (-) (*hangs up*) mardy bitch (–)
         6   giving me grief like it was my fault their fuckin [fʌkin] computers screwed up
         7   YOUNG MAN: what they say
         9   YOUNG WOMAN: (*mocking tone*) due to a computer error all payments scheduled
         10   for today will be delayed twenty four hours. You will receive payment tomorrow by one
         11   YOUNG MAN: Tomorrow (.) FUCK
         12   YOUNG WOMAN: Should have [av] heard [ɛrd] her [æ] (–)snotty cow *gesture to*
         13   *buggy* told her [æ] I got [gʊʔ] _im [ɪm] to feed and no money (.) you know what she said
         14   YOUNG MAN: what
         15   YOUNG WOMAN: can_t i get any help [ɛlp] off family or friends to tide me over
         17   YOUNG MAN: fuckin_ cheek (-) You have got baby food right
         18   YOUNG WOMAN: Yeah [yɛ] that_s [ðæʔ] not [aint] the point, they don_t know
         19   they don_t fuckin_ care (-) i asked about [abæuʔ] emergency payment (.) you heard [ɛrd]
         20   me right (-) I was polite like (.) no swearing [swɛːrin] or nothing [nʊθn] (-) way she
         21   reacted you'd think i_d shitted [ʃɪtɪd] on _er [ɛr] desk
         22   YOUNG MAN: some of them lot are really up themselves ain_t they
         23   YOUNG WOMAN: SOME (.) More than fuckin some (2.0)
         24   YOUNG MAN: (*With smirk*) guess you can_t spot me a tenner then
         25   YOUNG WOMAN: (*Un-amused*) Ha fuckin_ ha
              YOUNG WOMAN *hands phone back, checks baby in buggy grabs burger and fries from*
              bag and sits next to YOUNG MAN. *Eat in silence, calming down*

In this extract, g-dropping in the young woman's speech has been scripted, as she reports her conversation with the benefits agency and her frustration with the person she spoke to who she portrays as unsympathetic to her plight. T-glottaling is also evident throughout her speech, as is h-dropping the Birmingham pronunciation of tokens *what* and *gonna* in line 2 and *about* in line 19.

The third Act takes place the next evening during another night of rioting, where it becomes apparent that all three couples live in the same block of flats on the same estate where the shopkeepers' shop is bombed out; the lovers are smoked out of their flat and from where the chavs rush out of theirs into the street with the male shouting *I'm loving it*. In the final scene, all three couples and the two suits are on the stage, with the black suit holding a petrol bomb. There is a general reluctance on everyone's part to take the bomb and light its fuse, when a blacked-out person steps out of the shadows to light it as the lights go out. Having remained silent throughout the play, the audience clap enthusiastically yet mutedly for 41 seconds, a sure sign of their appreciation and approbation.

As with other performance discussed then, the setting of the play in Birmingham is used to explore a variety of social issues that are not unique to the characters, such as struggling small shop owners, young women on benefit and their unemployed partners and a couple having an affair getting caught up in unexpected events or events beyond their control such as a riot and the impact this has on the lives of people caught up in it. Again, mediatization and globalization are significant factors that contributed to its writing, as discussed in conversation with the playwright and some of the cast members.

5.4.1 In conversation with playwright Richard Green and members of the cast

In a conversation interview a day after a performance of the play had been attended, Richard explained that a major motivation for him writing the play was his annoyance at the way the riots in Birmingham had been portrayed in the media and by politicians. Particularly, he felt aggrieved at the ways in which people's behaviour had been portrayed as polarized as either right or wrong, with nothing in between. Only one character in the play, the young woman Tracey who played the character of the young chav hoodie, spoke with a Brummie accent. When why this was, and why none of the other characters did so Richard and Jayne, the actress who played Tacey explained:

(64)   as a group only one of us had a brummie accent (.) for the rest of us to create it and maintain it for the whole play would have detracted from the whole thing if our accents had been terrible (–) a couple of people did try brummie accents in rehearsals (.) did try to put it on especially (.) but this kind of thing (.) stereotype associated with accents (.) if you try to put on a brummie accent it can sound ridiculous (.) accents can differ on different levels and had that would have completely detracted from the seriousness of the material (mimicking Brummie accent) *people like [lɔik] talking [t ɔːrkin] like [lɔik] this all the time [taɪm]* (.) there_s something about the Brummie and Black Country accents that makes them more difficult to mimic than say Liverpool or Geordie.

Richard's comment echoes those also made by well-known actors Julie Waters and Mark Williams, who said that even great actors find it difficult to mimic the Birmingham and Black Country accents where normally they have no problem in mimicking others. Richard's and the actors' comments also echo those made by other performers such as Paul Jennings, namely that if accent got in the way of comic and dramatic effect then its role was deliberately diminished. As Jayne went on to explain:

(65) I definitely had her as a black country girl (.) I portrayed her as a particular person as opposed to being a face for a group of people yes quite specific in my mind she was definitely local a local girl my experiences are informed by me being from walsall (.) from the west midlands from the black country an_ i think that ran through the character a little bit [biʔ] which made it easier to relate to the character (.) you see people on the street like this and draw on that sort of character (.) yes, we went out into birmingham an_ yeah you can pick up from people all the time

Just as other performers have reported, in preparing for her character and taking part in the improvisations upon which the script was based, Jayne drew upon snippets of conversations she heard around her as part of daily life, encontextualising them from their original context, decontextualizing as a stored memory and recontextualising them into the dramatic, performance context. Jayne went on to talk about how in creating her character of the young hoodie, she worked backwards from choosing a chav stereotype upon which to base her character of a Brummie female chav, blurring the Black Country/Birmingham distinction to sound more Brummie. When asked if she was conveying the character of a Chav or Brummie Chav, she replied 'definitely Brummie chav.' Thus, Jayne's construction of a chavstyle character who also speaks with a Brummie accent is a double-voicing of two frames of rejection in mainstream British society: being chav and being Brummie.

(66) when my accent relaxes it can be broader [brɔ :dæ] (.) i mean i know richard wrote the script but there were parts i changed just to make it feel more natural to me so instead of *no* it would be *naa* you know (.) lots of little things like that [ðæʔ] in the script which felt more natural to me to speak (.) i didn_t necessarily think she was brummie (.) as for me the accent is natural it was for me enhancing something I have anyway being local (.) i think the main thing it was keeping it (the accent) consistent.

The fact that Tracey is the only character who speaks with a Brummie accent serves to accentuate her character as a Brummie and its accent features as part of the antilanguage of Chavspeak. She is also aware of the extent to which she enregisters specific features of the Brummie accent in her performance as a chav, and spoke specifically of her pronunciation of the word *no* as she describes above and others in the dialogue such as *mom* for *mum;* glottal stopping the t in words such as *better, later* and *what,* also pronouncing the *er* as *a; my* as *me* and *won't* as *wor,* as discussed in the context of the extracts given above.

5.5 Performance 3: The play *Too much pressure*

Too much pressure is a stage play by the playwright Allan Pollock who is also the play's producer, commissioned by and performed at the Coventry Repertory Theatre in 2011. It is the third play in a trilogy that spans turning points in Coventry's recent history, the first play, *One night in November,* centred upon the bombings Coventry suffered during the World War 11 and the second, *We love you city,* centred upon the city's football club, Coventry City, winning the Football Association cup in 1987. *Too much pressure* is set in 1979, during a time of industrial and social strife throughout the UK. In Coventry, that year marked the ending of manufacturing in the city, especially of cars, a corresponding rise in unemployment and the explosion of the rebellious punk generation, that brought with it the two-tone Ska movement that was instantly identifiable with the city. The play is set on a fictional version of the working-class estate where Pollock grew up and where his father worked as a family general practitioner. Many of the adults living on the estate at the time he lived there worked at one of the major car factories in the city, Standard Triumph, Jaguar and Massey Ferguson. Set against this back drop, it explores growing up as a teenager in this era with the older generation's world centred upon their work in the car factories, the younger on their music, and the fall out that occurs when one of the major car manufacturers, Standard Triumph, closed its factory with the direct loss of 8,000 jobs and a total of 23,000, that crippled the local economy.

The play thus centres upon family conflict set against the backdrop of economic and social change as well as generational clashes, with trade unionism on the left, racism on the right and macho-led culture in conflict with the youthful movement centred upon punks rejection of such attitudes. Each character in the play portrays a different aspect of the death of the car manufacturing industry in the city. At its heart is the Austin family who live on the working-class Canley Park estate in Coventry, where most of its inhabitants are employed by the Standard Triumph car factory, including father Cliff and eldest son, Terry. Austin itself is the name of a Standard Triumph car model. Cliff Austin, the father and his friend Nev together with Cliff's eldest son Terry, who followed in his father's footsteps to work at the factory, are both increasingly worried about the future of their jobs. In stark contrast with this older generation is Cliff's youngest son and Terry's brother Gary, who is more concerned with the music scene and forming a ska band with his newly found friends Nick and Sonya, who both attend grammar schools. 1979 was also the year in which both punk and ska music, the latter its origin in late 1950s Jamaica, hit the music scene in the UK and with which the region is associated. The title of the play is taken from the title of the first album by the British ska band *The Selector,* who formed in Coventry in 1979.

The play is set in the back garden of the Austin's house on a council estate complete with a 1959 Triumph Herald car on stage that Terry and Cliff are restoring, when the car industry was in its heyday in contrast with the urban decay and despair that characterises the year in which the play is set. Cliff and Terry cannot imagine a life outside Coventry and its car industry, whilst Gary, without the benefit of a grammar school education, sees music as a ticket to his way out of the kind of life his father and brother have lived. The theme of collectivism in the play is explored through the character of Terry and the left-wing union activism against the then newly elected Conservative government with Margaret Thatcher as prime minister, whilst the theme of individualism is explored through Gary and his friends and the personal dilemmas that arise when different cultures come together, in this case British and Indian. Much of the action happens off stage, as tensions build between Gary and his elder brother and father, with industrial relations reaching boiling point just as Gary's band begins to form. The play opens with Gary setting the scene with a short prologue off stage:

(67) 1 was it the people (.) place or the time do what [wʊʔ] _appened _appen because of nicky my
  2 [mɪ] brother (.) or would it _ave _appened anyway (.) you know they said it took the birds
  3 to make dylan listenable (.) the clash to make reggae accessible did it take nick to light the
  4 touch paper (.) one thing I know for [ʃɔː] sure [ʃɔːr] I met _im [ɪm] at the bus stop at the
  5 corner of charter avenue an_ marina close

Here, the Coventry accent shares many features with that of Birmingham and the Black Country, most notably in the pronunciation of /a/ in *what* in line 1 as /oo/ [ʊ]; the short /i/ in tokens such as *my* in Line 2; the pronunciation of *for* in line 4; t glottalling in line 1 , h- dropping in lines 2 and 4. Through the music references and those to street names, the play immediately takes its audience to Coventry in the 1970s. The audience would have known that the reference to the two streets is to ones that border the Canley estate in Coventry. Sounds of fighting are heard off stage and Gareth enters the stage with Nick, asking Gareth if he's alright, and that he recognises him as being new to the estate, with his family driving a Hillman Imp car. This reference immediately places the play in the 1960s or 1970s when the Hillman Imp was in manufacture and a very popular car at the time. Every characters' speech uses the shortened vowels heard throughout the region alongside h- and g-dropping and glottalling. Rhoticity is ...of all the characters' Gary's speech is clearly recognisable as being inflected with a Warwickshire accent, through h and g dropping and also the word *for* pronounced as *fouer*. Nick's on the other hand, is far less so. Gary immediately talks about the violent nature of the young men on the estate as a frame of acceptance:

(68) 1 (.) it_s like three _undred spartans swear to god there_s a boy on this estate _is
2 idea of fun is to capture a bumble bee right drug it [drʌgiʔ] (.) then tie a bit [bɪʔ] of [ɒ]
3 string round it [iʔ] when it wakes up run round the garden while it screams in agony another
4 couple of lads (.) ginger bollocks brother [brʌðæ] an_ his mate their idea of a wizard wheeze
5 their idea of a whackish prank found this kid drunk on the pavement right (.) picked _im
6 up (.) stripped _is [ɪz] clothes off him drove him to county Coundon left _im roped to a
7 lamp post with ira felt tipped to _is back
8 <<audience laughter>>

Spartans in line 1 refer to the feared Ancient Greek army that existed between 4th and 6th centuries BC who were popularised in the film *300* in 2006. The imagined construction of Coventry occurs here more through references to places than through any specific dialect features, other than ubiquitous h- dropping and glottalling. The token *like* in line 1, for example, that characterises the accent in Birmingham and the Black Country through its pronunciation as *liyek* [lɔːk] is pronounced here in a standard way. Coundon in line 6 is a reference to a neighbouring working-class area and *ira* in line 5 is to the Irish Republican Party, whose bombing campaign in the region was at its height at that time. The references in these first few lines then evoke violence throughout the ages linked to the Irish troubles of the time and in the context of 1970s council estates located in a specific place, Coventry. As the play progresses, in addition to the phonological features identified above, the phrase *down our/your end* is used when Nev refers to a man living in his street. Other dialect words heard in the play both in the same utterance are *twat* for a stupid person and *Brum: just some twats from brum* in referring to an altercation in the local pub. *Coventrian* is also used to describe someone who comes from Coventry with Coventry abbreviated to *Cov*. The inversion of *we was* for *we were* is used by Nev, and *who done it* in place of *who did it* by Gary. By contrast, Nev's speech is far more localised than Gary's. For example, when talking about the nature of his work:

(69) 1 what would you know about ard [aːrd] work [wɔik] eh all day boltin _ a bumper [bʌmpæ] on
2 the front of a fuckin car it_s like this chap just [jʌs] started [staːrtɪd] from down our
3 end a MINER type (.) from arley foreman shown _im the job on the first day _e said [sz]
4 listen [lɪsɛn] (.) it_s hard [aːrd] work [wɔik] and it_s borin_ _ard [aːrd] work [wɔik] he
5 says [sɛz] well let me tell you about _ard [aːrd] work [wɔik] _ard [aːrd] work [wɔik] on your

6   _ands and knees all day in the bowels of the earth grubbin_ coal [kʊʊl] out the ground
7   that_s what [wu?] _ard [a:rd] work [wɔik] is fuckin_ ard [a:rd] work [wɔik] (.) come
8   the end of the day (.) this lad is sobbin [sʊbm] _is arse is out of there before he can
9   touch the ground back to fuckin_ miner land

Here, Nev's repetition of the localised pronunciation of *hard work* as [a:rd wɔik] in lines 1, 4 5, and 7 serves to reinforce the relationship between manual labour and dialect, between work and language. He also uses the local expression 'down our end' in referring to a neighbour, and the past participle –n in place of –ed in 'shown' instead of 'showed.' When Sonya is introduced to the Austin family, she talks of the geographically diffuse nature of Coventry, which the Austin family acknowledge, though they themselves have lived in the city for several generations:

(70)   1   Sonya: it_s like everyone here_s from somewhere [sʌmwɛ:r] else
       2   Nev: somewhere [sʌmwɛ:r] else
       3   Sonya: yea (.) that_s why they reckon _ere_s so funny
       4   Cliff: well it_s tru isn_t it look at this estate (.) irish scots welsh posh gits Bangladeshis
       5   poles geordies
       6   Nev: I don_t think they count as a separate country
       7   <<audience laugh>>
       8   Cliff: they bloody well do we_ve got [go?] one lad from morpeth workin_ with us at the
       9   moment (.) if I can understand one word in three I count myself lucky

Nev mimics Sonya's pronunciation of *somewhere* in line 2 thereby signalling identification with her, while Cliff evokes the diverse backgrounds of people living in Coventry, not only from other countries in the UK and beyond in line 4 and from other social classes – namely upper-class ones, the *posh gits* of line 4 – but other regions in the UK such as Newcastle upon Tyne. 'Geordie' is the name given to people who come from that area that includes Morpeth mentioned in Line 8 and like the performance by *Fizzog* discussed in Chapter 3, is imagined in this extract as a different country by Cliff, as the world of 'posh gits' all as frames of rejection. Nev pointing out that Geordies are not from a separate country but by omission tacitly agrees *posh gits* are, evokes laughter on the part of the audience. The increasingly globalised nature of the world outside the estate in Coventry features large in the play through Sonya's references to the USA where one half of her family lives, musical references to American bands, the revelation that union activists were in the pay of the Soviets and newsreel recordings of the time playing in the background to events happening both in the UK and elsewhere in the world. The second half of the play witnesses the hopes and dreams expressed through the characters in its first half, with union activists revealed to be bullies and management plants, and the inevitable job losses facing Gary's father and brother foretold by the newsreel announcement of Standard Triumph cutting 23,000 jobs. Gary's plans of forming a band as a way of escaping Coventry also come to nothing, as Nick turns out not be whom he seems to be. Nick becomes involved in a fight one night that ends with him putting someone in hospital, just before the trio have an audition to play in a local *rock against racism* concert which he does not turn up for and dashing Gary's hopes of a first public performance. When Gary confronts Nick, Nick explains that his father was not killed in an accident but killed himself as a result of the ostracism he suffered when he blew the whistle on some of his workmates at Chrysler where he worked as a foreman. Some of his fellow foremen employed unqualified union activists in jobs that required skilled workmanship, with the result that one man suffered an accident where he nearly lost his head.

5.5.1 In conversation with playwright Allan Pollock

Allan Pollock was born in Manchester to a Scots father and Irish mother, but moved to Coventry in 1963 when he was one year old, which he called 'a classic immigrant profile for Coventry.' His father was a doctor, from a working-class background who had been the first of his family to attend university in the 1950s. Pollock attended a local grammar school before moving on to university and worked in the theatre for a number of years before moving back to Coventry in 2003 to pursue a career as a professional playwright. He talked of people 'taking the mickey' out of his accent when he was growing up though gave no specific examples. He also recalled that when he left Coventry in 1980 to attend university, it felt a tough and violent place that he was not sad to leave at the time, a toughness and violence he explores in the play. He had been very aware at school that most of his fellow pupils came from immigrant families not only from across the UK but also from Ireland, the Indian subcontinent or Eastern Europe, with very few whose families had lived in Coventry for more than two generations. The play, as Pollock explained in his conversation interview, reflects the diffuse nature of the city's population at the time. Whilst writing it, Pollock researched the events of the time in local newspaper archives and said that the majority of the headlines related to strikes, assaults and fatal car crashes. It also explores the shift from a working culture based on collectivism to one based on individualism, brought about by the oil crisis in 1973 and the subsequent rapid deindustrialisation through which Pollock had lived that brought with it a climate of brutality and violence. As he said:

(71) Coventry (.) the midlands as a whole really, is full of people from somewhere else (-)
          if you have got a group of people who came here for work from the four corners of
          the globe and suddenly there isn't any work then there's not so much to bind people
          together

He also recalled how the city was still in the late 1970s, recovering from the devastation and destruction wrought by suffering extensive damage through bombing
during the second world war that all but flattened the city and virtually destroyed
all its ancient buildings, including its medieval ones. When asked if the people of
Coventry have an affinity with their dialect, Alan replied by referring to the accent
which was more of a Warwickshire one than specific to Coventry, giving examples
of the long Northern pronunciation of /u/ in words such as *but* and *butter* that can
be heard across the region. He also observed that when a person from Coventry
was represented in media such as film and TV then invariably that person had a
Brummie accent which invariably upset people from Coventry. He also said that
exploring Coventry identity through accent and dialect was difficult to achieve,
and although he did try to get the actors in the play to incorporate a few accent
features in their speech, he echoed the words of others such as Paul Jennings in
Chapter 3 and Richard Green discussed above in relation to *The Riot* play saying:

(72) the second it gets in the way of acting then personally you would try to calm that down so
          long as nobody is speaking with a brummie accent or a cockney accent

Like the actors in the play *Riot,* the ones in *Too much pressure* were not coached
to speak in the dialect of the city where the play was performed, unless this
came naturally to them, as was the case with the character who played Gary.
Consequently, dialect use was not enregistered in the play to the same extent
as other, more locally based performances such as those discussed in Chapter 3
although h- and g-dropping and glottaling in particular, occurred throughout.
Pollock spoke of how the play juxtaposed notions of pride and unity that surface
out of all of the turmoil both within the family and the city in which they live,
against the economic and political background that destroyed car manufacturing
in the west Midlands at that time, and particularly in Coventry. The play he said,
is as much about working class experiences and solidarity as it is about Coventry
and collectivism versus individualism. However, when asked if the play would go
out on tour, Pollock said it would not, since its Coventry setting would mitigate
against it, with audiences asking why they were watching a play about a Midlands
city when their own had ones to tell, despite any universal element to its themes.

  This sentiment echoed that of another professional Midlands playwright
Malcolm Stent, who has lived and worked in Birmingham all his life, and all
his plays are set in Birmingham, including one called *Go Play Up Your Own*

End that is performed regularly at theatres across the region. The title refers to the local dialect expression used by children when playing in an alley way – 'entry' n Warwickshire dialect – that separates the backs of terraced houses from one another, telling each other when they fell out to move away back to the entry by their own homes. Stent recalled the well-known playwright and producer Willy Russell coming to see a performance of the play when it was first performed in the 1970s, saying to Stent how good he thought it was, and offering to stage the play in London. However, this was on the condition that the location of the play and references to places within it be changed to those of London, since audiences would be unfamiliar with the local references. This Malcolm refused to do and thus the play is only performed locally. Malcolm felt particularly aggrieved by this, particularly as some of Russell's own plays, notably *Educating Rita*, is set in the north and television dramas are often set in the north where no such compunction about unfamiliarity with local references seems to apply. He theorised that the reason for this was that London based producers felt threatened by Birmingham because of its proximity to London, whereas the North was far enough away from London not to pose a threat in the same way. When I mentioned this theory to the Director of Writing West Midlands, he also said that he thought the same way as Malcolm.

Pollock's play then, like those of Stent, is intended for a local audience who would understand local references in the play and the frames they evoked. This is in contrast to plays set in the North of England in the 1970s such as Willy Russell's *Educating Rita* and the TV series *Our Friends in the North* where the same concern about unfamiliarity with the region does not emerge as a concern when the performances are performed for national, rather than local, performances.

5.5.2 In conversation with members of the audience and celebrities

One member of the audience who agreed to be interviewed was a woman called Sue. She talked about how much she had enjoyed the play, its realistic portrayal of life in Coventry in the late 1970s, and the sound of the Coventry dialect in it. She cited the example of *Cov* in place of *Coventry*, which is how local people refer to the city when speaking to one another, and also the references to local places. Sue had been born in Glasgow to an English father and Scottish mother, but her family moved to Coventry in the 1970s when she was 13, because her father was transferred to a job at the car plant Rootes, a British firm, that later was owned by the American firm Chrysler before finally becoming the French-owned Peugeot before closing altogether in the mid 2000s.

Sue had lived in Coventry ever since moving to the city and married 'a Coventry lad.' Sue said she liked living in Coventry, and had not had any negative experiences of the kind portrayed in the play, but rather, she had welcomed the fact that there was so much more to do in a city such as Coventry than in the small Scottish village in which she had been born and spent her childhood. She recalled that she had had a Scottish accent when she moved to Coventry, but this changed, since as she explained:

(73)   when you go to school you tend to sort of when you_re younger you tend to take on accents a bit more easily or feel conscious of it an_ then you lose it

She also said that she thought there was more similarity between the Black Country and Birmingham dialect than between Birmingham and Coventry. When her children were growing up, she told of how her mother's family had mistaken their accent for being a Brummie one, to which she took exception, saying that people on the whole people did not like the Brummie accent, and when it featured in the media, the characters speaking it were portrayed as either sad or comic ones. Her children she reported, who all lived in the area, still spoke with a recognisable Coventry accent.

Mary was another member of the audience interviewed, and she too had thoroughly enjoyed the play. Mary had been born and brought up in Coventry in 1957 to parents who had come to the UK as refugees from Poland at the end of the second world war, had moved to Leamington Spa when she was 12 where she attended a grammar school before attending university, training to be a secondary school teacher of English, and moving back to Leamington Spa in her mid-twenties. She had been 22 in 1979, the year the play was set, so she recalled the Thatcher era extremely well, and the devastation it had wrought in Coventry. The council estate imagined in the play was very similar to the one in which she had lived in as a young girl, and the play plus its music evoked many memories of growing up in the city. In relation to dialect, she said she thought that the Warwickshire one was not particularly distinctive, citing the short vowel sound in words such as 'bath' as typical of the area, along with the long 'oo' sound in words like 'but' and 'she was sat' instead of 'she was sitting.' She had not thought that she herself had a distinctive Warwickshire accent, although she did hear herself saying words such as *up* and *but* with an /oo/ sound and *my* with the /ee/ sound. She also said she had been surprised when a friend had corrected her some years ago when she said *was sat* to *was sitting* as she had been unaware she had been using this form. Attending grammar school, university and her job as a teacher had, she said, 'smoothed out' any traces of dialect she may have once picked up in primary school. At the same time, she said she was not only aware of how

people modified the ways they spoke according to their social and cultural contexts but also the degree of stigma attached to the Birmingham accent, particularly. She said:

(74)   It really bugs me when TV shows such as *Crossroads* and *Auf Weidersein Pet* portray and
       stereotype brummies as dumb and thick

One prominent celebrity associated with the region is the actor and singer Hazel
O'Connor. Hazel was born in 1955 in Coventry on a working-class estate similar to
the one portrayed in the Pollock play, to an Irish father from Galway and English
mother whose family came from Birmingham. Her father had served in with
British army in Belgium and came to Coventry after being demobbed, working
at one of Coventry's car plants and mother became a hairdresser. She did not
recall being conscious of dialect as she was growing up except that her mother
did sometimes speak in an exaggerated Brummie accent to which she would draw
attention. When her mother began working as a hairdresser when Hazel was in
her early teens she noticed her mother's speech accommodating ever further
away from her Brummie accent. Tellingly, when Hazel spoke of her mother as
mum she pronounced it as *mom*.

Hazel said she had realised from a young age that singing was the career
she wanted to herself and in her teens, performed around the Coventry area with
her brother and his band. Her acting debut came in 1975 in a film called *Girls
Come First* but her real break musically and theatrically came in 1980 when she
was offered both the leading part and opportunity to write the soundtrack for the
film *Breaking Glass* that became a hit album with a chart-topping single. Hazel
spoke of the anger she felt during the late 1970s when Alan Pollock's play was set,
felt against the then right-wing Conservative government dissembling the urban
production in working class cities such as Coventry and dismantling everything
people had believed in during the last twenty years since the end of the second
world war. Although she had left Coventry in the early 1970s, she could see what
was happening to her father and men like him that inspired her to write songs
that were socially critical. She did not see herself primarily as an actress, but
used the opportunity given to her by acting in *Breaking Glass* to promote herself
as a singer. Her championing of the working class in her songs she attributed to
the part played by factories in communities such as the one from which she came,
where government policies of the day had pulled the working man to pieces and
the trade unions protecting their rights squashed.

Although Hazel had not lived in Coventry for a long time, she still retained
features of Warwickshire accent, such as the short [mi:], her pronunciation of
birmingham as *burmingum*; and evoking T-R in tokens such as *matter* pronounced

as *marrer*, glottalling and h and g dropping. She also used the term *back entry*, the local term for the alleyway between backs of terraced houses. Like Judas Priest discussed in Chapter 3, in singing her songs, Hazel did this in an RP accent, with *glass* in her well-known hit song *Breaking glass* pronounced with a long /a/ but in speech talking with the short /a/ vowel sound.

5.6 Performance 4: The Coventry Mummers

Creative performances performed by local performers for the local community were found only in the urban areas of Birmingham, the Black Country, Staffordshire Potteries and Coventry. By contrast, no such performances were found in any other areas, particularly more rural ones, as Chapter 1 has discussed. This is not to deny the kind of creative activity that does occur in rural areas, only that they are of a different kind. The one exception to this was the Mummers' plays, performed mainly in small Warwickshire towns such as Brinklow and Leamington Spa and neighbouring villages. Even so, the nature of the plays is such that they do not allow for any references to local, regionally based issues to form any part of their performances except as occasional asides. Mummers' plays are a rural activity, traditional amateur folk plays that take the form of seasonal ritual drama performed in a declamatory style by ordinary people rather than actors, for their community in homes, pubs or streets (Kirby 1971). Like the performances discussed throughout this book, performers were drawn from the local community and performed in local venues, but unlike all the others, their form and content linked to a very different tradition.

The origin of Mummers' plays is unknown, they are thought originally to be mime or dumb shows (the origin of the word mummers is said to stem from the Middle English word mum, meaning silent), with the performers dressed in disguise. They date back to at least the 15th century, since in 1511 Henry VIII passed a law banning them, on the grounds that they were believed to be responsible for an increase in crime during the times they performed as the masked players moved from house to house. As gatherings in pubs and streets, they also attracted pickpockets. Nevertheless, the plays continued to performed in spite of the threat of heavy fines and imprisonment. They became very popular in the 18th and well into the 19th century when they began to decline as the Industrial Revolution caused large numbers of farmworkers to migrate into urban areas. The Mummers also differ from other types of traditional folk groups such as Morris Men that they only act out seasonal ritual drama.

The plays were originally performed by troupes of hired farm labourers known as 'sides', performing in pubs, private houses and in the streets in as many venues as they could reach in one night on horseback carrying all their props, delivered in a bold, exclamatory style. Since the labourers would be known in their community, and more importantly to their employers, they disguised themselves by blacking their faces and making alterations to their clothing such as wearing a jacket inside out so that they would not be recognised by members of their audience, not least by their employers and the implication that he was not paying his farm workers and their families enough to keep them sustained throughout the winter. Mummers' Plays were revived in the 1960s, with the Coventry Mummers formed in 1966 being one of the oldest contemporary sides. They keep to the tradition of performing in towns and villages in pubs and streets and not so much in private houses and at the same times of the year as in the past, particularly at Christmas time. The difference today of course, is that the players are no longer farm labourers, although they are drawn from the local community.

Mummers Plays originate with tales about St George and the dragon and the struggle between good and evil. They normally fall one of three types: the Hero/Combat play which is the most popular, the Recruiting Sergeant play and the Sword Dance play. One character common to all plays is that of the Quack Doctor, since all three types involve miraculous resurrection of some kind. Each type has a skeleton plot with accompanying rhyming couplet script that can be adapted to, for example, incorporate fewer or more characters besides the bare minimum and to include reference to the locality in which they are played. For example, in his conversation interview discussed further below, one of the Mummers, Ian Pearson, tells a story he had heard that if it were thought that a pub landlord was watering down his ale, then their disguise made it possible for the players to refer to this.

Formed in 1966, the Coventry Mummers are one of the longest established contemporary societies in England and comprise a 'side' of 15 men. They are called the Coventry Mummers because of that city's prominence in the county despite being officially designated West Midlands, and a medieval town in times gone by. Today, they perform at small towns in Warwickshire such as Brinklow and Leamington Spa, and neighbouring villages. Roles in any play are often shared depending on how many are needed and there is no specific part that is only ever played by one member of the side. This is also in keeping with tradition, to minimise the risk of any performer being recognised. They keep to the criteria of playing at venues that are close together or that can be reached within 10 minutes on horseback, with four performances in a day ideal. They also carry on the tradition of collecting donations after each play that are given to designated charities.

The plays are short dramas spoken in rhymed couplets, traditionally performed in association with certain annual festivals, mainly around Christmas time but may also be performed at Halloween and Easter, depending upon the traditions of the region in which they are performed. The reasons for the original timings of the performances during the winter and early spring months was because this was when farm labouring work was at its scarcest and money was thus very tight. The plays were traditionally performed on *Plough Monday*, traditionally performed Plough Monday was traditionally the start of the English agricultural year, when work would resume after Christmas on the first Monday after the Twelfth Day in January, when the frosts on the ground are at their hardest and the fields could not be ploughed. The plays were performed around villages and landowners' houses in order to raise money in exchange for their entertainment with the monies they collected going to needy poor people such as a widow with a large family. One of the Mummers who was interviewed, Ian Pearson also recollected stories he had been told of Mummer's ploughing up the gardens of houses they had performed at if they did not receive what they deemed as sufficient payment.

The play performed was The Hero/Combat or St George's play, that involves St George as the hero fighting several different foes and surviving them all. The oldest record of the play is an 1823 version that comes from North Lincolnshire. Howkins and Merricks (1993) note that the language of the original plays has changed in more contemporary times since in the past they contained language that could be deemed obscene and offensive today, and the players were also often aggressive in their performance. Many incorporated dance into the play and adapted some of the content according to the locality in which they played, but the skeleton plot remains the same. The Coventry version of the play has seven characters with the customary fool, soldier, dame and doctor among others. It follows a rambling plot of children supposedly born out of wedlock, love tangles, jealousy, fight, death and through the work of the doctor, miraculous rebirth. Costumes are colourful but simple, made by the actors themselves. There is no scenery but there are props, including over-sized swords intended to bring a cartoonish element to the play. The players burst unannounced into the pub where they are playing, with the audience having no choice but to watch the performance given its loud declamatory style, and the close proximity of the performers to the audience. The performers also create a pantomime type of atmosphere, with the audience booing and cheering different characters; for example, booing The Turkish Knights and cheering St George.

All of the Mummers who acted the play when at the time of its recording lived in Warwickshire with many of them having done so for a number of years. Although performed locally with local players and for local audiences, the nature of Mummers' Plays is such that dialect use figures differently in these performances than the others discussed in this book. The plays themselves are prescripted in the sense that they have a standard allegoric plot of the death of the year in Winter to its rebirth in Spring, personified through a character dying and being resurrected back to life by the doctor and a number of other stock characters, with frames of reference evoking both aspects of myth and ways of life long gone by. Whilst some of the characters in the play recorded though, spoke with a recognisable Warwickshire accent that included features, particularly phonological ones already identified, no features appeared to be enregistered in the way they have been in other performances discussed in this book.

Mummers' Plays then, are very different in kind in many ways from locally based performances found in urban areas. Their origin is in a rural way of life that has long ago vanished and the imagined community they evoke has long passed into history and beyond the recollection of anyone living. There is no need any longer to support families through raising funds with lighthearted – and not so lighthearted – menaces, their scripts are formulaic and whilst there is space for it to be adapted to a specific locality, such adaptation is at the margins of the performance and not at its heart. The plays serve as an imaginative link to a rural past where dialect would have spoken as a matter of course by the farm labourers who performed them. Whilst today's performers of Mummers' Plays are no longer farm labourers, they nevertheless move into such personae when performing the plays. Their double-voicing centres upon playing the part of a particular stock character that would have been played by a farm labourer and thus inviting vernacular use that players can adapt regionally if they choose to so do. Their existence serves to throw into sharp relief the part played by dialect use in performance to be found in urban areas. Here, performances performed by white performers in particular centre around disruptive events in the recent past and in past living memory such as the 1970s and 2011 – and the changes they bring about over which ordinary working people have no control. Within these, dialect use is most prevalent in highly localised performance venues performed in front of highly localised audiences such as those found in the Black Country and Stoke on Trent in Staffordshire. Mummers' plays by contrast, serve to form a link with ways of rural life that have long since disappeared but nevertheless remain in the imagination and serve as a link to that past.

5.6.1 In conversation with Mummer Ian Pearson

One of the Mummers was Ian Pearson, who was in his late 40s at the time of the conversation interview, and had been a member of the Coventry Mummers for some time. He was born in Coventry, to parents who were also born there and lived in the city all their lives. His grandfather came to Coventry from Scotland where he had been serving as a soldier in the Highland regiment and when the city was a garrison town. He went to university in Birmingham and has lived in the region all his life. He reported that he had not been particularly conscious of Coventry dialect when he was growing up, since that was what he grew up with and would have considered it normal. When asked if the plays were adapted according to the audience demographic, Ian said that the very nature of the venues in which they were performed guaranteed a local audience. One example Ian gave of a character localising their origins is that when asked what his credentials are, the character of the Doctor says he has travelled. When asked where, he recites the names of train stations between Leamington Spa and Carlisle. The performances are also different in nature to others in that they are not always advertised in advance, and although the side gain a landlord's permission to perform in a pub, its clientele is unaware it is going to happen. The players burst into a pub and perform, make a collection and leave.

The tradition of Mumming has been followed by a son following their father, although Ian reported how this particular aspect of the Mumming tradition had been impossible to revive. All members of the side have families, but Ian said that like so many these days, his children go away to university and after that would gain employment that could be anywhere in the country. Ian was at pains to point out that Mummers' Plays were neither street theatre nor amateur drama, but were much coarser and although adaptive, the main dialogue of the play remains the same at each and every performance. Any identity construction that takes place then is away from the main dialogue and not linked to any enregistered features of dialect. If any character does draw upon their accent in an enregistered and indexical way, then Ian said it was a member of the side who is from Scotland, and delivers his lines in mimicry of the Scots actor Sean Connery.

5.7 Conclusion

This chapter has considered some of the ways in which dialect use is drawn upon in performance poetry and dramatic plays as active resources in creating identity for performance effect in ways that are similar to the more localized comedy sketches discussed in Chapters 3 and 4. They illustrate the ways in which constructing localness is not just a matter of using local code or evoking local places, but also using it in ways that link in with the wider historical and sociocultural contexts in which the performances take place. The subject matter of the stage plays *Riot* and *Too much pressure* centre largely upon the feelings of frustration felt by people, particularly those of the working class and low socio-economic status, to events over which they have no control but which directly affect the way they live their lives.

It is clear from the discussion in this chapter as in earlier ones that local performances performed in front of local audiences address the locality and the communities that live in it. They deal with issues that are pertinent to their highly localised audiences and a shared history that relates to the recent past, particularly from the late 1970s onwards in the Coventry play *Too Much Pressure* and in the Birmingham *Riot* play, set in 2011. This is especially true in urban areas such as the Black Country, Stoke-on-Trent in Staffordshire, Birmingham and Coventry, where the lives of ordinary people have changed radically through economic and social forces over which they have no control. The performances explore how such changes impact upon the lives of ordinary people and the varying ways in which they cope with them. By contrast, the Coventry Mummers' plays performed in Warwickshire are very different in nature, rooted in rural traditions that pre-date the 19th century and the industrial revolution. They are linked to place in so far as the players live locally and maintain the tradition of performing their plays within distances that can be reached within one evening in areas that are by and large rural or semi-rural. They thus evoke imagined communities of the kind who would have lived in the region in which they perform, and to which their present-day audiences might have belonged if they had lived in those times. They link to the an agricultural rural, rather than urban and industrialised past as experienced by farm labourers that existed long before the Industrial Revolution. They serve to maintain a heritage and tradition that keeps the memory of those times alive.

6 Agentive and situational dialect use: Place and identity in and beyond staged performance

6.1 Introduction

It is clear that within a region such as the West Midlands, like many in England, there is a wide range of performance activity linked to place. Such performances range from those given by local performers at mainly amateur or semi-professional venues in working class areas for an audience drawn largely from the immediate locality to professional performances performed in professional theatres to an audience drawn from much wider and mixed demographic. The performances discussed in the preceding chapters range from firstly, highly localised amateur 'open mic' nights in public houses, particularly in regions once associated with 19th century industrial working-class communities such as those in the Black Country and Stoke on Trent in the Staffordshire Potteries and where the audience is adult, mixed gender and white. Secondly, 'open mic' nights in a large city such as Birmingham where even in a suburb such as Northfield discussed in Chapter 3 as well as the city centre in *the Bluu Bar* discussed in Chapter 4 members of the audience comprise visitors to the city as well as local people and where the audience is adult, mixed gender and mixed ethnicity. Thirdly, performances at subsidised venues such as *The Drum* that cater for adult, mixed gender audiences drawn from a specific Afro-Caribbean ethnic group. Fourthly semi-professional or professional plays performed in a traditional theatre style or repertory theatre as discussed in Chapter 5 and finally traditional Mummers' Plays performed in local public houses at specific times of the year to a pre-determined story outline in small towns and villages in Warwickshire.

Localness, however, can be configured and/or imagined and constructed in differing ways. The extent to which any of the performances draw upon dialect use in enregistered ways to index specific aspects of regional and social identity appears to depend largely upon the performers' audiences attending their performances in terms of their demographic makeup. The more locally oriented the performance in terms of its venue, especially outside of city or town centres, the more dialect use is prevalent. It is true to say that the world in which we now live is very different from all kinds of pasts that have been attributed largely to the twin forces of media and migration to which globalisation can also be added, and communities from which performers and their audiences are drawn can no longer be assumed to be bound by local, national or regional spaces. However,

https://doi.org/10.1515/9781501506796-006

when it comes to performers enactments in front of live audiences, then certain assumptions can be made about the spaces from which audiences are drawn depending upon the location of the venue. This in turn, allows performers to annexe the forces of media and migration through the prism of the local, including the local dialect, in attempting to make sense of modernity and its impact upon audience's and performers' lives, often in comic and semi-serious ways. Performers are well aware that their performances cannot of themselves promote social change. However, their carnivalesque nature, particularly those given by comedians, serve to help local communities to understand or to make sense of the modern world, acting as a coping mechanism, a means of understanding the current social order and one's place in it. Performers show themselves to be well aware of the indexical nature of language use, particularly as it pertains to dialect, and their greatest degree of enregistration is in front of audiences who are most familiar with the dialect in question.

In Birmingham and the Black Country in particular as discussed in Chapter 3, the performances took the form of semi-improvised sketches and turns, where the more locally placed the venue in relation to the intended audience, the more likely the performers enregistered a range of dialect features indexically and more frequently than in venues where the audiences were not drawn from so localised an area. In the case of performances given by Afro-Caribbean performers in Birmingham discussed in Chapter 4, the degree of enregisterment of features drawn from a Black Brum multiethnolect varied, since the demographic nature of the audiences discussed was very different, with the performers 'speaking to' different kinds of audiences. In the case of scripted performances performed in theatres in Birmingham and Coventry discussed in Chapter 5, their nature is such that enregistered dialect features are drawn upon selectively in relation to specific performers who hail from the region, rather than being required as part of character representation. In the Warwickshire Mummers' plays, also discussed in Chapter 5, dialect use was largely irrelevant given the nature of the performances enacted. The performers were also, with the exception of the women's theatre group *Fizzogg*, all male, with the imaginative communities constructed through performance centred upon the effects of wider economic and social changes wrought about through modernity upon the local communities affected by them.

The extent to which performers enregistered dialect use features in their enactments varied according not only to the locality, but also to the type of performance venue in which they took place and the content and subject matter of the performance. Performers from the Black Country discussed in Chapter 3 and of Afro Caribbean heritage discussed in Chapter 4 enregistered features most frequently, followed by some performances in Birmingham, the Staffordshire Potteries and lastly Coventry. A common theme running throughout conversations with actors and playwrights was that where dialect use was thought to interfere with an audience's understanding or the requirement for an actor to speak in a specific accent sounding unauthentic, then such use was less frequent. Equally pertinent is the fact that performers, particularly in highly localised comedy acts, enregistered features were most evident the most at punchlines to jokes or comic turns. The degree to which enregisterment was most evident also depended upon the locality: the further away from the place they represented, the fewer features were reportedly enregistered. In comedy acts in particular, performers' enregistered dialect features the most. In the performances by white performers in Birmingham, the Black Country and Stoke on Trent, performers who were from the region enregistered features of dialect associated with those regions. In contrast to this, performers by Birmingham born Afro Caribbean performers drew upon a range of dialects from within England and also elsewhere in the world, to create the multiethnolect of Black Brum.

By contrast, locally based performances in the shire counties as opposed to those in urban areas were of a very different nature, and mainly centred around folk clubs and folk festivals where the performers were drawn from all over the country and not necessarily local. The exception to this was the Mummers' Plays discussed in Chapter 5, where dialect enregisterment is absent, possibly because the time in history to which they relate are beyond those of living memory. In such performances, performers may perform with a distinctive regional dialect and enregister certain features of it if it their first one, but it may not necessarily be the one of the region in which they are performing, but from where they themselves hail, which can be from anywhere in the UK.

Such accommodation can be viewed as double-voicing on the part of its speakers, since it is clear people such as the performers and others interviewed, are well aware of altering their linguistic style according to the situations in which they find themselves. They are also aware of the degree to which they enregister dialect features according to their situational context. Dialect use in performance contexts occurs mainly in densely populated urban areas such as Birmingham, The Black Country, Coventry and Stoke-on-Trent. These regions comprised largely working-class communities that once centred upon local manufacturing, and where people once either lived where they worked or close to their work. The more local the area from which the audience is drawn, the more evidence there is of dialect use, such as in the Black Country comedian Paul Jennings', the Black Country women's theatre group *Fizzogg*'s and the Staffordshire Potteries performance poet Mark Vale's performances. The venues are public houses, with members of the audience living largely nearby. In Birmingham, locally based performers are often one amongst a range of others drawn from different areas, such as Craig Deeley, the Birmingham comedian and Tracey, the Birmingham actress.

The demographic of Birmingham and other cities in the region is such that social networks are looser and not as dense as those to be found in the Black Country, with far more people-flow into the cities from elsewhere in the UK or from across the world. The exception to this is the Jamaican performers who form a distinct social group within Birmingham. For them, the concept of 'place' or 'where are you from?' as discussed in Chapter 4 and later in this chapter, encompasses not only one place or region, but several, including Jamaica and London as well as Birmingham.

The plays performed in theatres in Birmingham and Coventry, *Riot* and *Too much pressure* respectively, although dealing with local issues, are enacted in front of diverse audiences, where day to day experiences rooted in the local area act as vehicles for examining social issues that go beyond the immediate locality. Outside of cities, in towns and villages, local entertainment is less place bound and more generic in nature, centring upon folk clubs and festivals, the former drawing in performers from across the West Midlands region and beyond whilst the latter attract performers and audiences from across the country. Apart from the Mummers' Plays in Leamington Spa and surrounding villages, no locally based performances for local audiences were found in cities, towns and villages of the shire counties of Shropshire, Warwickshire or Worcestershire, and not through any lack of effort in trying to find any. The nature of the Mummers' Plays is also such that any dialect enregisterment within them is redundant in terms of constructing any sense of localness.

The extent to which people's use of dialect is indexical then – or double-voiced – varies from person to person and situation to situation. Reflexivity about dialect use on behalf of the general public at large though, provides the conditions whereby performers, particularly when performing in local venues to highly localised audiences and in a region such as the Black Country, can exploit their linguistic awareness for both comic effect and in relation to identity construction simultaneously.

6.2 Staging identity and place through dialect use

It is clear, that regional dialect use, particularly in urban areas of England, is still very much in prominence within the localities with which they are associated, and that such use in performance is highly indexicalised and enregistered, linked to performative content. In addition, there is also the emergence of a multieth-nolect exemplified by 'Black Brum' as discussed in Chapter 4 where language use is 'designed' to draw upon a range of regional identities with which the perform-ers identity. As conversations with performers and members of their audiences' attest, adults are well aware of the prejudices associated with dialect use and thus are more likely to accommodate away from it and towards standard English when in mixed company away from their immediate locale, and particularly in relation to public spaces and places such as the workplace. Savage et al's (2013) analysis of a survey into social class undertaken by the British Broadcasting Corporation (BBC) has shown how the traditional triangle representation of social class has changed in shape to resemble more that of an onion. Since the 1970s, membership of the working classes has shrunk whilst that of the middle classes has expanded, with more nuanced strata within the classes identified. However, whilst the class structure in England may have changed over the last forty years or so, nevertheless the annual *British Social Attitudes* (BSA) reports show that 60% of people continue to describe themselves as working class (Devine 2016). As Devine and Sensier (2017: 35) say: 'It seems, then, that working-class identification is not declining in tandem with the shrinking size of the working class.' Savage (2016) states that there has been a dramatic revival of interest in social class since the turn of the 21st century. His central argument is that the concept of social class owes its distinctiveness to the fact that it straddles both academic and popular discourse. He also points to the ways in which social class is currently theorised has changed since the 1970s, and identifies four fundamental underpinnings. Firstly, the dramatic rise in inequality in the UK since the 1980s; secondly, that class still matters to people; thirdly, the growing interest in research approaches to inequality that are granular than large-scale studies previously undertaken and finally, the French theorist Bourdieu's influence upon British sociology. This has been particularly so in relation to his concept of 'mis-recognition,' the ways in which power works through 'naturalising' social relations and serves to explain how people in even a highly class divided society, might not be class conscious themselves. Bourdieu has also been influential in taking attention away from class a discrete social variable and towards '...class as the contingent outcome of the operations of capitals, habitus and fields. Rather than fixing class as one discrete entity, it was thus seen as a more fluid outcome of other mechanisms, in a way which permitted more flexibility in how the concept could be used, and furthermore could engage with public debates' (Savage 2016: 67).

Bourdieu's work of course has also influenced linguistics, with his idea of linguistic capital being part of cultural capital, and the processes through which power is transmitted through language as discussed in Chapter 2. It is clear that the performers discussed throughout this book are well aware of the cultural capital afforded to standardized versions of a language such as standard English. They also can be said to award cultural capital to dialect use in their performances that undercut the power relations associated with standard language ideology. As the preceding chapters of this book have shown, where performers and artists from working class backgrounds have moved into the middle class by virtue of education and employment, they retain a sense of working class identity through their language use that includes dialect features. As Devine and Sensier (2017: 35–36) say:

> People know about class, although they dislike it...people still make sense of the world by drawing boundaries and making judgements. The easy binary class divide has been replaced by subtle judgements about cultural tastes and activities with class undertones. Confirming what you are not rather than who you are, and keeping a clear distance from those at the bottom, prevails. Thus class snobbery has gone underground.

A major way in which people today identify with the working class is through their use of dialect. As chapter 1 has discussed, the traditional distinction between dialect and register is no longer as clear cut as it once was, since the use of (some) distinctive formal patterns characterising a regional, working class dialect can be shown to be motivated by interactional circumstances, such as creative performances. It is not so much that dialect use is dying out then, but that accommodation is on the increase and people's relationship with dialect has changed. Drawing upon even a single distinctive dialect feature in speech that is otherwise in standard English and RP such as the velar nasal plus in pronouncing *Birmingham* or elongating vowel sounds in pronouncing *Dudley* as *Doodleigh* is sufficient for people to 'place' the speaker both in relation to those localities and to a social class identity. Equally, the tag *ennit* is sufficient to index an Afro-Caribbean identity and a comment such as *I'm brummie ennit* indexes both being from Birmingham and a Jamaican heritage. Pan- national and regional working-class social identities can also be said to be evoked on speakers' parts through such features as t-glottaling, h- and g-dropping and the T-R rule which has been ubiquitous across the data discussed in preceding chapters. Class snobbery then may be said to have gone underground in a political or sociological sense, but people may linguistically subvert that snobbery by continuing to self-identify with the working class once they have moved across to the middle class through dialect use associated with that class.

Performers from what were once dense, tightly knit urban communities that centred upon local manufacture such as those in the Black Country and the Staffordshire Potteries retain more dialect features in their performances and speech in general, than those from Birmingham, Coventry and Warwickshire. This is not surprising, given that the former communities have been in existence for much longer than the latter. Even so, the range of dialect features they draw upon is a restricted one, that have become highly indexicalised and enregistered. Social identities that once centred upon the workplace in traditional working-class communities can be said to have shifted the locus of place identity from work to language. Dialect use can also signal racial identity in multifaceted and complex ways as Chapter 4 has shown in relation to performers of Afro-Caribbean heritage. Here, performers continue to draw upon patwa to index their colour and colonial past, whilst at the same time drawing upon features of the Birmingham dialect and to a certain extent, MLE in constructing or 'designing' as one of the performers said, their identity.

The post-war period of manufacturing boom that ended with the 1973 oil crisis is a key period in recent British political and social history that has also impacted upon its linguistic one. Predictions of working class affluence fell away towards the end of the 1970s with the 1980s being a different decade that witnessed the collapse of manufacturing and the defeat of trade unions (Devine and Sensier 2017). Since the 1980s, the decline in manufacturing that relied largely upon manual labour corresponded with an increase in educational access as the demands of the workplace changed, especially for the younger generation where sons in particular, stopped following their fathers' footsteps into manual, unskilled labour as illustrated by Allan Pollock's play *Too much pressure* discussed in Chapter 5. For such boys and men, the prospect of white collar work made accessible through education meant a corresponding shift in social class status from working class to middle class. Thus, many of the performers and others interviewed, hailed from a family background where their parents were working class but where they themselves, by virtue of their occupations, had moved into the middle class. Dialect use thus functions as a link with a working-class heritage that no longer exists but lives on in people's memories and in the imagination. The dialect loss that occurs through dialect levelling and mainly through education, can feel akin to a betrayal of their family heritage on such people's parts, a feeling to which those interviewed testify. Performers, members of the audience and the celebrities interviewed were all well aware of the degree of accommodation in which they engage – or not, as the case may be – outside of the immediate circle of family and friends.

Evoking place and imagined community through dialect use in performance is multifaceted and complex, and involves taking account of performers' linguistic as well as social histories as well as those of their audiences. The linguistic or feature pool upon which performers draw is taken from a wider contact pool that may consist of dialects drawn from more than one language. In white communities of the kind found in Birmingham, the Black Country, Coventry and Stoke on Trent for example, dialect links to a specific geographic region and a working-class industrial past and, in some cases such as Mark Bailey the Trent Vale Poet, present. Such performers interweave or integrate aspects of local dialect associated with their region into standard English to varying degrees. In the more affluent towns and villages of the shire counties, dialect use in performance is far less prevalent: indeed, virtually non-existent. Performances here such as the Mummers Plays discussed in Chapter 5 date back centuries to pre-Industrial Revolution times and serve to form a link with imagined communities of that time. In Afro Caribbean communities of the kind found in Birmingham, the linguistic or feature pool is more complex. The range of places and dialects drawn upon is diverse, crossing continents and retaining a link with a colonial past and a time of African slavery. It is thus not so much that dialect use or linguistic conservatism as it is sometimes termed is used by performers in an agentive, enregistered way to resist change, but more as a way of making sense of or coming to terms with the rapidly changing world and the forces of mediatization and globalisation in ways that do not deny people's linguistic and social roots. As one performer put it, deliberately choosing to incorporate aspects of dialect into their social interaction both as a performer and an individual, was to his mind an act of conservation, not preservation. That is, people wish to conserve dialect as a way of retaining a link with a past way of life and working-class identity that is fast disappearing or has already. It is also telling that publicly funded charities such as the Lottery Heritage Fund include dialect projects under their remit, where dialect is perceived as an important part of the fabric of English cultural heritage and worthy of being recorded.[1]

6.3 Dialect use, linguistic style and identity construction

In contemporary English usage, it is clear that dialect can be used to creative and ideological effect to give voice to particular kinds of identity construction. This is particularly so when the performers or other artists such as the celebrity category that feature in this book are themselves local to the region. The performers come from a traditional working class background or, in the case of Allan Pollock, from a middle class family but grew up on a working class estate. They hail from sections of society who benefited from widening access to education in the 1970s and 1980s that included access to public examinations which in turn gave access to further or higher education and subsequent employment that has been, in most cases, very different from that of their parents. All – with one exception – the Warwickshire Mummer Ian Pearson – attested to the levelling effect education and employment had upon their dialect use. Performers also draw upon dialect in performance to varying degrees through the personae they portray related to the working class, with many performances set – or referring to – pivotal points in recent social history, namely the late 1970s and early 1980s.

---

1 The outcomes of one such Lottery Heritage Fund project can be seen at: http://talkyamyam.com/

It is clear from the data considered in the three preceding chapters, that some dialect features are shared across the region: those of Coventry and Staffordshire are evident in the Birmingham dialect with phonologically the addition of the velar nasal plus that is also found in the Black Country, which in turn, has the highest proportion of dialect specific features from all of those in the region. Performers from across the region who do enregister dialect use are also aware of the fact that they so do – the more contemporarily oriented and localised the performance, the greater the enregistration. On the whole, performers from Birmingham and the Black Country say that the further away from the locality they are, the less dialect features they enregister in their enactments but those they do, are highly indexed in relation to place. The exception to this is Mark, the Trent Vale Poet, who makes no such accommodation. Performers who write their own material such as Paul Jennings discussed in Chapter 3, and playwrights who are also producers such as Pollock and Green discussed in Chapter 5, all shared the same view that dialect can be a powerful indexical feature in performances. However, they are also cognizant of the ways in which dialect use can 'get in the way', either through the performer drawing upon it in ways that impede audience understanding or actors not familiar with it unable to replicate it and thus not sounding authentic or natural to the audience. Thus, where performances constitute a cast of actors in a theatre space, such as the plays *Too Much Pressure* and *Riot,* and the audience who attends them are drawn from a much wider area than the more localised ones, then the role of dialect use is less evident for the reasons given above.

6.4 Dialect, performance and agency

The notion of agency is key to the ways in which performers engage with dialect use. Whilst factors such as gender, ethnicity, occupation and audience undeniably have an impact upon how people and especially adults talk, performers are very adept at treating such factors as resources to create not only unique voices as first identified by Johnstone (1996) but also stereotypical, predominantly working-class characters and personae. As discussed above, this is because in their performances they evoke a working-class heritage and past that no longer exists in the ways in which it once did, but lives on in the imagination. It may also be way, despite having moved into the middle classes economically, many people from a working-class background continue to self-identify in sociological surveys as working class. It is clear from conversation interviews with performers and audiences that they index aspects of their identity through enregistering specific dialect features linked to place (- or not -). As discussed above, the processes of indexicality have made people more aware than ever before of how they speak. Performers exploit this in their enactments, both through the content itself and the way it is linguistically realised with, for example, the greatest intensity of dialect use featuring at the end of a punchline in a comic turn. Or, in the case of the womens' theatre group *Fizzog*, through their caricature of women who are a generation older than them. A striking feature of the conversation interviews with not only performers and playwrights but also celebrities and members of audiences, is the degree to which people in general are aware of the – largely negative – attitudes and prejudices associated with the dialects of the region and the cultural capital value of standard language versus dialects. Members of the audience have also shown how they react to dialect use in their own speech along a cline associated with past largely negative linguistic experiences that has caused them to accommodate away from their dialect as much as possible to maintaining aspects of dialect use in spite of negative associations. The degree to which any individual accommodates their speech away from dialect and towards standard English, or enregisters specific features then, clearly depends upon not only interactional and situational context but also linguistic experience.

A common thread running through all the performances (Mummer's Plays apart) is of coming to terms with and trying to make sense of the impact of the media, migration and increasing globalisation have had upon people's lives in recent times and particularly from the 1970s onwards. Traditionally, regional dialect use has correlated with social class, particularly the working class. However, the forces of modernity over the past forty years or so have served to alter the nature of that social class, arguably more than any other. Where working class communities were once tight knit, such as the one portrayed in the play *Too much pressure*, they have splintered and fragmented. Dialect use, once unnoticed in such communities has, through modernity, become indexicalised and through linguistic hegemony, to a certain extent demonised in the eyes of the general – middle class – public at large, as discussed in Chapter 5. At the same time, dialect can be used agentively to link to a recent cultural and industrial heritage and past that have all but disappeared and is historically distant, but lives on in linguistic use, as discussed above.

The question *where are you from?* and as discussed in Chapter 4, crystallises an individual's agentive relationship with their language use particularly if it shows any traces of dialect other than standard English as it simultaneously evokes aspects of identity at various levels – ethnicity and social class as well as nation and region. All Birmingham and Black Country performers of white ethnic origin reported that they pre-empted the negative comments that inevitably arose when self-identifying with those regions by 'getting in first', with a 'confession' that they hailed from them. Within the region itself, there is also an irritation that in the media, people from the west Midlands in general are all portrayed as being from Birmingham, whereas performers and playwrights from the Black Country, Coventry and Staffordshire Potteries were at pains to say that they were not 'from' Birmingham. Performers of Afro Caribbean heritage had a more complex relationship with the answer to that question, since it included the dimension of a place of birth of either themselves or their parents that is not in England. Roy McFarlane in the pome of the same name and the performance given by Deci4Life and Moqpal Selassie demonstrate the complexities wrought about by modernity when that question is asked of any one from that background. They illustrate the ways in which a question such as this in everyday conversational interactions is an example of nationality and ethnicity talk (NET) (Hua and Wei 2016). As discussed in Chapter 4, NET as an act of identity calibration involves categorisation and positioning of one's self and others and also stance-making, on the part of both the performer and his interlocutors. Although the question 'where are you really from' does not of itself contest immigrants' entitlement, it does in relation to people's perceptions of whether the speaker is an 'interloper' or 'outsider' and thus not wanted and how they position themselves in relation to the tangled history, memory and expectation that is imbued and fuelled by power inequality. McFarlane's poem exemplifies such an entanglement, and the complex socio-cultural and historical complexities of what counts as 'home' as discussed above and in Chapter 4 when an immigrant is asked the question: 'where are you from?'

6.5 Dialect, performance, creativity and imagination

Linked to agency, is the issue of creativity and imagination. It is clear that the degree to which dialect use is incorporated into creative and spoken word performances depends largely upon the locality and venue in which they take place. Each enactment is in turn, set against the background of the wider historical and socio-political contexts within which it is performed and the sets of beliefs, values, assumptions or ideologies that underpin these contexts and specific use of language. Thus, within even the most highly localised performances given at *The Holly Bush* in Cradely Heath in The Black Country, performers make reference to the world beyond, be it Muslim terrorists, the closing of factories or taking people out of their comfort zone on package holidays in Spain. Such performances are characterised by mocking self-reflexivity, which evoke a kind of *schadenfreude* on the part of the audience. All are acutely aware of the social stigma accorded to the dialects they may still speak or of which they have a memory, whilst at the same time acknowledging the subversion of linguistic hegemony at play in them.

Performers creatively and imaginatively evoke a set of shared experiences to which the members of the audience may react either positively or negatively depending upon their own personal experiences. For some, dialect use evokes a frame of rejection based upon past negative experiences; for others, it evokes a frame of acceptance in that they deliberately resist accommodating their speech entirely away from any trace of dialect in it. The localised nature of venues means that performers are able to evoke a working-class past that is shared collectively by the majority of their audience in self-reflexive ways, bringing time and space together through a sense of a specific place. It also allows for performers to relocate social institutions and day to day activities that have become increasingly dislocated from local communities – such as the police, holidays and football – in ways that embed them back into the community. What all performers and their performances have in common, is the ways in which they construct imagined communities that are conjured up in relation to the locality in which they are performed to places or spaces not only from within England but across the whole world, whether that be a European location such as a beach in Spain further afield as in references to the United States and China or evoking a homeland such as Jamaica.

Performers draw on dialect use and localised references in carnivalesque and self-reflexive ways to evoke imagined communities centred upon the region in which they live and the performances take place, and through such use subvert or mock contemporary cultural norms, including linguistic ones. They do so in ways that are also received differently by members of their localised audiences. Either they find them amusing or uncomfortable, depending upon individuals' past experiences. The performances also exemplify the underlying sociocultural contexts within which they occur as a means of juxtaposing the norms and values of those 'within' the community from those 'outside' or 'beyond' it, in ways that subvert traditional notions of linguistic and social hierarchy, and particularly by poking fun at them. Performers thus consciously interweave a specific set of dialect features in ways that relate, connote or signify imaginatively specific geographic places and the (speech) communities that inhabit them. Such conscious choice is indicative of an understanding on the part of both performers and their audiences of the underlying hegemonic cultural and social forces associated with the use of a sociolect such as standard English and regional dialects. For performers of Afro Caribbean heritage, their use of Patwa or Jamaican language is indicative of a link with the past as well as with the country of their forefathers that lives on in collective imagination. For many poets and performers, it is also a way of keeping alive the memory of past injustices and struggles, and illustrates the ways in which dialect switching may be metaphorical in nature.

Local performances performed by locally based performers deal with issues that are pertinent to their highly localised audiences and a shared history that relates to the recent past, particularly from the late 1970s onwards in the Coventry play *Too Much Pressure* and in the Birmingham *Riot* play, set in 2011. This is especially true in urban areas such as the Black Country, Stoke-on-Trent in Staffordshire, Birmingham and Coventry, where the lives of ordinary people have changed radically through economic and social forces over which they have no control. The performances explore how such changes impact upon the lives of ordinary people and the varying ways in which they cope with them. By contrast, the Coventry Mummers' plays performed in Warwickshire are very different in nature, rooted in rural traditions that pre-date the 19th century and the industrial revolution. They are linked to place in so far as the players live locally and maintain the tradition of performing their plays within distances that can be reached within one evening in areas that are by and large rural or semi-rural. They thus evoke imagined communities of the kind who would have lived in the region in which they perform, and to which their present-day audiences might have belonged if they had lived in those times. They link to an agricultural rural, rather than urban and industrialised past as experienced by farm labourers that existed long before the Industrial Revolution. They serve to maintain a heritage and tradition that keeps the memory of those times alive.

6.6 Conclusion

A common theme that links all the performances is that their subject matter by and large evokes frames of reference that are often specific to the localities in which the venues are located. Comedic performances 'poke fun' at prevailing social orders and evoke a kind of 'us' and 'them', where 'us' is the local region – or in the case of performances at *The Bluu Bar* and *Drum* the local region and Jamaica – and 'them' everyone beyond it. In dramatic performances then, dialect use, far from portraying any kind of parochial insularity, serves to give voice to the experiences of a specific, locally based community at a time of significant social change. A discursive and interactional approach to dialect use thus interrelates four aspects or dimensions of language study:

– Firstly, studying dialect use in relation to linguistic style has to take account of (a) the individual and the social networks to which they belong and may have belonged to in the past; (b) the discursive genre within which language use occurs and (c) the wider socio-historical and cultural contexts of that use. It also takes account of the ways in which individual voices may be polyphonic, as with the Caribbean performers discussed in Chapter 3. Indeed, in today's mobile, global and technological world, polyphony is fast becoming the linguistic norm, as people seek to construct social identities that also index the place(s), past and present, from whence they came.

- Secondly, there is the identification of the actual dialect features in any particular dialect of English that contribute to linguistic style. In contemporary spoken English usage, dialect can be used to creative and ideological effect to give voice to particular kinds of identity construction.

- Thirdly, there is the issue of agency: the degree to which any language user is aware of the aspects or dimensions above, and chooses to index or 'mark' their identity through enregistering specific dialect features linked to place (-or not-), thereby linking to a recent industrial heritage and working-class past that have disappeared or a cultural heritage that is both geographically and historically distant, but lives on in linguistic use.

- Finally, linked to agency, is the issue of creativity and imagination: the degree to which dialect is incorporated into creative and spoken word performances in tune with the locality in which performances take place, set against the background of the wider historical and socio-political contexts within which language is used and the sets of beliefs, values, assumptions or ideologies that underpin these contexts and linguistic use.

Dialects associated with urban regions of England such as those in the West Midlands serve a sociocultural purpose in that individuals draw upon them to link with a historic, manual working-class past and, in the case of Afro Caribbean performers, a colonial past. The identity once inherent in social networks that centred around neighbourhoods where people worked, lived and socialised has transferred, through the processes associated with indexicality, to language instead. Performers exploit underlying forces of mediatization and globalisation that underly contemporary society's transformation since the 1970s in relation to their own and their audiences' experiences of that transformation. They localise experiences through the imaginative worlds they create on stage, subverting standard language ideologies as part of their creation, largely by reversing accepted frames of acceptance and rejection. For performers of Afro Caribbean heritage, their inclusion of Patwa or Jamaican language into their speech also serves as a way of linking with the past, not wanting society at large to forget that past and their struggle against past injustices. The common link between all the performances discussed is that regional dialect or a multiethnolect serves as a link to the past that lives on in collective imagination and gives voice to it, particularly in performances enacted in highly localised venues.

References

Adams, Michael. 2009. Enregisterment: a special issue. *American Speech* 84(2). 115–117.

Akram, Sadiya. 2014. Recognizing the 2011 United Kingdom riots as political protest: a theoretical framework based on agency, habitus and the preconscious. *The British Journal of Criminology* 54(3). 375–392.

Agha, Asif. 2003. The social life of cultural value. *Language and Communication* 23. 231–73.

Agha, Asif. 2005. Voice, footing, enregisterment. *Journal of Linguistic Anthropology* 15(1). 1–5.

Agha, Asif. 2007. *Language and social relations*. Cambridge: Cambridge University Press.

Anderson, Benedict. 2006 [1983]. *Imagined communities: reflections on the origin and spread of nationalism*. London and New York: Verso.

Antroutsopoulos, Jannis. 2010. The study of language and space in media discourse. In Peter Auer and Jurgen E. Schmidt (eds.), *Language and space: an international handbook of linguistic variation vol 1: theories and methods*, 740–758. Berlin: De Gruyter Mouton.

Antroutsopoulos, Jannis. 2014. (ed.). *linguae & litterae: Mediatization and Sociolinguistic Change*. Berlin: De Gruyter Mouton.

Antroutsopoulos, Jannis. 2016. Theorising, media, mediation and mediatization. In Nikolas Coupland (ed.), *Sociolinguistics: theoretical debates*, 282–302. Cambridge: Cambridge University Press.

Appadurai, Arjun. 1996. *Modernity at large: cultural dimensions of globalization*. Minneapolis: University of Minesota Press.

Attardo, Salvatore. 2001. *Humorous texts: asemantic and pragmatic analysis*. Berlin: Mouton de Gruyter.

Auer, Peter. 2011. Dialect vs. standard: a typology of scenarios in Europe. In Bernd Kortman & Johan van der Auwera (eds.), *The languages and linguistics of Europe: a comprehensive guide*, 485–500. Berlin: De Gruyter Mouton.

Auer, Peter 2013. The geography of language: steps toward a new approach. https://portal.uni-freiburg.de/sdd/fragl/2013.16 (accessed 11 September 2016).

Auer, Peter. 2014. There's no harm in glossing (but a need for a better understanding of the status of transcripts). *Research on Language and Social Interaction* 47(1). 17–22.

Back, L. 2003 [1995]. X amount of Sat Siri Akal!: Apache Indian, Reggae music and intermezzo culture. Reprinted in R. Harris & B. Rampton (eds.), *The language, race and ethnicity reader*, 328–345. London: Routledge.

Bakhtin, Mikhail. 1981 [1971]. *The dialogic imagination: four essays*. (trans. C. Emerson and M. Holquist). Austin: University of Texas Press.

Bakhtin, Mikhail. 1984a [1965]. *Rabelais and his world*. Bloomington: Indiana University Press.

Bakhtin, Mikhail. 1984b [1963]. *Problems of Dostoevsky's poetics*. (ed. and trans. Caryl Emerson). Minneapolis: University of Minnesota Press.

Bauman, Richard. 1986. *Story, performance and event: contextual studies of oral narrative*. New York: Cambridge University Press.

Bauman, Richard. 2000. Language, identity, performance. *Pragmatics* 10(1). 1–15.

Bauman, Richard. 2001. The ethnography of genre in a Mexican market: form, function and variation. In Penelope Eckert & John Rickford (eds.), *Style and sociolinguistic variation*, 57–77. Cambridge: Cambridge University Press.

Bauman, Richard & Charles L. Briggs. 1990. Poetics and performance as critical perspectives on language and social life. *Annual Review of Anthopology* 19. 59–88.

https://doi.org/10.1515/9781501506796-007

Baxter, Judith. 2014. *Double-voicing: power, gender and linguistic expertise*. Basingstoke: Palgrave Macmillan.

Beal, Joan C. 2009. Enregisterment, commodification, and historical context: "Geordie"versus "Sheffieldish." *American Speech* 84(2). 138–156.

Bell, Allan. 1984. Language style and audience design. *Journal of Sociolinguistics* 13(2). 145–204.

Bell, Allan. 2011. Falling in love again and again: Marlene Dietrich and the iconization of non-native English. *Journal of Sociolinguistics* 15(5). 627–656.

Bell, Allan & Andy Gibson. 2011. Staging language: An introduction to the sociolinguistics of performance. *Journal of Sociolinguistics* 15(5). 555–572.

Bell, Nancy. 2016. Introduction. In Nancy Bell (ed.), *Multiple perspectives on language play*, 1–10. Boston: De Gruyter Mouton.

Bennet, Joe. 2012. Chav-spotting in Britain: the represenations of social class as private choice. *Social Semiotics*. 23(1). 146–162.

Berry, Liz. 2014. *Black country*. London: Chatto & Windus.

Biber, Douglas & Susan Conrad. 2009. *Genre, register and style*. Cambridge: Cambridge University Press.

Bigham, Douglas S. 2012. Emerging adulthood in sociolinguistics. *Language and Linguistic Compass* 6. 533–544

Birmingham City Council, 2011. Ethnic groups. http://www.birmingham.gov.uk/cs/Satellite?c=Page&childpagename=Planning-and-Regeneration%2FPageLay-out&cid=1223096353923&pagename=BCC%2FCommon%2FWrapper%2FWrapper (accessed 4 March 2014).

Blackledge, Adrian & Angela Creese. 2010. *Multilingualism: a critical perspective*. London: Continuum.

Blommaret, Jan. 2010. *The sociolinguistics of globalization*. Cambridge: Cambridge University Press.

Bonstetter, Beth E. 2011. Mel Brooks meets Kenneth Burke (and Mikhail Bakhtin): comedy and burlesque in satire film. *Journal of Film and Video* 63(1). 18–31.

Britain, David. 2017. Wich way to look?: perspectives on urban and rural in dialectology. In Chris Montogomery & Emma Moore (eds.), *Language and a sense of place: studies in language and region*, 171–188. Cambridge: Cambridge University Press.

Bucholtz, Mary. 2000. The politics of transcription. *Journal of Pragmatics* 32(1). 1439–1465.

Burke, Kenneth. 1984 [1959][1937]. *Attitudes towards history*. Berkely, Los Angeles, London: University of California Press.

Butler, Judith. 1990. *Gender trouble: feminism and the subversion of identity*. London: Routledge.

Butler, Judith. 1997. *Excitable speech: a politics of the performative*. London and New York: Routledge.

Charmaz, Kathy. 2014. *Constructing grounded theory*. London: Sage.

Charmaz, Kathy & Richard G. Mitchell. 2007. Grounded theory in ethnography. In Paul Atkinson, Amanda Coffey, Sara Delamont, John Lofland & Lyn Lofland (eds.), *Handbook of ethnography*, 160–174. London: Sage.

Cheshire, J. & S. Fox. 2009. Was/were variation: A perspective from London. *Language Variation and Change* 21(1). 1–38.

Cheshire, J., P. Kerswill, S. Fox & E. Torgersen. 2011. Contact, the feature pool and the speech community: The emergence of multicultural London English. *Journal of Sociolinguistics* 15(2). 151–196.

Clark, Urszula. 2001. *War words: language, history and the disciplining of English*. Oxford: Elsevier Science.

Clark, Urszula. 2004. The English West Midlands: phonology. In B. Kortmann & E. Schneider (eds.), *A handbook of varieties of English*, volume 1, 134–162. Berlin: Mouton de Gruyter.

Clark, Urszula. 2007. *Researching language: English in action*. Basingstoke: Palgrave.

Clark, Urszula. 2013a. *Language and identity in Englishes*. London: Routledge.

Clark, Urszula. 2013b. "er's from off: the indexicalization and enregisterment of Black Country dialect. *American Speech* 88(4). 441–66.

Clark, Urszula & Esther Asprey. 2013. *West Midlands English: Birmingham and the Black Country*. Edinburgh: Edinburgh University Press.

Clifton, Jonathan. 2012. A discursive approach to leadership: doing assessments and managing organizational meetings. *Journal of Business Communication* 49(2). 148–168.

Clyne, Michael. 2000. Lingua franca and ethnolects in Europe and beyond. *Sociolinguistica* 14. 83–89.

Cohen, Anthony Paul. 1985. *The symbolic construction of community*. London: Routledge.

Copland, Fiona, Sara Shaw & Julia Snell (eds.). 2015. *Linguistic ethnography: interdisciplinary explorations*. Basingstoke: Palgrave Macmillan.

Couper-Kulhen, Elizabeth & Margaret Selting. 2018. *Interactional linguistics: studying language in social interaction*. Cambridge: Cambridge University Press.

Coupland, Nikolas. 2001. Dialect stylization in radio talk. *Language in Society* 30(3). 345–375.

Coupland, Nikolas. 2007. *Style: language variation and identity* Cambridge: Cambridge University Press.

Coupland, Nikolas. 2009. The mediated performance of vernaculars. *Journal of English Linguistics*. 37(3). 284–300.

Coupland, Nikolas. 2012. Bilingualism on display: the framing of English in Welsh public spaces. *Language in Society* 41(1). 1–27.

Coupland, Nikolas. 2014. Sociolinguistic change, vernacularization and broadcast British media. In Jannis Androutsopoulos (ed.), M*ediatization and sociolinguistic change*, 67–98. Berlin: De Gruyter Mouton.

Coupland, Nikolas & Peter Garrett. 2010. Linguistic landscapes, discursive frames and metatcultural performance: the case of Welsh Patagoia. *International Journal of the Sociology of Language* 205. 7–36.

Crowley, Tony. 1991. *Proper English: readings in language, history and culture*. London & New York: Routledge.

Crowley, Tony. 1996. *Language in history: theoriesand texts*. London & New York: Routledge.

Crowley, Tony. 2003 [1989]. *Standard English and the politics of language*. Basingstoke: Palgrave Macmillan.

Crul, Maurice. 2016. Superdiversity versus assimilation: how complex diversity in majority-minority cities challenges the assumptions of assimilation. *Journal of Ethnic and Migration Studies* 42(1). 54–68.

Devine, Fiona. 2016. The working class, middle class, assimilation and convergence. *The Sociological Review* https://www.thesociologicalreview.com/blog/the-working-class-middle-class-assimilation-and-convergence.html (accessed 15 July 2017).

Devine, Fiona & Marianne Sensier. 2017. Class, politics and the progressive dilemma. *The Political Quarterly* 88(1). 30–38.

Dray, Susan & Mark Sebba. 2011. Practices, ethnicity and authenticity: 'Creole' and youth language in a British inner-city community. In L. Hinrichs & J. Farquarson (eds.), *Variation in the Caribbean: from creole continua to individual agency*, 231–250. Amsterdam: John Benjamins.

Dubios, Sylvie & Barbara Horvath. 2002. Sounding Cajun: The rhetorical use of dialect in speech and writing. *American Speech* 77(3). 264–87.

Eckert, Penelope. 2000. *Language variation as social practice: the linguistic construction of identity in Belten High*. London: Routledge.

Eckert, Penelope. 2008. Variation and the indexical field. *Journal of Sociolinguistics* 12(4). 453–476.

Ensink, Titus & Christoph Sauer. 2003. Social-functional and cognitive approaches to discourse interpretation: The role of frame and perspective. In Titus Ensink & Christoph Sauer (eds.), *Framing and perspective in discourse*, 1–21. Amsterdam: John Benjamins.

Fairclough, Norman. 1992. *Critical discourse analysis: the critical study of language*. London: Longman.

Fauconnier, Gilles & Eve Sweetser. 1996. *Spaces, worlds and grammar*. Chicago: University of Chicago Press.

Figueroa, E. & P. Patrick. 2002. Kiss-teeth. *American Speech* 77(4). 383–97.

Foucault, Michel. 1972. *The archeology of knowledge and the discourse on language*. New York: Pantheon Books.

Garcia, Ofelia. 2009a. *Bilingual education in the 21st century: A global perspective*. Malden, MA and Oxford, UK: Wiley-Blackwell

Garcia, Ofelia & Li Wei. 2015. *Translanguaging: language, bilingualism and education*. Basingstoke: Palgrave Macmillan.

Gibson, Andy. 2011. Flight of the Conchords: recontextualising the voices of poular culture. *Journal of Sociolinguistics*. 15(5). 603–626.

Giddens, Anthony. 1991. *Modernity and self-identity: self and society in the Late Modern Age*. Oxford: Wiley.

Gilroy, P. 1991. 'It ain't where you're from, it's where you're at...' The dialectics of diasporic identification. *Third Text* 5(13). 3–16.

Gilroy, P. 1993. *The Black Atlantic: modernity and double consciousness*. London: Verso.

Glaser, Barney G. & Anselm L. Strauss. 1999 [1967]. *The discovery of grounded theory: strategies for qualitative research*. Chicago: Aldine Publishing Company.

Goatly, Andrew. 2012. *Meaning and humour*. Cambridge: Cambridge University Press.

Goffman, Erving. 1981. *Forms of talk*. Philadelphia: University of Pennsylvania Press.

Gramsci, Antonio. 1995 [1971]. *Selections from a prison notebook*. London: Lawrence and Wishart.

Grant, Tim, Urszula Clark, Gertrud Reershemius, David Pollard, Sarah Hayes & Garry Plappert. 2017. *Quantitative research methods for linguists*. London: Routledge.

Green, Judith, Maria Franquiz & Carol Dixon. 1997. The myth of the objective transcript: transcribing as a situated act. *TESOL Quarterly* 31(1). 172–176.

Gumperz, John. J. 1982. *Discourse Strategies*. Cambridge: Cambridge University Press.

Hackert, Stephanie. 2012. *Emergence of the English native speaker: a chapter in nineteenth century linguistic thought*. Berlin: De Gruyter Mouton.

Hall, S. 1992 [1978]. 'What is this "black" in black popular culture?' In S. Hall et al., *Policing the crisis: mugging, the state, and law and order*, 100–115. London: Macmillan.

Halliday, M.A.K. 1978. *Language as a social semiotic: the social interpretation of language and meaning*. London: Edward Arnold.

Hammersley, Martyn. 2006. Ethnography: problems and prospects. *Ethnography and Education* 1(1). 3–14.

Hammersley, Martyn. 2007a. The issue of quality in qualitative research. *International Journal of Research & Methods in Education* 30(3). 287–305.

Hammersley, Martyn. 2007b. Reflections on linguistic ethnography. *Journal of Sociolinguistics* 11(5). 689–95.

Hesse, B. (ed.). 2000. *Un/settled multiculturalisms: diasporas, entanglements, transruptions*. London: Zed Books.

Heyd, Theresa. 2010. How you guys doin'? Staged orality an emerging plural address in the television series *Friends*. *American Speech* 85(1). 157–175.

Hodson, Jane. 2014. *Dialect in film and literature*. London: Routledge.

Hoey, Brian A. 2013. *Opting for elsewhere: lifestyle migration in the American middle class*. Nashville, TN: Vanderbilt University Press.

Howkins, A. & L. Merricks. 1993. " we be black as hell:" ritual, disguise and rebellion. *Rural History*. 47(1). 41–53.

Hua, Zhu & Li Wei. 2016. "Where are you really from?:" nationality and ethnicity talk (NET) in everyday intercations. *Applied Linguistics Review* 7(4). 449–470.

Hutchison A. J., L. H Johnston & J. Breckon. 2010. Using QSR-NVivo to facilitate the development of a grounded theory project: an account of a worked example. *International Journal of Social Research Methodology* 13. 283–302.

Jaffe, Alexandra. 2012. *Stance: sociolinguistic perspectives*. Oxford: Oxford University Press.

Jaffe, Alexandra. 2015. Staging language on Corsica: stance, improvisation, play and heteroglossia. *Language in Society* 44(2). 161–186.

Jaffe, Alexandra, Jannis Androutsopoulos, Mark Sebba & Sally Johnson (eds). 2012. *Orthography as social action: scripts, spelling, identity and power*. Berlin, Boston: De Gruyter Mouton.

Jaffe, Alexandra, Michelle Koven, Sabina Perrino & Cecile B. Vigouroux. 2015. Introduction: heteroglossia, performance, power and participation. *Language in Society* 44. 135–139.

Johnstone, Barbara (1996) *The Linguistic Individual: self-expression in language and linguistics*. New York: oxford University Press.

Johnstone, Barbara. 2002. *Discourse analysis*. Oxford: Blackwell.

Johnstone, Barbara. 2004. Place, globalization and linguistic variation. In Carmen Fought (ed), *Sociolinguistic variation: critical reflections*, 65–83. Oxford: Oxford University Press.

Johnstone, Barbara. 2009. Pittsburghese shirts: commodification and the enregistration of an urban dialect. *American Speech* 84(2). 157–175.

Johnstone, Barbara. 2011. Dialect enregisterment in performance. *Journal of Sociolinguistics* 15(5). 657–679.

Johnstone, Barbara. 2013. *Speaking Pittsburghese: the story of a dialect*. Oxford: Oxford University Press.

Johnstone, Barbara. 2014. Commentary: sociolinguistics and the news media. In Jannis Androutsopoulos (ed.), *Mediatization and social change*, 457–460. Berlin: De Gruyter Mouton.

Johnstone, Barbara. 2016. Characterlogical figures and expressive style in the enregisterment of linguistic variety. In Chris Montgomery and Emma Moore (eds.), *A sense of place: studies in language and region*, 283–300. Cambridge: Cambridge University Press.

Johnstone, Barbara. 2019. Enregisterment: linguistic form and meaning in time and space. In Beatrix Busse & Ingo H. Warnke (eds.), *Handbook of language in urban spaces*. Berlin: De Gruyter. https://works.bepress.com/barbara_johnstone/66/(accessed 15 November 2016).

Johnstone, Barbara, Jennifer Andrus & Andrew E. Danielson. 2006. Mobility, indexicality and enregisterment of Pittsburghese. *Journal of English Linguistics* 34(2). 77–104.

Johnstone, Barbara & Scott Kiesling. 2008. Indexicality and experience: exploring the meanings of/aw/monophthongisation in Pittsburgh. *Journal of Sociolinguistics*. 12(1). 5–33.

Jorgensen, Normann J. 2008a: Polylingual languaging around and among children and adolescents. *International Journal of Multilingualism* 5(3). 161–176

Jones, Owen. 2012. *Chavs: the demonization of the working class*. London: Verso.

Kerswill, Paul. 2014. The objectification of 'Jafaican: the discousal embedding of MLE in the British media. In Jannis Androutsopoulos (ed.), *The media and social change*, 428–455. Berlin: De Gruyter Mouton.

Kerswill, P., E. Torgersen & S. Fox. 2008. Reversing 'drift': innovation and diffusion in the London diphthong system. *Language Variation and Change* 20. 451–491.

Kerswill, P., J. Cheshire, S. Fox & E. Torgersen. 2012. English as a contact language: the role of children and adolescents. In Marianne Hundt & Daniel Schreier (eds.), *English as a contact language*, 258–282. Cambridge: Cambridge University Press.

Khan, A. 2006. *A sociolinguistic study of Birmingham English: language variation and change in a multi-ethnic British community*. Lancaster University, unpublished PhD dissertation.

Kirby, T.E. 1971. The origin of the Mummers play. *The Journal of American Folklore* 84 (333). 275–288.

Kristeva, Julia. 1996. *Word, dialogue and the novel*. Oxford: Blackwell.

Lapadt, J. C. & A. C. Lindsay. 1999. Transcription in research and practice: From standardization of technique to interpretive positionings. *Qualitative Inquiry* 5. 64–86.

Levitt, J. H. 1968. *North Staffordshire speech*. Keele: University of Keele.

Llamas, Carmen & Dominic Watt (eds.). 2009. *Language and identities*. Edinburgh: Edinburgh University Press.

Lyotard, Francios 1979 [1984] '*The postmodern condition: a report on knowledge* (theory and history of literature). Manchester: Manchester University Press.

Macaulay, Ronald. 2006. *The social art: language and its uses*. Oxford: Oxford University Press.

Markus, Hazel Rose & Moya, Paul M. L. 2010. *Doing race: 21 essays for the 21st century*. New York: W.W. Norton.

Martin, Vivian B. & Astrid Gynnild. 2011. *Grounded theory: the philosophy, method and work of Barney Glaser*. Boca Raton, FL: BrownWalker Press.

Moller, Janus Spindler. 2008. Polylingual performances among Turkish-Danes in late-modern Copenhagen. *International Journal of Multilingualism* 5(3). 217–236.

Montgomery, Chris & Emma Moore (eds.). 2017. *Language and a sense of place: studies in language and region*. Cambridge: Cambridge University Press.

Och, Elinor. 1979. Transcription as theory. In Elinor Och and B. Schiefflin (eds.), *Developmental pragmatics*, 43–72. New York: Academic Press.

Och, Elinor. 1992. Indexing gender. In Alessandro Duranti & Charles Goodwin (eds.), *Rethinking context: language as an interactive phenomenon*, 335–358. Cambridge: Cambridge University Press.

Otsuji, Emi & Alastair Pennycook. 2010. Metrolingualism: fixity, fluidity and language in flux. *International Journal of Multilingualism* 7(3). 40–254.

Paizza, Roberta, Monika Bednarek & Fabio Rossi. 2015. *Telecinematic discourse: approaches o the language of film and TV*. Amsterdam: John Benjamins.

Patrick, Peter. 2014. Jamaican Creole. In Marianna Di Paolo & Arther Le Spears (eds.), *Languages and dialects in the US: focus on diversity and linguistics*, 126–136. London & New York: Routledge.

Pennycook, Alastair & Emi Otsuji. 2015. *Metrolingualism: language in the city*. London: Routledge.

Preston, Dennis. 1982. Ritin' Fowklower daun 'rong: Folklorists' failures in phonology *Journal of American Folklore* 95. 304–26.

Preston, Dennis. 1983. 'Mowr bad spellun': a reply to Fine. *Journal of American Folklore* 96. 330–39.

Preston, Dennis. 1985. The Li'l Abner syndrome: written representations of speech. *American Speech* 60(1). 328–36.

Queen, Robin. 2015. *Vox popular: the surprising life of language in the media.* Oxford: Wiley Blackwell.

Rampton, Ben. 1995. *Crossing: language and ethnicity among adolescents.* London: Longman.

Rampton, Ben. 2011. Style contrasts, migration and social class. *Journal of Pragmatics* 43(5). 1236–1250.

Rampton, Ben, Janet Maybin & Celia Roberts. 2015. Theory and method in linguistic ethnography. In Fiona Copland, Sara Shaw and Julia Snell (eds.), *Linguistic ethnography: interdisciplinary explorations*, 14–50. Basingstoke: Palgrave Macmillan.

Ruhi, Sukriye, Michael Haugh, Thomas Schmidt & Kai Worner. 2014. *Best practices for spoken corpora in linguistic research.* Newcastle upon Tyne: Cambridge Scholars Publishing.

Sali, Sara. 2002. *Judith Butler.* London: Routledge.

Savage, Mike. 2016. The fall and rise of class analysis in British sociology 1950–2016. *Tempo Social* 28(2). 57–72.

Savage, M., N. Cunningham, M. Taylor, Y. Li, J. Hjlibrekke, B. Le Roux, S. Friedman & A. Miles. 2013. A new model of social class? Findings from the BBC's great British class survey. *Sociology* 47(2). 219–250.

Schilling-Estes, Natalie. 2002. On the nature of isolated and post-isolated dialects: Innovation, variation and differentiation. *Journal of Sociolinguistics* 6(1). 64–68.

Schmidt, Thomas & Kai Worner. 2016. *Multilingual corpora and multilingual corpus analysis.* Amsterdam: John Benjamins.

Scollon, Ron & Suzanne B. Scollon. 2003. *Discourses in place: language in the material world.* London: Routledge.

Scott, Jeremy. 2016. Midlands cadences: narrative voices in the work of Alan Sillitoe. *Language and Literature* 25(4). 312–327.

Sebba, Mark. 2004. British Creole: morphology and syntax. In B. Kortmann & E. Schneider (eds.), *A handbook of varieties of English: a multimedia reference tool (vol 2)*, 96–208. Berlin: Mouton de Gruyter.

Sebba, Mark. 2007. *Spelling and society: the culture and politics of orthography around the world.* Cambridge: Cambridge University Press.

Selting, Margaret, Peter Auer, Dagmar Barth-Weingarten, Jorg Bergmann, Pia Bergmann, Karin Birkner, Elizabeth Couper-Kuhlen, Arnulf Deppermann, Peter Gilles, Suzanne Gunthner, Martin Hartung, Friederike Kern, Christine Mertzlufft, Christian Meyer, Miriam Morek, Frank Oberzaucher, Jorg Peters, Uta Quasthoff, Wilfried Schutte, Anja Stukenbrock & Susanne Uhmann. 2011. Gesprächsanalytisches Transkriptionssystem 2 (GAT 2). http://www.gespraechsforschung-ozs.de/heft2009/px-gat2.pdf (accessed 6 September 2016).

Silverstein, Michael. 1992. The indeterminancy of contextualization: when is enough enough? In. P Auer & A. di Luzio (eds.), *The contextualization of language*, 55–76. Amsterdam: John Benjamins.

Silverstein, Michael. 1993. Metapragmatic discourse and metapragmatic function. In J.A. Lucy (ed.), *Reflexive language: reported speech and metapragmatics*, 33–58. Cambridge: Cambridge University Press.

Silverstein, Michael. 2003. Indexical order and the dialectics of sociolinguistic life. *Language and Communication* 23. 193–229.

Simpson, Paul. 1993. *Language, ideology and point of view*. London: Routledge.

Trester, Anna Maria. 2012. Framing entextualization in improve: intertextuality as an interactional resource. *Language in Society* 41. 237–258.

Turner, Graeme. 2010. *Ordinary people and the media: the demotic turn*. London: Sage.

Tusting, Karin & Janet Maybin. 2007. Linguistic ethnography and interdiscplinarity: opening the discussion. *Journal of Sociolinguistics* 11(5). 575–583.

Vertovec, Steven. 2007. Super-diversity and its implications. *Ethnic and Racial Studies* 6. 1024–1054.

Vigourouz, Cecile B. 2015. Genre, heteroglossic performances and new identity in modern French society. *Language in Society* 44. 243–272.

Walker, Traci. 2014. Form versus function: the independence of prosody and action. *Research on Language and Social Interaction* 47(1). 1–16.

Wei, Li. 2011. Moment analysis and translanguaging space: discursive construction of identity by multilingual Chinese youth in Britain. *Journal of Pragmatics* 43(5). 1222–1235.

Index

https://doi.org/10.1515/9781501506796-008

CPSIA information can be obtained
at www.ICGtesting.com
Printed in the USA
LVHW11084530721
693878LV00003B/199

9 781501 524509